REVELATION AND

Colin Ewart Gunton 1941–2003

Revelation and Reason

Prolegomena to Systematic Theology

Colin E. Gunton

Transcribed and Edited by
P. H. Brazier

t&t clark

Published by T&T Clark
A Continuum imprint
The Tower Building, 11 York Road, London SE1 7NX
80 Maiden Lane, Suite 704, New York, NY 10038

www.continuumbooks.com

All royalties go to the Colin Gunton Memorial Fund at King's College London

British Library Cataloguing-in-Publication Data
A catalogue record for this book is available from the British Library

Typeset and graphics by P. H. Brazier

Printed and bound in the U. S. A.

ISBN-10:	0567033554	(hardback)
	0567033562	(paperback)
ISBN-13:	9780567033550	(hardback)
	9780567033567	(paperback)

Revelation and Reason

Prolegomena to Systematic Theology

Part One : From Reason and Revelation to Revelation and Reason

Part Two : The Modern Problem in an Historical Context

Part Three : Aspects of Karl Barth on Faith And Reason

Contents

PART TWO : THE MODERN PROBLEM IN HISTORICAL CONTEXT

Tables and Graphics

Foreword

This is a work based on tape recordings of a seminar programme for MA students given by Professor Colin Gunton at King's College, London (the recordings – for personal study – were made in the Michaelmas terms of 1999 and 2000: this programme is listed in the appendix). The aim of the course was to turn those attending from being students into theologians: men and women with a critical ability to lay out what constitutes the intellectual content of the Christian faith, and, to a degree, to develop the ability to answer the questions and doubts that are so often thrown at Christianity not just by the faithful – the often puzzled faithful – but also from detractors of various belief systems, particularly self-confessed atheists from the academy (usually philosophers and scientists, university dons, who repudiate and deny all religion, but are blind to the religious beliefs – often pagan atheistic religious beliefs and ethics – that they espouse with a fundamental certainty that beggars belief). The course was not about apologetics; neither was it primarily about theological history: the objective was in many ways to be able to explicate, to lay out, illuminate and elucidate in as systematic and methodical a way as possible, what constitutes the Christian faith and how it coheres. In this Colin Gunton did not compromise with modernity or postmodernity! This book is in some ways about the relationship of theology and the Christian faith with modernity/postmodernity.

This book represents Colin Gunton's profound insights into the nature of theology through a consideration of faith, Revelation and reason; the material is from prepared lectures and extemporary material from discussions. This material is a unique insight into Colin Gunton's highly valued and original style of teaching which here exhibits profound understanding and reflection upon God's Revelation and humanity's use of reason. Colin Gunton was a world-renowned scholar, systematic theologian and Reformed Church minister. Approximately one-third of the work is a direct transcript and analysis of the three lectures Colin Gunton gave at a breakneck speed at the beginning of the course each year, each was of two hours duration: 1. 'From Reason and Revelation to Revelation and Reason'; 2. 'The Modern Problem in an Historical Context'; 3. 'Aspects of Karl Barth on Faith and Reason'. These lectures were a history, analysis and critique of Revelation and reason in systematic theology and philosophy, culminating with Karl Barth. These three lectures form the titles and contents of the three parts of this book; each lecture is subdivided into three chapters and expanded with material that is a transcript of the unrehearsed, unscripted, extemporary responses Colin Gunton gave to MA students' papers on set topics in the course, seamlessly integrated, where relevant, with the material from the main three lectures. For example, Colin Gunton's response to a paper on John Locke is integrated into Chapter 2; responses to a paper on Von Balthasar are also integrated into Chapter 2; material on Frei and Lindbeck, Chapter 3; Hegel, Chapter 7; Barth and Schleiermacher, Chapter 8; Barth and Brunner on natural theology, Chapter 9, and so forth. Many of these student papers appeared superficially to be satisfactory, but Colin Gunton was merciless at exposing any flaws and faults in the research or argument presented: the students were on a steep learning curve! Although Colin Gunton would not have made a politically correct, liberal, humanist infant school teacher – thank God – he was kindness itself if a student could concede the perceived flaw/fault. Credit must, therefore, be given to the anonymous students (note, none of the material from the students' papers is included here) who provided the stimulus and trigger for Colin's mind to generate relevant material, facts, ideas, from a variety of theologians and philosophers, make links/connections, pursue several lines of argument – all at once – and present as tight and logically coherent an argument as was possible. He would also congratulate a student and concede a point when appropriate!

Colin Gunton presented a paper entitled, 'I Know that My Redeemer Lives: A Consideration of Christian Knowledge Claims' to the Research Institute in Systematic Theology at King's on the morning of 28 September 1999, the day the MA course transcribed here started in the afternoon. This is an early version of a paper that was published in a volume of essays by T&T Clark a year later (*Intellect and Action: Elucidations on Christian Theology and the Life of Faith*, reissued by Continuum in 2005). This material was highly relevant, and indeed was discussed during the first MA session that afternoon, and is here integrated into Chapter 1 (§. 2 The Christian Claims to Knowledge, §§. i–vii: Gunton scholars might want to compare this material with the published version to see how Colin's ideas developed as a result of the questions and discussion in the seminar).

Colin Gunton's understanding is here presented as systematically as possible, with the use of charts and graphics to give clarity, based on the illustrations he drew on the whiteboard during the seminars. Whether he was lecturing or responding to a seminar discussion, he gave space to the free rein of his mind when analysing a particular strand of a theologian's thought: he was a creative teacher and a deeply read theologian; this is shown in his unscripted and extemporary responses to the students' papers: what drove him was a passion for truth, a love of the God who revealed himself in Christ Jesus – knowledge forged almost as a by-product of our salvation wrought on the Cross. These responses showed the breadth of his learning, and his genius spontaneously to bring to mind relevant ideas from a wealth of theologians and philosophers, while incisively and piercingly exposing the flaws as well as the strengths under consideration. Because it is intended that this book is read not just by postgraduate specialists, I have added explanatory details to key names and movements in references where necessary. Any writer/theologian or book/article referred to by Professor Gunton is referenced, where possible, in the note and linked to the bibliography where all the works Colin cited or referred to however obliquely or explicitly are listed.

It is often forgotten by those who read and support Colin's later work with its heavy emphasis on the unique self-revelation of the one triune God in Christ that originally he graduated in 'Greats' from Oxford, and for the first ten years or so at King's (before he was appointed Professor of Christian Doctrine in the early 1980s) he taught history of philosophy and philosophy of religion: he knew philosophers and their arguments in a way that many theologians – whether Catholic, Reformed or Evangelical – do not. Thereafter Colin Gunton taught the 'Revelation and Reason' course to MA students for nearly twenty years. Early on he produced a series of lectures – The 1993 'Warfield Lectures' given at Princeton Theological Seminary – on Revelation and reason, which were published by T&T Clark (*A Brief Theology of Revelation*, reissued by Continuum in 2005). This was the closest he came to producing a textbook for the course, but he always warned the students

> *the material in this course has changed much since those lectures were given ... and this course changes each year according to the students on the course, but, yes, I would certainly recommend you read that book, but what we say together here, now that's important! But it's more than that; this course is not really about textbooks, it is about reading the actual people – Descartes and Locke, Kant, Schleiermacher and Hegel, Torrance and Barth, all these people who had so much to say about whether theology was possible and how we valued reason, our capacity, you see, to reason things out. Read these people; read them and argue with them.*

Therefore, these seminars are essentially an introduction for students and general readers to Colin Gunton's understanding of reason and Revelation; this topic is important and lies at the heart of theology and the Christian faith. Christoph Schwöbel, commenting on this work, asserted how these seminars are an important engagement with the biblical and doctrinal dimensions of Revelation and reason, and they are a sustained reflection on the philosophical issues involved in the truth-claims of Christian faith. As such Christoph commented that

> [They may be seen] *as a prominent and inspiring example of engaging the main philosophical positions since the Enlightenment in a dialogue about the claims of reason and the insights of revelation. On the British (and to a certain extent also on the American) scene there is relatively clearly defined division between philosophical analysis and discussion of religious truth claims as it is conducted by philosophers and the theological exposition of the rationality of faith in the context of the church pursued by theologians. In these lectures (and probably because of his philosophical training and early teaching experience as a lecturer in philosophy of religion) Colin has successfully overcome this division with regard to the material he refers to and with regard to the debates he gets involved in.* [This is] *a courageous attempt at identifying those strands in contemporary discussions (e.g. on foundationalism and postfoundationalism) which clarify general aspects of the relationship of reason and revelation, dealing with them critically in such a way that they open up a constructive approach for Christian theology.*

> [They can be seen] *as a further testimony of Colin's style of doing theology in an important field which, because of his early death, was never fully espoused in his writing ... I would see the lectures both as a complement and counterpoint to* The Barth Lectures. *(Generally speaking, people who would claim to be Barthians don't have much time for engaging with Locke, Kant and, say, Hegel and tend to repeat Barth's often idiosyncratic statements in* Theology of the Nineteenth Century. *Colin is a very unusual Barthian in this way. Conversely, the Locke-, Kant- and Hegel-specialists normally have no time for Barth, deterred by his rather fulsome statements about philosophy. Colin's work is the interesting example of the work of a philosophically interested and competent, Barth-inspired theologian.* [1]

The material here presented is testimony to one of the greatest British theologians of the late twentieth century. *Revelation and Reason* is a complementary volume to Colin Gunton's posthumously published *The Barth Lectures* (Continuum, 2007), and a true prolegomena to Colin's unfinished *Systematic Theology*, which he was working on at the point of his unexpected death, and which is to be published also by Continuum.

My acknowledgement and thanks go to Colin himself with whom I had many discussions relating to the nature of theology and philosophy, and therefore Revelation and reason, but also to Colin's wife, Jenny, and his daughter Sarah, who made me welcome and allowed me to go through Colin's papers, unearthing much material and understanding which complements the lectures/seminars represented in this book.

Paul Brazier
July 2008

1 E-mail, Christoph Schwöbel to Paul Brazier, 22 September 2007.

APOCALYPSIS ET RATIO

... let my mind meditate on you,
let my tongue speak of you,
let my heart love you,
let my soul hunger for you
... until I enter into the joy of the lord,
who is God, Three in One,
blessed for ever.

ANSELM OF CANTERBURY
PROSLOGION

INTRODUCTION

Stephen R. Holmes

Tuesday was postgraduate student day at the Research Institute in Systematic Theology at King's College London. In the morning, doctoral students and taught postgraduates would gather to hear and to respond to a seminar paper. The discussions would continue over lunch, and at 2.00 p.m. the taught postgraduates would gather for class. The second semester, this might be one of several offered modules, taught by different staff members, but from September to Christmas, unless he was on research leave, the slot belonged to Colin Gunton and his course on Revelation and reason.

'The aim of this course', he would announce at the beginning, 'is to teach you to think like theologians...' The words might vary slightly from year to year, but the sentiment was always the same. As befits almost any course in higher education, and certainly any course at postgraduate level, the material studied in those weeks was almost incidental (more about that 'almost' later). This time was not about mastering a body of knowledge, but about learning habits of thought, ways of arguing, methods of evaluating evidence that were appropriate to Christian theology.

What is being explored here is the material proper to any taught postgraduate course, the question of the academic nature of theology. A discipline belongs in the university if it is able to carry out a self-critical discourse about its own sources and methods. The question is not so much whether it is right or wrong (most academic disciplines accept with some cheerfulness that their best insights are only approximations to the nature of reality, and that many of their current hypotheses are likely to be proved false), but whether it knows how to ask and answer that question: What sort of evidence is needed to prove or to disprove a hypothesis in this discipline?

Of course, this conception of the nature of a proper academic discipline is not uncontested. An alternative, and powerful, idea suggests that 'objectivity' or 'neutrality' is the core of any discourse that is truly academic. On this account, what makes a discipline proper to the university is its willingness (or, rather, the willingness of its practitioners) to put aside any personal preferences or commitments, and to attempt dispassionately to come to a balanced view of the evidence. The scholar may acknowledge that she would like X to be true, but that preference is checked at the door of the university, so to speak, and scholarship is pursued in a scrupulously neutral manner.

There is a sense in which deciding between these two ideas of what it is to be properly academic was the heart of Colin's lectures on Revelation and reason. In theology, more so perhaps than any other discipline, they simply stand in contradiction to one another. An investigation into the self-understanding of Christian theology's own methods and sources cannot but show that, for most of its history, theology has understood its basic claim about knowledge to be that knowledge is non-neutral. Revelation is not a form of knowledge that is passively presented for human investigation, available in proportion to the seeker's ingenuity. Rather it comes as a gift, and so depends fundamentally on the disposition of the giver. And if it is the Father's good pleasure to hide these things from the wise and learned while revealing them to little children (Mt. 11.25–26), then the knowledge will be in the possession of the little children, not the scholars.

For many years in British universities the notion that true academic study was objective and neutral reigned supreme. This was the world of the university that Colin began to teach in, first as a lecturer in the philosophy of religion in King's College London. There was nothing wrong with his decision to be ordained to the ministry (of the newly formed United Reformed Church, although he remained a thoroughgoing Congregationalist at heart) in the college chapel; but almost all around would assume that it should not and must not affect what he taught in any way.

I began my doctoral studies under Colin's supervision in 1996, not many weeks after my own ordination, to Baptist ministry. By then Colin had been teaching in King's for something over twenty years and had migrated from the philosophy of religion to systematic theology, via 'Christian doctrine' along the way. I was able to assume, and Colin certainly assumed, that what was expressed in baptismal and ordination vows, a personal commitment to the truth of the Christian faith in one of its historical expressions, was an intrinsic, and perhaps even necessary, qualification for working in Christian theology. What had changed in the meantime?

In part, the culture had changed, within and without the academy. Colin was rather impatient with the fashion in humanities departments in universities for embracing 'postmodernism', and even criticized the term itself heavily and pertinently. Whatever the rights or wrongs of such criticism, fashionable postmodern suspicion has meant that, in my generation of humanities scholars, and mostly in the one above it, no– ne believes in even the possibility of academic neutrality anymore. It was pretences to neutrality that justified racism, colonial oppression and the subjection of women in Western culture. A supposedly objective account of the order of things shored up entrenched privileges, and so formed a bastion against the progress of justice. Our instinctive reaction is that the person who comes seeking to recruit us to a programme that proclaims itself to be academically neutral and objective is seeking to impose a hegemonic power claim, and to disguise or obscure that fact.

As I say, Colin was, probably rightly, rather impatient of such claims. Academic fashions come and go, and none of them should be considered that hospitable to the strange and ever new claims of the Christian gospel. You will search in vain in the lectures that follow for any celebration of Lyotard's proclamation of our incredulity towards metanarrative. But if Colin finds his reasons for rejecting claims to academic neutrality in a different place, this context is, I suspect, not irrelevant to understand why these claims were increasingly found convincing by others. For Colin, however, the key data lay not in changing culture, but in unchanging gospel. It is an analysis of the nature of Revelation, building on and supported by the fathers and doctors of the church, that leads to the conclusion that theological knowledge is only comprehensible on its own terms. The attempt to make theology 'objective', to argue from reason to Revelation, beginning in some supposedly shared, and so neutral, rationality, was simply a mistake. This is not how theological knowledge has been pursued, and so any attempt to pursue it that way is alien to the discipline's own self-understanding of its methods and modes of argument. To argue from reason to Revelation is to fail to be properly academic, in the first sense of the word defined above.

What is theological knowledge? That is the primary question addressed at the start of these lectures. Colin traces the long-standing Christian hesitation with valuing knowledge: against the Gnostics, Irenaeus insists that the facts of the gospel, not our knowledge of them, is what makes the difference; Calvin thinks that knowledge without obedience is a dangerous irrelevance. Nonetheless, theology explores the knowledge of the Christian. This is never, however, obscurantism; there is never any suggestion that knowledge does not matter, rather a careful and chastened account of the nature of that knowledge.

It is careful because of the ever present danger of Gnosticism, of pretending that our knowledge, not God's action, is the decisive fact of life and death; chastened because aware of its own multiple limitations. The old Reformed scholastics stressed that the only complete knowledge of God is God's knowledge of himself; this is archetypal theology, of which all other knowledge of God is merely an ectype. Even ectypal theology, however, exists on various levels: the knowledge of the saints in heaven is more complete than the knowledge of those still journeying, and so there is an eschatological limitation to our theological knowing (cf. 1 Cor. 13, and as Colin comments here at the opening of Chapter 2, §. 2.ii); even the best theology we may hope to possess 'on the way' is beyond our individual reach, because our minds are limited and our hearts are sinful.

In stressing the limits of our theological knowing, however, we must never make the mistake of thinking that limitation necessarily implies inadequacy. If we ask 'Is our theology adequate?' the answer must take the form of another question: 'Adequate for what?' We never know enough to give an exhaustive account of God's act and being – of course not – but we trust that we know enough to speak adequately of God, and, more particularly, to hold firmly to the faith necessary for salvation.

Colin traces the history of such questions, stressing how much they are characteristic of the modern age. It was not that theologians of previous ages were uninterested in the relationship between Revelation and reason: Irenaeus, Origen and Thomas all appear to make that point; but they lived in a context where the fact of Revelation could be assumed. It is the modern doubt about Revelation that makes the contrast with reason vital.

The reasons for that doubt are well enough known: the appalling experiences of the wars of religion were understood, rightly or wrongly, to be a result of the impossibility of judging between differing claims to Revelation without resorting to violence, and so Europe's intellectual elite gave themselves to the search for a shared rationality which was not tradition–specific. This was the Enlightenment (or this was one strand held more or less in common by the several national enlightenments, if you prefer). The search was for a firm foundation, an intellectual basis which no one could doubt.

Following T. F. Torrance, Colin was throughout his career fiercely critical of this intellectual programme; they both were required to deploy all their (remarkable, in both cases) intellectual powers to overcome the assumption that this must be right. Living in a context which is less inclined to assume the simple correctness of such ideas, I wonder if we should be more generous to our forebears? The quest was, after all, a noble one: if there happened to be such a foundation, it would be well worth finding. The problem was not the quest itself, nor even its failure (assuming that by now we can all agree that it has failed), but the assumption that gradually arose that what was being sought would be the basis on which the adequacy of theological claims would be judged. Academic theology was being given a different and, as Colin shows in these lectures, a foreign account of how its claims are justified. It was being rendered a less academic discipline.

I think the history of this is a bit more complicated than Colin allows in these lectures (I could say the same about several other matters…): Descartes and Locke and the rest were not consciously trying to supplant Christian theology, so much as assuming that the best dictates of reason would inevitably accord with the content of Revelation, and then struggling to cope when it appeared to them that this assumption was not well founded. Colin's telling of intellectual history is often enough impressionistic, offering heightened contrasts, bold colours and stark lines; like a great painting, however, if it distorted the appearance of reality somewhat it was only to reveal more clearly the essence of what was being looked at. Colin gets right to the heart of the problem that the 'Enlighteners' created for Christian theology with stunning clarity; if he slightly misrepresents this or that figure along the way, this is no doubt a fault, but in the context of a lecture course designed 'to make you think like theologians', the big picture, the essential intellectual issue, was the thing, not nice historical details.

After the Enlighteners, liberals and existentialists, once again, the reality of the matter is exposed in merciless clarity. In Schleiermacher or Bultmann, it is just another form of 'foundationalism', another way of looking for justifications alien to theology on which the discipline may establish itself – or at least an apparently acceptable parody of itself. Deriving theological justification from a claimed universal religious experience is no different, at heart, to deriving it from a claimed universal rational basis. Once again, the discipline is being asked to be un-academic, to ignore its own coherence and its own native methodology in order to appear more acceptable to the surrounding culture. The point, finally, of all this is precisely coherence. Theology claims to be speaking about ultimate reality, and to be dealing with texts and people, and particularly an institution – the Christian church – that claim a privileged insight into the nature and intentions of ultimate reality. These claims may be right, or they may be wrong, but they cannot be irrelevant to the way theology proceeds. No discipline can rationally make a claim about the basic nature of reality, and then seek to found it on a different claim: simple logic demands as much.

T. F. Torrance's investigations of the idea of 'theological science' (discussed in Chapter 2, §. 2) trace these arguments most effectively, and get us back to the question of objectivity. The argument above defends the self-sufficiency of theology but not the place of faith commitment within it. Torrance, following Polanyi, stresses the personal component of any human knowledge; he also stresses the necessity for an academic discipline to be shaped according to its subject matter. On the one hand, Polanyi gave to Torrance, and to Gunton (for Colin's early interest in Polanyi see the much-neglected *Enlightenment and Alienation* from 1985), the idea that knowledge presupposes a knower, and that Locke's notion of the knowing mind as a mere blank sheet, a tabula rasa, was inadequate. I bring the sum of my experiences and intuitions about life to the evidence I amass; I cannot do otherwise. Generally, the truly great scholars in any academic discipline are those whose intuitions are well-shaped from the point of view of the discipline; they are characterized by their ability to be right more often than not in their hunches and 'gut-feelings'. On the other hand, Torrance, surely rightly, pressed the demand for coherence that I have sketched above and derived much more from it: if theology is to be properly academic, 'scientific' in Torrance's terms, then its claimed modes of knowing must align with its claims about the nature of things. This brings us back to Revelation.

There is a sense in which these two conceptions (Polanyian 'personal knowledge' and Torrance on the 'scientific' nature of theology) coalesce, and they coalesce around the notion that faith commitment is important in thinking like a theologian. In Polanyian terms, one who is accustomed to living in ways shaped by the Christian gospel is likely to have well–formed intuitions about the way that gospel will work out. In more theological terms, if Revelation is understood as a gift, a gift related to response in faith, to faithful Christian practice, to life within ecclesial fellowship, then all these things should, by straightforward logic, be assumed to be important for the practice of theological reasoning.

* * *

Concretely, where is Revelation to be found? The united Christian answer is 'scripture'. This might be glossed in various ways, and other locations for Revelation might be added alongside, but on this point there is at least unanimity. The exploration of the doctrine of scripture takes up Chapter 3 in this volume.

The doctrine of scripture is first put in context: in recent theology, the point has been made repeatedly that the primary locus of Revelation is the person of Jesus Christ. (Colin's students didn't make this point the year these lectures were recorded, but we might ask, would the Fathers, Schoolmen and Reformers have disagreed? I think the answer is slightly complicated: they might have agreed with the statement, but they would have understood something sufficiently different by it that they would not have drawn the same consequences from the statement as we do. The key to this is the word 'person': this carries a very particular connotation for anyone after the Romantic period. The Fathers would have been more interested in the nature of Christ's being; the Reformers in the history of his actions.) We need to take another step backwards again, however – and here we are in the territory Colin mapped out in his 'Warfield Lectures', published as *A Brief Theology of Revelation.*[1] What do we mean by 'Revelation'? Coleridge shows the way: we mean knowledge that is received as a gift, and so all truth is a species of Revelation. When we turn to the scriptures, again we are following Coleridge,

[1] Colin E. Gunton, *A Brief Theology of Revelation* (Edinburgh: T&T Clark, 1995). This work contains the series of six lectures Colin Gunton gave at Princeton Theological Seminary in 1993, the Warfield Lectures.

the posthumously published *Confessions of an Inquiring Spirit.*[2] The gift is given first to the writers of scripture, who record as they are inspired to do; but the words themselves are not the gift – they are the record of, and can be again the occasion for, God's sovereign gracious act of revealing.

Obviously Karl Barth is behind all this somewhere, but this is not straight Barth: Colin suggested that Barth is rather too focused on what happens to the reader of scripture, and needed a more adequate account of what scripture is in itself because God inspired its writers, not just what it might become for us as God meets us through it. (In recent terms, Colin believed Barth was overly actualistic in his account of scripture, and needed a better account of its enduring substance…) But whatever account we give of scripture, for Colin its importance was as a locus of mediation. This book is a place where God graciously gives himself in the person of his Son to his people.

A writer from a different ecclesial tradition might have had more to say about tradition under this head; Colin covered the Roman Catholic view fairly sketchily, with several rather sweeping assertions that might be considered misrepresentations by those more knowledgeable about that tradition. The Creeds get the merest nod (Chapter 4, §. 3.ii), oddly, given the importance attached to them at the beginning of the lectures (Chapter 1, §. 2.vi). I think Colin was more comfortable with the earlier notion of a 'rule of faith', defined by its content, not by a strict verbal rule, and permitting some creative re-statement by individual teachers to meet the needs of the day. I am sure that there was nothing in the Nicene Creed he disagreed with (excepting the later Western addition of the filioque, of course); but the mind of the church, the apostolic deposit that has been passed down, is both more and less than a verbal formula.

* * *

Much of these lectures are taken up with examinations of the history of theology. Colin's approach to the history deserves comment. He was master of the grand historical narrative, and would tell big stories spanning centuries to illustrate what he regarded as the key historical developments. Examples in this book are not hard to find. For Colin 'history', particularly the history of theology, meant something: it was a series of lessons in how beliefs propagate and distort, how a wrong emphasis that enters the tradition grows and evolves to produce serious consequences centuries later, or how a brilliant mind might cut through all the cultural accommodations of his (almost always…) time and recall the church, or at least those parts of it that would listen, to the gospel.

2 *Confessions of an Inquiring Spirit* was published in London by W. Pickering in 1840. For a contemporary edition see, Samuel Taylor Coleridge, *Confessions of an Inquiring Spirit and some Miscellaneous Pieces* (Lennox, MA: Hard Press Editions, 2006).

To say that these big stories needed nuancing is to miss their point: Colin was not trying to give a full and adequate narrative in the history of ideas, but trying to illustrate the nature of systematic theology. Ideas make a difference to each other; one wrong note echoes down through the symphony, affecting every theme in surprising and significant ways. Of course, this basic understanding of history might be felt to be unacceptable by one or another reader: perhaps it appears too simplistic; perhaps the notion that ideas connect quite so straightforwardly may be doubted. Consider, however, the effect on the students. Colin's grand narratives would give them both a map, however lacking in detail, against which they could plot figures in theological history, and, much more importantly, it gave them a sense of why the things they were studying mattered. Theology, on Colin's telling, has consequences; it is worth giving time and effort to; it is a way, an important way, of serving the churches, and of serving the church.

I have admitted elsewhere in print that I do not find all of Colin's big stories convincing. Here, I confess to wincing somewhat at the characterization of the medieval period. Greek and Hebrew mindsets are held to be fundamentally opposed (the day will come when theologians stop believing Von Harnack on this, and it cannot come too soon); Greece offering a quest for God by our own (rational) effort, and Israel God's gracious gift of himself. In Augustine (of course…) the two are married, into a strange semi-Pelagianism: whereby we ascend as far as our reason will take us, and then God rewards our efforts with the gift of Revelation. And this is the view that characterizes the Middle Ages.

For myself, I do not suppose Augustine was any more Pelagian here than in his strictures about salvation. *De Trinitate* is clear enough on the matter: 'This is my faith, because it is the faith of the church'. *Fides quaerens intellectum* is characteristically Augustinian, and surely a more adequate picture of the whole scholastic enterprise (Aquinas as well as Anselm) than the one Colin offers in these lectures. But at worst, at least Colin offered something worth disagreeing with!

To the knowledgeable reader, when the details of the various accounts of the history of theology are perused, it is also not hard to find examples of – politely, we might say over-simplification; less politely, distortion or even sometimes actual error. Please remember, these are transcripts of lectures, and of 'off-the-cuff' responses in seminars. Sometimes, no doubt, Colin's comments were phrased unfortunately; sometimes he might have been reaching for a fairly hazy memory. I do not suppose any of us would be very comfortable having verbatim reports of our conversations with students published without being able to check facts and references fully first; but that is all we have here.

Finally under this head, anyone who knew Colin would have to admit his willingness to be corrected from the text. Whatever ideas he had, he always showed an admirable respect for the scholarly evidence. Confronted with a quotation that contradicted his interpretation, he would readily concede the point. This, incidentally, is one of the reasons for some of his idiosyncratic interpretations: Colin was never content with knowing and repeating the 'standard scholarly line' on anyone; he always went to the primary texts, read them, and came to his own judgements about what they said. When he began as a young lecturer in the philosophy of religion, he simply read through the history of Western philosophy, thinker by thinker, text by text, and taught what he read there.

The third major division of these lectures is Barth. I have written elsewhere about the importance of Barth for Colin's theology, and about aspects of his interpretations of Barth. Here the point to note is this: if Colin was trying in this course to teach his students to 'think like theologians', Colin believed he learnt this skill himself primarily from reading Barth. The influence of his Doktorvater, for a year at least, Robert Jenson, should not be discounted, of course; but basically it was Barth.

Why Barth? Why not Calvin or Irenaeus – or indeed St Paul or St John? The reason is in these lectures: the section on Barth begins with lengthy discussions of Kant, Hegel and Schleiermacher. Barth, alone among the truly great theologians in Colin's opinion, is one of us, he is modern, and does theology while conscious of that. In fact, for Colin, this might be precisely Barth's greatness: he is the one person in the modern era who actually grasped what it is to do theology. If the rest of us do theology after Barth, then that is only because he has shown us that it is possible, and what it looks like. Once again, many readers will be crying out for nuance and qualification: What of those from whom Barth learnt – Dorner, perhaps? And is Barth's apparently lifelong commitment to Herrmann's demolition of metaphysics really the only way forward? But, and again, these are lectures to students beginning their graduate studies: for Colin, always, the big idea was the thing; nuance and qualification could come later. And so a familiar tale is told of Barth's destruction of his liberal inheritance, based in pastoral experience and the shock of the war, followed by politicization and then the return to scripture in Romans. Paul Brazier weaves in material on Bultmann here, as a counterpoint to the existentialism of Barth's early dialectical theology. Colin ran the parallel of Bultmann with Heidegger rather than with Barth, which throws into sharp relief what is Christian in Bultmann's theology, rather than focusing, as so many theologians do, on what is judged to be inadequate.

From Anselm, we get the core notion of 'the epistemological priority of God'. God is true rationality; theology is rational insofar as it corresponds to the truth, God. From the debate with Brunner, we get the single focus on Christ. And so Barth provides the model for Colin's account of the relationship of Revelation and reason: reason is dependent on Revelation, on God's own act and being, and on God's revelation of himself in Christ.

* * *

These raw transcripts of lectures, seminars and discussions, of unprepared responses and of quick oral surveys, are obviously unpolished and contain many flaws of emphasis and even of fact. Paul Brazier has done a remarkable job in making something connected out of them, but they remain what they are, with all the inevitable imperfections. To focus on these imperfections, however, would be to miss the point. Colin aimed to enable the students to think like theologians; overly general historical claims, questionable interpretations or assertions, could all be corrected later; what was at stake was a habit of mind, a way of understanding theology as the church's science, that is only authentically itself, and so only properly academic, when it is prepared to assume the rightness of the gospel. In a recent online discussion about the vocation of a theologian I wrote these words:

> *I think a good theologian prays well, first. No theologian who doesn't has even begun to understand the discipline. And then s/he serves the Church, and his or her particular part of it (down to a local congregation) in humility and faithfulness. Theology belongs to the Church; any theologian divorced from the Church is a bad theologian, however brilliant or knowledgeable. A good theologian has a grasp of gospel values, and would swap everything s/he has written to see one sinner repent, or one broken life healed. A good theologian writes and speaks only to help the Church be more faithful to the gospel, bringing whatever knowledge of the tradition, whatever insight into contemporary modes of thought, and whatever native cleverness s/he may possess, all into service of this one end. A good theologian is marked by humility and cheerfulness, knowing how far short of the mystery of God and God's works his/her best efforts fall, and knowing that in the good grace of God something of lasting worth may still come from them. A good theologian, finally, does know something, and has some capacity of thought, and so can make a contribution through his/her God-given vocation.*

This was written quickly, and expresses an instinctive understanding of what it is that we, as academic theologians, do. It is an understanding that was formed in me more by Colin's precept and example than anything else. Since I wrote this, enough people have commented that it expresses something helpful that I repeat it here, because if there is anything of worth in it, it is no more than an expression of some of what Colin sought to teach and to model for all his students in his annual lectures on Revelation and Reason.

Stephen R. Holmes
St Mary's College, St Andrews

Part One : From Reason and Revelation to Revelation and Reason

Chapter 1

CHRISTIAN DOCTRINE AND SYSTEMIZATION

1. Revelation and Reason

Right, so, 'From Reason and Revelation to Revelation and Reason': the aim of this course is to make you think like theologians. You will by Christmas think theologically! You may all have started this course for various reasons but that is what this particular course is about: to make you think theologically. Yes, undergraduates will start to think theologically – one hopes – but this is where you really should start to think seriously and deeply, and develop your own skills. So, why Revelation and reason? For that matter why the title: 'From Reason and Revelation to Revelation and Reason'? Well, theologically, for much of the twentieth century religious belief has been seen as going from reason to Revelation, from reason towards Revelation, starting with reason, you see. Nowadays many would prefer, I believe, to see the priority and the debate going not from reason but from revelation to reason. Are the two alternatives? You might ask are there really two alternatives. Well, not necessarily so. You might ask should Revelation be all–encompassing – not necessarily so.

Now, is there a textbook you ask; if there is a textbook for this course then I suppose I would recommend you reading my book on Revelation. It's not really a textbook and the material in this course has changed much since those lectures were given – which was in a different context to this course; and this course changes each year according to the students on the course, but, yes, I would certainly recommend you read that book, but what we say together here, now that's important![1] But it's more than that; this course is not really about textbooks, it is about reading the actual people – Descartes and Locke, Kant, Schleiermacher and Hegel, Torrance and Barth, all these people who had so much to say about whether theology was possible and how we valued reason, our capacity, you see, to reason

1 Colin E. Gunton, *A Brief Theology of Revelation* (Edinburgh; T&T Clark, 1995). This work contains the series of six lectures Colin Gunton gave at Princeton Theological Seminary in 1993, the Warfield Lectures.

things out. Read these people; read them and argue with them. That's what this course is about.

So, Revelation and reason; it seems to me not that the two have to be treated as alternatives but that putting it as from Revelation to reason has the significance of embracing everything under a theological rubric, a single theological rubric. To say that reason, as it were, operates within the sphere of Revelation is to say that this is not a philosophical course; it's not actually a philosophical course, it's a theological course, a course in theology even though you cannot avoid the philosophical dimensions of it.

So what is systematic theology? – well for a start it's what we're doing. But anyway, systematic theology is what happens when theology engages with philosophy: therefore reason should be discussed theologically. Although people think they know what reason is, by and large they are not clear. This is, I think, yes, very important: reason should be discussed theologically.

Paul Tillich's systematic theology shows that there are many ways in which reason can be understood.[2] What does Tillich say? – Tillich distinguishes between two forms of reason: instrumental reason and ontological reason.[3] This is all well and good but Tillich does not come up with a clear-cut answer as to what Revelation or reason is.

i. Systematic Theology

So what is systematic theology? What is it to be systematic? This is something I suppose we need to sort out right from the start. By and large people can only speak about what they think it may mean initially, they can then go on to say what others think. Systematic theology is, to me at least, not to do with the construction of systems; it's not about reducing Christianity to a system or ordering it into such a neat manner that it is all tied up. It is more about being systematic in a general way. You can lay a dinner table in a systematic way: this means laying it out in the best possible way so that it is clear, comprehensible, functional – all the elements, cutlery and so on, relate and function together. So it seems to me that you can be systematic without having a system. But where does the concept come from? Where does the concept of systematic theology come from in the first place? On the whole, systematic theology is a modern concept: systematicity is a modern

2 Paul Tillich, *Systematic Theology* (3 volumes; Chicago, IL: University of Chicago Press, 1951–63. Volume 1: *Reason and Revelation, Being and God* (1951); Volume 1: *Existence and the Christ* (1957); Volume 1: *Life and the Spirit: History and the Kingdom of God* (1963). See: Volume 1: *Reason and Revelation, Being and God*, Part 1 Reason and Revelation, ch. III 'The Structure of Reason', pp. 79–118. See also, generally, ch. I 'The Nature of Systematic Theology', in particular 'Theology and Philosophy: A Question', pp. 21–25; also, ch. II 'The Method and Structure of Systematic Theology', in particular 'The Rational Character of Systematic Theology', pp. 59–67.

3 'Ontological reason can be defined as the structure of the mind which enables it to grasp and to shape reality', Paul Tillich, *Systematic Theology*. Volume 1:*Reason and Revelation, Being and God*, p. 83. See also, Part 1 Reason and Revelation, ch. III 'The Structure of Reason', pp. 79f. The two concepts of reason are dealt with on pp. 79–80, inc. ontological reason, p. 81; in addition, Tillich deals with the concept of subjective and objective reason on pp. 83–87.

concept. It arises about the same time as modern culture, about the same time as modern philosophy, historiography and science arise.[4]

If you want a history of it, a history of systematicity and how it arose, then Nicholas Rescher's book, *Cognitive Systemization*, that will give you a history of the, well, the idea as we can call it. [5] The origins of the concept of system, systemizing, derive from the Greeks – from Greek cosmology, possibly from the Stoics who talked about a world system. You see, you have to note the objective here: a systematic organization of reality; you see, a systematic ordering, organizing of reality, well, what they took to be reality. And you see for the Stoics this was essentially pantheistic – because the world was fundamentally divine, OK, they saw the world as fundamentally divine, so it is fair to say that for them this world view was pantheistic. And Rescher, in his work, charts the movement away from the objective to the subjective. So, you see, the system, any system, is now a construct of human thought, rather than a description of reality, therefore it becomes subjective. I think he's right, quite right; you see this is absolutely characteristic of modernity. Hence you have thought rather than observation: it is the organizing mind that comes into play here, no longer reality.

ii. Kierkegaard

This is, of course, characteristic of the eighteenth and nineteenth centuries. This is typical of Schleiermacher in theology and Hegel in philosophy; they are characteristic of this, they are both characteristic of this approach. You see Hegel is the great systematizing philosopher. For Hegel, the whole of human culture was to be organized into a philosophical system that expressed the movement of the world spirit. For Hegel the key to this was the human mind before it, in front of, or comprehending it: the human mind was before the world, comprehending and systemizing it. The problem with this, in fact there are lots of problems with this approach, but the main, the key problem, I think, is that the word 'God' is resistant to systematizing – if not the word 'God' (as 'god' means different things — note 'god' with a lower case 'g') then the Christian Gospel. The Christian Gospel is always resistant to pigeonholing. I think it is fair to say, it is fundamental, yes it is fundamental, that if you think you have got the Christian world view organized, then you haven't. This is the view of Karl Barth. Once you fully organize your theology into a system, then it becomes a philosophy and it is no longer open, it is no longer an eschatologically open gospel which it has to be.

If we look at this further, deeper, then there are at least two reasons for this; there are two reasons in particular for this and they are expressed by Søren Kierkegaard: they are first, intellectual and second, moral (figure 1).

4 Colin E. Gunton, 'A Rose by any Other Name?', in *International Journal of Systematic Theology* 1.1 (1999), pp. 4-23.

5 Nicholas Rescher, *Cognitive Systematization. A Systems–Theoretic Approach to a Coherentist Theory of Knowledge* (Totowa, NJ: Rowman and Littlefield, 1979).

First, the intellectual reason; you see it means one thing to be God, quite another to be human. Because Christianity's centre is Jesus Christ who is both God and human, it means that if you think you have organized Christianity into a system, you haven't. There is something intrinsically resistant to systematizing in any theology based upon the doctrine of the Incarnation – or the doctrine of God-and-man in Christ. That's Kierkegaard's view, and it is not a view about the absurdity of Christianity. It is often made to be that, but it is not Kierkegaard's view that Christianity is absurd. If you read Murray Rae's book on Kierkegaard you'll see this spelt out very clearly.[6] It is part of the logic of Christianity that the givenness of God and man side-by-side requires a certain openness of concept, because it is simply not possible to incorporate the divine and the human into one philosophical system. Kierkegaard's chief opponent in this was Hegel: Kierkegaard believed that Hegel turned the gospel into its opposite. He is right; I think he – Kierkegaard – is right in his criticism of Hegel.

Second, moral: not only is the subject matter of theology impossible, but the human being is incapable. Why? – because the human being is finite and, of course, the key to this finitude, this limit is heightened by human sin; so that the human moral reality militates against organizing completely accurately: we are incapable of a full and accurate systematizing of the gospel. So we cannot do truly systematic theology, we cannot truly be systematic.

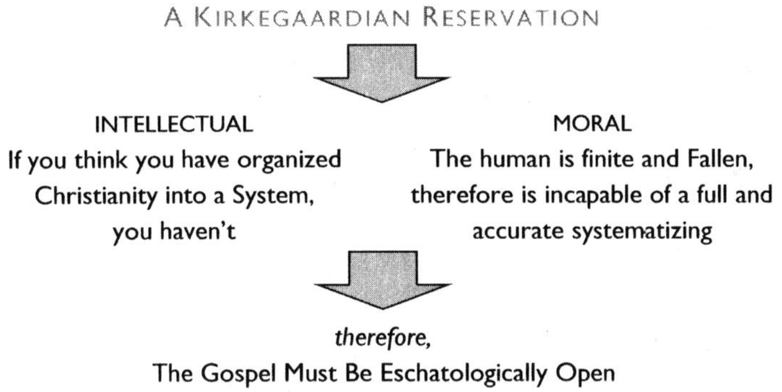

Figure 1

6 Murray Rae, *Kierkegaard's Vision of the Incarnation: by Faith Transformed* (Oxford: Clarendon Press; Oxford University Press, 1997).

2. The Christian Claims to Knowledge [7]

If we cannot be truly systematic then what is the basis of Christian doctrine? For that matter what is the basis for a Christian claim to know? *'I Know that my Redeemer Lives'* (Job 19.23-7): What is the ground to the Christian claims for knowledge? The Letter of James says *'You believe that God is one; you do well. Even the demons believe – and shudder'* (Jas 2.19). Calvin asserts that all right knowledge of God is born of obedience[8] – that is important, crucially important, if we are to understand how we can know God, we must be obedient and respectful to the object of our study – to God, we must be open to how *He* has revealed *Himself*.

i. Between Gnosis and Doubt

There are a number of difficulties facing Christian claims for truth – claims that we know things others do not. Some of these things will be culturally contingent, others intrinsic to the faith. There are intrinsic difficulties surrounding the verb, 'to know'. This is related to the problem of knowledge – these problems are yet to be resolved. Different meanings of the word confuse the matter. Human relationships to God, different cultures and traditions, mean that concepts of 'to know' will be manifold. Then, you see, knowing someone well is not the same as knowing a set of statistics. And however well you know someone there will always be something of them you don't know; we can never disclose our true selves, fully. We also need to understand the biblical uses of the term 'to know'.

Theologically there are two chief problems: Gnosticism is one problem; in addition the dogmas of the unknowability of God are the other side of Gnosticism. Certain claims for knowledge are simply ruled out for Christians, an argument pursued at length by the early Fathers in the refutation of the heresies since known as Gnostic. Gnosticism is simply, perhaps too simply, the possession of a knowledge perhaps hidden from others and involves at the same time a claim to a sort of esoteric or superior knowledge transmitted by a secret tradition.

Condemning this is one thing, but how do you justify theological knowledge that is outside of the perception, or seemingly outside the perception, of ordinary people. You see, that's the question. And where is election? – Are some given to know some things about the mystery of God, things that are hidden from others?

[7] This section is derived from an early version of a paper Prof. Gunton presented to the Research Institute in Systematic Theology at King's College London on the morning of 28 September 1999. A fuller version of the paper, including changes as a result of the questions and discussion, was published a year later: Colin E. Gunton, '"I Know that my Redeemer Lives": A Consideration of Christian Knowledge Claims', in Colin E. Gunton, *Intellect and Action: Elucidations on Christian Theology and the Life of Faith* (Edinburgh: T&T Clark, 2000), pp. 46–65.

[8] *'Omnis recta cognitio del ab obedientia nascitur'*, John Calvin, *Institutes of the Christian Religion*, Vol. 1 (ed. John T. McNeill; Library of Christian Classics; Louisville, KY: Westminster John Knox Press, 2006 [1960]), Bk. I. Ch. vi. §. 2, p. 72.

You see, this is what Paul is dealing with when he is writing to the Christians at Corinth: the Corinthian correspondence, it's dealing with this question of knowledge, hidden knowledge, and how we relate and behave to those who do not 'know' the faith. Paul's polemics: if the polemics of the Corinthian epistles are understood to be directed against some form of proto-Gnosticism, the eschatological dimensions of the issue become apparent. Paul's opponents claim that by virtue of being raised to a higher life they are already above the usual requirements of holy living. This is undoubtedly the case with Irenaeus' opponents. They believe themselves to be enlightened with knowledge different and more superior to that which is available to those who only hear of the established tradition.

The heart of the Irenaean counter to all, or partial, Gnosticisms is that salvation is not by the possession of some knowledge, but only by the publicly proclaimed Incarnation: the objective content of the gospel rather than the hold of the subject upon it. The limits of the human knowledge of God are also set by the attribute that there has always been: *His* unknowability. This is a doctrine, which has had a serious effect upon the history of theology.

We can all too easily talk about God in terms of mysticism, but, the *doctor ignorantia* can easily lead to agnosticism; here again the antidote is the Incarnation. If Jesus Christ is the revelation of God the Father then a claim for revelation contains a corresponding claim for knowledge on the part of those who acknowledge the Incarnation.

However, we must affirm the subjective knowledge. This leaves open the status of such knowledge. How though do we relate this on the one hand to Gnosticism and on the other to God's unknowability? The extrinsic difficulties for those who would lay claim to theological knowledge arise from the cultural dimensions of the problem which, I believe, Paul shows in 1 Corinthians:

> *For Jews demand signs and Greeks desire wisdom, but we proclaim Christ crucified, a stumbling-block to Jews and foolishness to Gentiles, but to those who are the called, both Jews and Greeks, Christ the power of God and the wisdom of God.* 1 Cor. 1.22

Being loosely glossed this might read –

> *Modernists seek certainty; postmodernists deny it, but we? What do we claim and proclaim?*

What do we claim and proclaim? Does faith expect a kind of certainty, an assurance? Calvin commented that the knowledge of faith should be in assurance, rather than comprehension. How are we to avoid on the one hand salvation by doubt, and on the other an over–confidence in our certainty.

Too much may be made of the postmodern suspicion of knowledge that it hides a will to power and domination. Many Enlightenment claims are solved by reason and science – this is different from traditional forms of knowledge. This does, however, bear the hallmarks of Gnosticism. However, we must remember that Christian claims to knowledge have been, and still are, employed repressively. Our intellectual enterprises will be marked by the context within which they are carried on. Barth affirmed we cannot avoid using the concepts of the philosophers because we operate on the same field of contention as they – classically.[9]

Similarly there are knowledge claims even in modernist denials that we can know theologically in the way we once claimed to do. Or similarly in postmodernism there are strong affirmations that there is no knowledge: this is implicitly a denial of postmodernist claims – though their epistemology even denies this! We may be in danger of being a generation that loses knowledge in a welter of useless information. Yet to convey information is to convey what is known. It is interesting in the age when the market economy dominates all, and when many universities claim to be marketing or selling knowledge, that Justin Martyr claimed that at least Christianity, unlike the other philosophical schools, did not charge for its knowledge.[10] To Justin Martyr this was one of the characteristics, which confirmed the authenticity of Christianity. But once again we are, are we not, at the knife-edge of gnosis and doubt?

ii. Aspects of Biblical Teaching

Knowledge as teaching: according to the Bible, aspects of the knowledge of God are teachable. Brian Haymes sees this in the Old Testament: 'Hear O Israel, the Lord our God is One Lord...'.[11] Hearing this is important, it becomes knowledge. Haymes comments that to be taught these things about God was to have knowledge about God. It is this knowledge rather than any particular acquaintance or experience that is foundational for most of the people of Israel.

So we are concerned with various forms of knowledge. There is also the instance of the knowledge of self-knowledge in David's experience before Nathan the Prophet (2 Sam. 11.27–12.15): the fruit of revelation through parable. David hears a story, but the meaning is clear: he is the man. Similarly Jesus in the synoptic gospels demonstrates in no uncertain terms that certain things about the grace and sovereignty of the God of Israel are teachable beyond peradventure. Jesus knows things: facts. John's Gospel theologizes the matter – Jesus often says '*are you a teacher of Israel and you do not know these things*' (Jn 3.10). Jesus communicates the knowledge of God in what can only be called propositional terms: '*we speak of what we know and bear witness to what we have seen*' (Jn 3.11). So also it is with the apostles teaching: the faith, once and for all delivered to the saints.

9 See, for example, Karl Barth, 'Fate and Idea in Theology' (English translation of 'Schicksal und Idee', lecture delivered at the Hochschulinstitut in Dortmund, February to March, 1929), in H. Martin Rumscheidt (ed.), *The Way of Theology in Karl Barth: Essays and Comments* (Intro. Stephen W. Sykes; Allison Park, PA.: Pickwick Publications, 1986), pp. 25–62.

10 See, Justin Martyr's *First Apology*, specifically §. 1–12: Karen O'Dell Bullock, *Shepherd's Notes: Writings of Justin Martyr* (Nashville, TN: B&H Publishing Group, 1999).

11 Brian Haymes, *The Concept of the Knowledge of God* (New York, NY: St Martin's Press, 1988). Note, this is the opening of 'The Shema', a series of readings from the Pentateuch which are prayed on a daily basis by Jews: Deut. 6.4-9 and 11.13-21, and Num. 15.37-41. (Editor.)

This is to be conveyed through the ages as knowledge of God and salvation. We can scarcely begin to quantify the volume of knowledge available for teaching in the pages of scripture, and the theological tradition which stems from it. This knowledge is saving knowledge: it is revealed, it is given – to know it is to know something of the source and content of salvation.

We need to remember again Justin Martyr's contention that Christianity is the true philosophy. We must again consider what type of knowledge it is that is given. This knowledge can be distinguished from other forms of knowledge as it is *revealed* knowledge. That is to say, knowledge that is not intrinsic to the knower because it is given by God: in other words it's distinctive form is that it is given by God.

Paul hands on what he has received: what was vouchsafed to him above all in the revelatory self-presentation of the Lord to him on the road to Damascus, and in the instruction he received subsequent to it. However, once committed to writing, this is a knowledge which can be obtained by reading; those who fail to read and learn are simply culpable: those who fail to read, fail to know, fail to recognize and understand what is there. Scripture needs to be interpreted.

Take the story of Philip and the Ethiopian in Acts: although Jesus is set forth in the words of Isaiah, the Ethiopian does not understand, he does not know: he has to be taught with the authority of one who does know[12] – however objective the word of God is it has yet to become so for the believer. We are here in the realm of knowledge by divine revelation. As the words in the story of Peter's confession demonstrate.[13] This combines an essential teaching of the unknowability of God with a definite claim for revelation. God's only Son has made him known.[14] Paul speaks in his Letter to the Ephesians of knowing the love of Christ, which surpasses knowledge. The control is Christological, yet it involves remarkably confident claims. Paul speaks of the assurance of this.[15]

You see, the theological pitfall is that this form of knowledge can destroy as much as it edifies. Take Paul's dispute with the Corinthian followers over their knowledge that idols do not exist, this dispute is particularly instructive. He concedes in one sense to their knowledge: the gods and demons do not exist, and therefore meat offered to them is indistinguishable from meat slaughtered other ways. Yet it remains the case that, quite apart from these subtleties, it was clear to Paul that sharing in the festivities of the Pagans risks going into the realm of the demonic, in the same way as deviant sexual practices do.

There is therefore a knowledge, which puffs up rather than builds up. Therefore we should place our forms of knowledge on a hierarchy and acknowledge that this, though important, is not at the top of the pile.

12 Acts 8.27-38.

13 'And Jesus answered him, "Blessed are you, Simon son of Jonah! For flesh and blood has not revealed this to you, but my Father in heaven"' (Mt. 16.17).

14 'No one has ever seen God. It is God the only Son, who is close to the Father's heart, who has made him known' (Jn 1.18; cf. 1 Jn 4.12).

15 'I want their hearts to be encouraged and united in love, so that they may have all the riches of assured understanding and have the knowledge of God's mystery, that is, Christ himself' (Col. 2.2).

iii. Knowledge of the Heart

We are at the point where we need to acknowledge that there is knowledge of God which is of the heart and is superior to knowledge as set out so far. For example, Jeremiah conveys to Israel that the Lord will put *His* law within them, and will write it on their hearts and will be their God, and they shall be *His* people, they shall *all* know me.[16]

This is about the teaching of the new covenant – not through teaching knowledge, but that all will know in the heart. Job's confession is similar. He says, *'I had heard of you by the hearing of the ear, but now my eye sees you; therefore I despise myself, and repent in dust and ashes'* (Job 42.5).

This knowledge has to be understood as knowledge in relation, in relationship. This is classically expounded in the fourth gospel. We will talk more about knowledge, revelatory knowledge and relationship later – it is important. In the fourth gospel this is knowledge mediated by the Incarnation. Central to this is John's pneumatology, which makes it clear that knowledge is being brought into relation with God the Father through the mediation of Jesus Christ: the Spirit leads into all truth.[17]

But we are told elsewhere in the gospel that truth is not primarily propositional. We must not forget that there are many propositions in this gospel. However, to know the kind of Jesus presented in this gospel is to know the truth. In other words what we are concerned with here is a kind of personal knowledge. Knowledge in the fourth gospel is indwelling. The relation of God the Father and God the Son is of a mutual indwelling which is expressed in the terms of personal knowledge rather like that which philosophers call 'knowledge by acquaintance'.

John's Gospel also makes the further point that the mutual indwelling of the Father and the Son is related to the indwelling of the Holy Spirit in the life of the church. We find the same ecclesiological connotations in Paul's use of the phrase 'in Christ'. Knowledge here is related to friendship, as in Abraham's relation to God. This personal knowledge has two dimensions:

relational
eschatological

Knowledge which is mediated by the spirit is a gift rather than possession, because it is a bringing into being by relation of the Father and the Son. Does this kind of

[16] 'The days are surely coming, says the Lord, when I will make a new covenant with the house of Israel and the house of Judah. It will not be like the covenant that I made with their ancestors when I took them by the hand to bring them out of the land of Egypt – a covenant that they broke, though I was their husband, says the Lord. But this is the covenant that I will make with the house of Israel after those days, says the Lord: I will put my law within them, and I will write it on their hearts; and I will be their God, and they shall be my people. No longer shall they teach one another, or say to each other, "Know the Lord", for they shall all know me, from the least of them to the greatest, says the Lord; for I will forgive their iniquity, and remember their sin no more' (Jer. 31.31-4).

[17] Jn 16.13.

knowledge incorporate and marginalize the propositional? For example, Frances Watson comments –

> *This 'knowing-that' is inseparable from the 'knowing-of' the Father as 'the only true God and Jesus Christ whom you have sent', which is presented here as the definition of 'eternal life' (17.3). How could one know the Father who sends and Jesus Christ who is sent without knowing that the Father sends and Jesus Christ is sent?* [18]

This is presented as a definition of eternal life: How can one know the Father and Jesus Christ who is sent without knowing that the Father sends and that Jesus Christ is sent? This implies propositional claims, though this is not what it entails: γνῶσις (gnosis) as a noun in John's Gospel and in Paul's epistles is almost entirely subordinated to verbal forms – knowing is something that is done because of a relation to God in Christ. This should lead to a diminution of the kind of boasting of knowledge of God and salvation of which Paul is so critical.

The Trinitarian matrix is also clear from 1 Corinthians. Paul's claim in 1 Corinthians that we have the mind of Christ – and surely this is an apostolic *'we'* – is almost certainly not an ironical quotation but an assertion made positively: those in this relationship may confidently claim a certain kind of knowledge because God has given it to them – hence the pneumatological.

The eschatological dimension is often brought out by Paul in that it is more important to be known than to know. To know that one is known is a form of knowledge. However, the form of the relation is the condition of those who are now known as they are known. Hence this is another defence against a sort of Gnosticism: we know in part.[19] As everywhere in theology, you see, pneumatology and eschatology are inseparable in so far as the part anticipates the whole.

This is a confirmation not just of knowledge but also of wisdom. The modern world tends to equate knowledge with wisdom, but wisdom is far more to do with the knowledge of the heart, and with the embodied and patiently tested knowledge of the heart: Christian knowledge is inseparable from the wisdom that takes the form of love exercised in community. The whole of the Corinthian correspondence demonstrates this.

iv. Towards a Theological Synthesis

Knowledge as the knowledge of faith: the creedal or confessional nature of all our beliefs is summarized to a degree in church dogmas, the nature of the knowledge

[18] Colin Gunton is quoting from Francis Watson, 'Trinity and Community in Johannine Theology'. This is presumably an earlier version of a paper because the wording is slightly different from the published paper: Francis Watson, 'Trinity and Community: A Reading of John 17', in, *International Journal of Systematic Theology* 1.2 (July, 1999), pp. 164–84. A similar quote is to be found on p. 171.

[19] 1 Cor. 13.9.

with which we are concerned is somewhere between faith and sight. There still is a realm beyond faith to which we cannot go. Faith is a kind of personal knowledge, which by virtue of the fact that it is given, passively, remains outside of the control of its recipient.

It should not therefore be understood voluntaristically – as in the so-called 'leap of faith' (after Kierkegaard). This is because it is the instrument by which the human knower is related to God the giver. Faith is the only appropriate focus of the human knowledge of God because it is that which responds to the creator-creature relationship: faith, you see, faith – I am summarizing from the Congregational Union's declaration of faith here – faith in God is more than the affirmation of certain beliefs, it is a confident trust in God: it is the response of a whole person's life to God's claims and it finds its expression in worship.[20] It is important to remember that we worship God and this worship is equally as important as knowledge.

However, this begins to point to human fallibility, human wavering and sin. That is why faith will fall short of sight. This anticipatory and instrumental nature of faith can be found in Hebrews 11: faith celebrates the objective reality of the blessings for which we hope, a demonstration of events as yet unseen. Listen –

> *Now faith is the assurance of things hoped for, the conviction of things not seen. Indeed, by faith our ancestors received approval. By faith we understand that the worlds were prepared by the word of God, so that what is seen was made from things that are not visible.* Heb. 11.1

William Lane comments, that this interpretation is rhetorical and aphoristic in character, it offers not a form of definition, but a recommendation and celebration of the faith that results in the acquisition of life.[21]

Christians are in a form of relationship, rightly characterized as 'knowledge', which is the gift of the eschatological Spirit, and therefore not necessarily shared by those without that faith. Because this is only knowledge by gift and anticipation, it remains subject to the limits imposed by the human condition.

v. The Incarnational Ground of Knowledge Claims

The God made known through scripture, through the election of Israel, and through the Incarnation, is known through strict limits set by God: the creator is known only insofar as he interacts with the creation. That he does so in human beings indicates that he can be known, but this is, in Kierkegaard's famous description, *incognito.* It is important to remember that the human intellect cannot

20 Colin Gunton is summarizing from *A Declaration of Faith* (London: The Congregational Union of England and Wales, 1967), p. 9.

21 William L. Lane, *Hebrews 9–13 Word Biblical Commentary*, Vol. 47 (Dallas, TX: Word Books, 1991), pp. 325 and 328.

break through this *incognito*. It is the Incarnation that determines both the reality and the limits of the knowledge of God. Therefore, we must accept that the limits to the knowledge of God are set Christologically, not philosophically. That is so important. The Incarnation also sets the eschatological limits: his promise of the *parousia* is that there will be a universal and inescapable knowledge of God: so Christian knowledge is necessarily faith knowledge (figure 2).

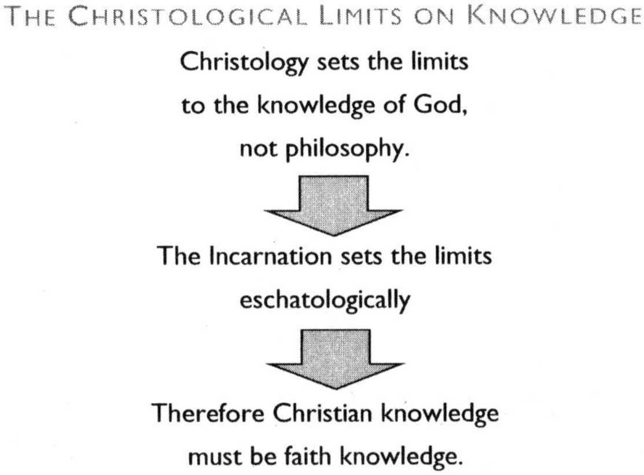

Figure 2

So, to summarize: the intellectual component – for there must be an intellectual component, otherwise how can we do theology let alone systematic theology and how else can we discuss revelation and reason – to summarize, the limitations on knowledge are:

personal – human weakness and sin
theological – the unknowability of God
eschatological – we know in part, and only as we are known

This is all seen in connection with scripture. This form of knowing necessarily involves an intellectual component as in the doctrine of creation: the word is creation because, and in so far as, it becomes the gift of God for us, whether we perceive it or not.

Perceiving things as what they are is part of our theological responsibility; this is seen as a concern for the internal coherence in the meaning of things known. This is true despite the limitations of the human mind's capacity to know and the limits on the human mind's capacity to order the things of God into systems: that is why we must be so wary about how we do systematic theology and how we discuss Revelation and reason.

Expressing and ordering the truth has nearly always been seen as the responsibility of the theologian. It has always been believed that the truth of things can be penetrated and expounded – to a degree. It is important to remember that, as Tom Torrance said, God's revelation of himself is not thwarted by our littleness or incapacity (figure 3).[22]

THE REVELATION OF GOD

God's revelation of *Himself*,

is not thwarted by our littleness

or by our incapacity.

Figure 3

Revelation is God making *Himself* knowable; more than that, it is making the human intellect able to appropriate this knowledge. It is important to remember that the Christian faith has always had an intellectual component. The Christian church has a proud tradition of producing outstanding intellects. However, it must be remembered that it is the intellectuals and those who have power in the church who are in the greatest danger of following forms of Gnosticism.

The limits of the intellectual are attested to by the notion of heresy – the premature solution of problems, or the claiming to know too much, too confidently! Many disputations were arrived at from claiming too confident a knowledge of the divine essence – claiming to penetrate to the heart of God's inner being. Once again this is about the limits of the human capacity to know. To know that we are known implies a propositional articulation, but woe to those who too confidently claim to possess knowledge. This is the greatness of Barth that he sees that propositional knowledge has its limits.

A modern example of this danger is an excessive confidence in the human capacity to systematize that which by virtue of God's unknowability is resistant to system. But; a serious but: despite all the provisos we must not deny the Incarnation.

The second aspect of the intellectual component concerns knowledge not of the internal truth and coherence of that which is revealed but of its implications for human knowledge of the world, that is its bearing, by virtue of its distinctive content on matters beyond its immediate subject matter.

The fact that God is made known through the mediation of his two hands – the Son and the Holy Spirit – has a direct bearing on the world and human life within it. There have therefore been unnecessary clashes with fashionable scientists when an acknowledgement of the limits of human theological knowability would

22 T. F. Torrance, *Transformation and Convergence within the Frame of Knowledge. Explorations in the Interrelations of Scientific and Theological Enterprise* (Belfast: Christian Journals, 1984), p. 292. Colin Gunton acknowledged that this source was from Matthias Clausen, 'Proclamation and Communication. Apologetics After Barth?', *International Journal of Systematic Theology*, 1.2 (1999), 203–19, p. 206.

have helped. Yet without Revelation we should lack knowledge of the human condition.

One of the implications of Revelation, says Barth, is to know the world as it is.[23] We know the world has been created because we observe the renewal of the world. The presence of God becomes known through actuality and possibility. To know that the world has been created and to know that God has visited and continues to visit it, to redeem it, this is a form of knowledge, which is there to those who have perceived it – is it not?

Despite all we have said of the limits to the knowledge of God and the unknowability of God, we must not deny the implications of the Incarnation, that God gives himself in Barth's words, to –

> *'...a real human viewing and conceiving.'*[24]

Knowledge is contingent. Knowledge is dependent upon an event: the Incarnation. We can speak of the needle eye of the Incarnation and the cross. You see, we as finite and fallen human beings know only contingencies. We may ask, 'Is all human knowledge fallible?' Despite the extremes of postmodern negation, which negates the ability to know, the stress on fallibility is important. We must avoid the impossibility of high standards. Often modern concepts have overstressed the ability to know, as in mathematics and science. Hence the over–realized eschatology of the Enlightenment is now in retreat; this must be seen as an encouragement. All other forms of knowledge can now see the position claimed by theology in the past – we are those who have not yet arrived at our destination.

You see, I think we can fairly say that knowledge is given to those who are bodily finite and in time and space. Holmes supports Coleridge's view that some knowledge can only be gained after a period of doubt as distinct from a rapid, logical unfolding.[25] Examination and self-questioning is important; examination and the ability to question yourself and your assumptions are important.

So where is the knowledge of the heart? It is not intellectual rationalism; the knowledge of the heart is not intellectual rationalism. But, then it is not experiential — neither is it experiential. It represents the whole person, compact of will, emotion and imagination to name but a few of what can be called our faculties.

So, where is God-given wisdom? We can fairly assert that we may hold firmly to what we believe to be true, even though I know that it may conceivably be false.

Uniqueness: there is uniqueness to this. Christian knowing will from the point of view of the knower, be just another form of relation to reality. Robert Jenson has commented:

[23] Karl Barth, *The Church Dogmatics* (eds G. W. Bromiley and T. F. Torrance; Edinburgh, T&T Clark, 1957), Vol. IV/3, §.72 'The Holy Spirit and The Sending of the Christian Community', p. 769.

[24] Karl Barth, *The Church Dogmatics* (eds G. W. Bromiley and T. F. Torrance; Edinburgh, T&T Clark, 1957), Vol. II/1, §.27 'The Limits of the Knowledge of God', p. 194.

[25] Richard Holmes, *Coleridge: Darker Reflections* (London: HarperCollins, 1998), p. 205.

> *Theology is ... 'metaphysics'. That is, it claims to know elements of reality that are not directly available to the empirical sciences or their predecessor modes of cognition, but that yet, must be known – if only subliminally – if such lower–level cognitive enterprises are to flourish. Theology claims to know the one God of all and so to know the decisive fact about all things, so that theology must be a universal and founding discipline or a delusion.* [26]

Hence the uniqueness of the Incarnation: it is a unique event available for all, not another object of inquiry. The Incarnation was brought about by the Spirit, hence it can only be known by the Spirit. We need to get away from the mechanics of knowing to that which is known.

vi. The Ecclesial Dimension

Does the Church know more than ordinary individuals? It is not so much Christians who know but the church! Now that's an interesting assertion, isn't it? If the church mediates revelation then this is an important question. You see, creeds and confession are set in the first person plural, aren't they: We believe. But do individuals believe? Do they know more in part than the community of faith which represents them in the world and before God?

This may be an idealist picture – indeed it may be seen to be a Catholic picture – but we need to acknowledge unknowing and fallibility. The Council of Chalcedon was divided as well as united; it divided those of theological difference. Even today, despite the heresy of much modern theology, the apostolic tradition has still been passed on relatively intact. Individuals falter and doubt – they are individuals, but the church as a community over time and space has confessed, more or less, confidently and united.

My former teacher Robert Jenson quotes Maximus the Confessor. This is an important quotation:

> *The one who knows the mystery of the cross and the tomb, knows the reasons of things. The one who is initiated into the infinite power of the resurrection knows the purpose for which God knowingly created all.* [27]

Jenson then comments –

> *Maximus' knowledge is that of a mystery into which initiates are baptised. Those who are baptised into Christ's death and say 'Amen' to the Eucharistic prayers, and who hold a*

[26] Robert Jenson, *Systematic Theology*, Vol. 1 (Oxford: Oxford University Press, 1997), p. 20.
[27] Maximus the Confessor, *Centuries*, 1108A–B. See: Polycarp Sherwood (ed.), *St Maximus the Confessor: The Ascetic Life, The Four Centuries on Charity* (Ancient Christian Writers; Mahwah, NJ: Paulist Press, 1955).

> *fraction of the bread, these are those who know the goodness of the creation. The great 'never-the-less' cannot finally be resolved from the conceptual outside, but it can be liturgically inhabited.*[28]

Therefore, we can say that cultic and personal knowledge are both important. Being in Christ involves a form of personal knowledge in God realized by participation in the worship and life of the church.

However, this – what might be called the cultic dimension of the matter – requires supplementing by a recurrence to the notion of personal knowledge, in order to bring out its broader participatory aspects. Being 'in Christ' involves a form of personal knowledge of God realized by participation in the worship and life of the church. This means that this knowledge cannot be reduced to propositional form. It generates true propositions, perhaps even some timelessly true ones – 'God is love' – but the knowledge of which we speak is the knowledge of those placed in the life of a community centred on and ordered around one whose presence-in-absence implies a certain status for the knowledge.

vii. An Uncomfortable Observation

Right, OK, so what can we conclude? Well, we can say that the creeds and confessions of Christendom contain reference to the church. This entails that those who accept the gospel message submit at least part of their judgement to an authoritative teaching which is mediated by an institution and a tradition or traditions.

Calvin is surely right to say that we do not believe in the church as we believe in God; it is preferable to say that we believe the church.[29] And yet even in that form there are contained two offences against the spirit of the age, against political correctness even. Modern individualism is offended that individuals should submit themselves to the dogmas of an institution, with the possible – and highly significant – exception of the State; while the ideology of tolerance is offended by the categorical claims for truth which the gospel makes. Much modern tolerance is, to be sure, little more than a means of the repression of uncomfortable opinion.

What needs to be reiterated is that all positions, including relativism, are positions, and thus far they are exclusive and intolerant of those positions which are logically incompatible with them. This is well illustrated in Gavin D'Costa's critique of the concept of religious pluralism.[30] All ideologies and theologies take some institutional or communal form. Christian exclusivism, insofar as it maintains an awareness of the eschatological limits of its own knowledge claims – and the historical weakness of its position is that it has not always done so – Christian

28 Robert Jenson, *Systematic Theology*, Vol. 2 (Oxford: Oxford University Press, 1997), p. 24.
29 John Calvin, *Institutes of the Christian Religion*, Vol. 2 (ed. John T. McNeill; Library of Christian Classics; Louisville, KY: Westminster John Knox Press, 2006 [1960]) Bk. 4. Ch. i. §. 2, p. 1012.
30 Gavin D'Costa, 'The Impossibility of a Pluralist View of Religion', *Religious Studies* 32 (1996), pp. 223–32

exclusivism ought to be able to maintain a due balance of tolerance and intolerance.

3. Early Examples of Systematic Theologians

So, we need to recognize the limits to the knowledge of God, yet the stress has to be on knowledge mediated by the Incarnation. Without the Incarnation as God's self-revelation there is no true knowledge of God. Yes, that is a strict and to some a narrow position, and yes the Incarnation does not, for some, leave space for a debate between Revelation and reason, but the Incarnation is given to us all. The Incarnation itself represents a kind of relentless intolerance: a refusal to tolerate the rule of sin and evil. The value of such passages as Jesus' expression of invective against certain forms of religiosity – *'woe to you, scribes and Pharisees, hypocrites!'* – this is uttered several times in Matthew 23 and it shows that he was not a tolerant man. And yet the means of its expression was from beginning to end not repressive, even to the cross. So, systematic theology is about asserting the truth, the givenness of truth revealed by God in the Incarnation – is it not?

So, if the debate between Revelation and reason must be qualified by the Incarnation then we can look to two early examples of Patristic theologians to illustrate the point: Irenaeus of Lyons and Origen. These two are examples of early systematic theology, theologians that systematize.

i. Irenaeus of Lyons

Irenaeus was active around the year 180. Irenaeus is important, very important, for developing an emerging systematization of theology; you see, Irenaeus' theology is predicated on the unity of God. Irenaeus's system all comes from his work against the Gnostics who held that the Old Testament God and the New Testament God were different deities. What did Irenaeus do? [31] He held that God is one, and therefore the Creator God of the Old Testament, the so-called Creator God of the Old Testament, and the Redeemer God of the New Testament were actually one

31 Irenaeus (Greek: Εἰρηναῖος, c.110–c.190), was a second-century bishop of Lugdunum in Gaul (now Lyon, France) whose writings were influential, formative and crucial in establishing the sound doctrinal basis of the faith. In terms of the early development of Christian theology he is an important Father of the Church, notable as a Christian apologist. He was also a disciple of Polycarp, who was said to be a disciple of John the Evangelist. Irenaeus wrote many works but the most important is the five-volume *Adversus Haereses* (*Against Heresies*; often called *On the Detection and Overthrow of the So-Called Gnosis*), which was a systematic refutation of the Gnostic heresy. See: Alexander Roberts, James Donaldson, Philip Schaff and Henry Wace (eds) *Ante-Nicene Fathers* (10 volumes) (Peabody, MA: Hendrickson Publishers, new edn, 1994), specifically, see Volume 1: *Apostolic Fathers, Justin Martyr, Irenaeus*, containing Irenaeus' extant works.

and the same deity; and therefore what you get in Irenaeus is a unity of the economy of God.[32]

Irenaeus showed how there is a constant thread running through, a thread of God's acts with the world, with his people. Therefore there is a sort of systematization in Irenaeus because everything is thought of as being in the action, or under the aegis, of this one God. And for Irenaeus God's ordering in the world is through himself and the Son. Therefore, to Irenaeus, any theology that must be, must follow from God's acts in the world, and the fact that through them he makes himself known.

The leading feature of Irenaeus, despite the fact that his thought seems to jump all over the place in the five books, is an emerging systemization: he seems to think systematically, he really does. Irenaeus does not order his work like a modern systematic theologian beginning with knowledge of God and moving on to doctrine, creation, etc. He does not attempt to organize Christianity into a system. This is because his work was directed at refuting heresy, the Gnostic heresy, Gnosticism. There is no attempt to organize his material into a systematic whole, but he knows what belongs where. You see, listen to this,

> *Irenaeus is a systematic theologian in the sense that he knows the relation of ideas, which belong to which.* [33]

Brunner notes that you can't treat creation apart from Christ, and you can't treat Christ apart from the Father, and the Father's eschatological action; he knows that you can't treat the Christian life apart from the Incarnation. This is what systematic theology is about: he knows what belongs where, what things have to be said, and what kind of weight they have to each other. The key to thinking theologically is a matter of weight: what weighting you apportion to different elements. For example, if you overweight the doctrine of creation at the expense of the doctrine of salvation you fail to understand the reasons for the Incarnation and the Cross. If you overweight the Incarnation and the Cross at the expense of creation then you tend to have a conception of salvation out of the world, rather than in the world.

So much depends upon what you emphasize against what. Systematic theology is about how you order, how you set out, how you weight different elements of Christian doctrine.

32 The economy of God: economy, as in housekeeping, God's ordering and maintaining of the world. The economy of God is seen as from creation through to the eschaton: creation is the call of Israel, Jesus, and the church; then finally there is the eschaton.

33 Emil Brunner, *The Mediator. A Study of the Central Doctrine of the Christian Faith* (Philadelphia, PA: Westminster Press, 1947), p. 262. See also, Gunton, Colin E., 'Using and being Used: Scripture and Systematic Theology', in *Theology Today* 47.3, October 1990, pp. 248–59.

ii. Origen

Origen of Alexandria was essentially the next generation, active in the first half of the third century. He is the first theologian who tries to organize the faith into a system. He was a brilliant theologian. Origen is regarded by Robert Jenson as the first world-class thinker. You see he established his Christian doctrine by moving from the basis of elementary foundation principles, through clear and cogent argument, to a single body. That is so important, he moved from the basis of elementary foundation principles, a ground, thereby through clear cogent arguing, to arrive at a single body of doctrine (figure 4).

Origen is a sheerly brilliant theologian – that may be almost to his own cost – and what he tried to do was this: on the basis of elementary foundation principles (this is almost a definition of the modern understanding of system – it is almost as if the moderns have taken it from the Origenist model, and he possibly got it from the Stoics), take elementary foundation principles, and from there by clear and cogent argument, move to a single body of doctrine. This was the first attempt to be systematic.

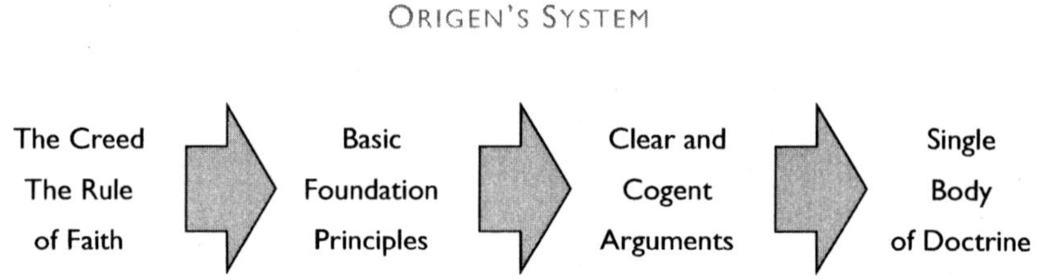

Figure 4

So what were Origen's elementary principles? Origen is not a modern; that's important to understand, he is not a modern theologian. What drives him is not what drives a modern. This is because he starts with the rule of faith, the doctrine of the creed. A modern thinker moves from what he perceives as self-evident principles. You see, systematic theology can be seen to be the establishment of Christian doctrine by moving from the basis of elementary foundation principles – creedal principles – through clear and cogent arguments, to a single body of doctrine, which in itself relates to revelation and is revelatory in a sense. That, if you like, is a definition of systematic theology not the only one, certainly not the only one, but, certainly one you could work with, one you could use.

Origen's great work is Περὶ Ἀρχῶν (*Peri Archōn*) – often called *De Principiis*, in English *On First Principles.*[34] It is, I believe, the first real example we have of

[34] Origen of Alexandria, Περὶ Ἀρχῶν c. 212 and 215. It exists today only in the translation by Rufinus, along with fragments preserved in the *Philokalia*, and smaller citations in Justinian's *Letter to Mennas*. See Origen, *On First Principles: Being Koetschau's Text of the De Principiis Translated into*

systematic theology, it is often rated as such, as certainly important, whatever the detractors say, the opponents – and there are plenty! So what does Origen say? What does he do? Well he starts with the creeds as the ground of his doctrine. There is a balance, on the one hand the creed, which is the starting point which you may not go beyond, and on the other, you have the attempt to organize it into systematic principles. History has for the most part decided that he did go beyond the creed, beyond the orthodox: especially in the adoption of universalism – ἀποκατάστασις (apokatastasis). Yes, it is fair to say that he formulated much that was outside of what became orthodox.

You see, for Origen, the material world was secondary, an afterthought, and a way for the fallen from the pre-Genesis world to be redeemed. To Origen the world was subordinated to salvation. Origen is accused sometimes of just playing with ideas and, yes, he is something of a speculative thinker, that is a fair criticism.

So, systematic theology is the intellectual side of Christianity, showing how the beliefs of the church relate to one another as a single body. In summary, systematic, to be systematic, is the intellectual side of the Christian faith. Well, it certainly seems so to me; it seems to me that it is showing how the beliefs of the church relate to one another as a single – as in some sense, either relatively or absolutely – a single unified body of truth. I believe, obviously, that it can only be a relatively, a relative unified body of truth because of the problems (because of what I outlined earlier about Kierkegaard's reservation – the intellectual and the moral). Systematic theology is also about how this body of doctrine relates to other truths, other sources, especially, today, science, the natural sciences so often. Therefore this is about the inner coherence of the faith and how the faith coheres with other sources.

In the time of Irenaeus and Origen the question was how Christianity cohered with philosophy; today, the question is how Christianity coheres with science. You see, Origen was concerned with showing how theology was beyond the Middle Platonic, how it went beyond Middle Platonism. You could say that Irenaeus' agenda seemed to be solely to deal with the Gnostics. If that is true it is because he was a theologian of crisis: Irenaeus is like Barth, a theologian of crisis. This is the Barth model, in other words you answer the questions thrown to the faith: you answer the crisis of belief. Origen and Tillich are by contrast theologians of culture who are concerned with how the gospel integrates with the best insights of the culture of their day.

4. Revelation

Both Origen and Irenaeus are dealing with a theology of Revelation in the broadest sense: something has been given. There is givenness about theology, about

English (trans. G. W. Butterworth; Introduction, Henri De Lubac; Gloucester, MA: Peter Smith Publisher inc; new edn, 2002 [1985]). A different translation can be consulted online at: http://www.newadvent.org/fathers/0412.htm.

doctrine, about our beliefs. Even for Origen, the more philosophical of the two, the rule of faith was important. Irenaeus uses the rule of faith against the Gnostics, but not in the same manner or with the same force or placement as Origen. To Irenaeus, the rule of faith had been handed down from the apostles; to Origen it was given as a summary of Christian teaching, but in neither is there an explicit theology of Revelation.

Therefore, you see, it is this focus on Revelation and reason that marks us as modern, as a modern group rather than in the mould of the patristic writers. Patristic writers were not as self-conscious about Revelation as we are today. The early patristic writers did not treat Revelation as explicitly as we do today. Ignatius of Antioch, even before Irenaeus, talks of God revealing himself, he talks about the revealed God, the God revealed in Jesus, but there is not the self-conscious emphasis there is today. So although Revelation is used by these patristic theologians it is simply taken as a matter of course that truth is given to the church as direct Revelation.

Yes, you see, these early patristic theologians were not as hot on Revelation as a theological truism. The modern view is often that the juxtaposition of Revelation and reason comes from Aquinas. However, in the *Summa Theologiae*,[35] there is no treatise on Revelation. Thomas has a view of Revelation, but there is no explicit treatment of it. He starts with the knowledge of God, but not Revelation, he then moves to the content, he does not agonize as to whether it is revealed or not. The preoccupation with Revelation is a characteristically modern concern. It arises, of course, precisely from the fact that so many modern philosophers have denied it. When everybody assumes it, you don't need to talk about it too much, you can rely on it. Once philosophers begin to deny it, then of course – you see the problem. When Kantian philosophers say that God can't be known through historical or worldly action, or from the created order, then people get worried.

5. Foundationalism

Nicholas Wolterstorff wrote an article in *Modern Theology* in 1998 entitled 'Is it Possible or Desirable for Theologians to Recover from Kant?'[36] This is exactly the question: Do we need to devise against Kant a theology of Revelation? Do we need to recover from Kant (we'll actually talk about Kant next week, and certainly the

[35] Thomas Aquinas, *Summa Theologiae* (the complete paperback set, 60 volumes, plus one index volume; dual language, Latin-English; Cambridge: Cambridge University Press, 2006 [1962–76]).

[36] Nicholas Wolterstorff, 'Is it Possible and Desirable for Theologians to Recover from Kant?', in *Modern Theology*, 14.1 (1998), pp. 1–18. Wolterstorff notes how Kant is a watershed in theological history, resulting in the anxiety–ridden question, 'Can we speak of God? How can we?' He notes how modern theologians are 'compelled not to say about God what they want to say without first establishing that they are justified or entitled in saying those things; therefore theologians have experienced both frustration and anxiety'. Wolterstorff challenges this Kantian agony. He claims we can reject the 'mental representationalist picture required by [Kant's] account of intuitions and concepts'.

week after when we look at Barth)? This raises the question, what is a doctrine of Revelation, and why do we need one? Ronald Thiemann in *Revelation and Theology* argues for one, but some regard his argument as somewhat inconclusive.[37] Thiemann argues that modern theology uses the concept of Revelation in an attempt to cross over an epistemological bridge that cannot be crossed. Thiemann describes this as 'Faith seeking Foundations'.

Where does this lead? Where does this take us? – foundationalism; you see, Thiemann is talking about foundationalism.[38] He details three writers who are dealing with this: John Locke, Friedrich Schleiermacher and T. F Torrance. Thiemann wants to avoid the notion of Revelation as an attempt to cross over the epistemological divide. He argues that Lock, Schleiermacher and Torrance all try to use Revelation in this way. To Thiemann, Revelation should not be of independent interest; rather it should be part of the doctrine of the function of God. What is interesting is God: we can only speak of Revelation as something that implicates God. In some ways this is a Barthian approach, but only in some ways; only in some ways. Revelation, you see, is part of the function of the doctrine of salvation. This is in some ways a Barthian approach, but don't take that as whole, complete, there are significant differences. You see, Barth argued to those who said we could have no knowledge of God that we can, because God actually does reveal himself to us.

To make a more general Barthian point, it seems to me that we can say that, perhaps, Revelation is a function of the doctrine of salvation. In other words it is because God reconciles the sinner to himself, or however you put it, that it is right to say that he, in so far as he does, that he reveals himself too; that is to say, he overcomes our moral or religious opposition and our intellectual opposition and reveals himself *as a function of salvation*. OK, you see, Revelation is in the process of our being saved. It is the relation to God wrought through the salvific act that is prior; Revelation, revelatory knowledge, is but a secondary concern. It's important to remember that the doctrine of Revelation is not the creeds: the creeds narrate God's actions, but they are not Revelation in themselves; they are very important, they certainly were for the patristic theologians.

i. Evidentialism: Grounding in the Prior, the External

Foundationalism as the term suggests is about the foundations upon which belief systems are built – the comparison with building is obvious, the foundations or

[37] Ronald F. Thiemann, *Revelation and Theology: the Gospel as Narrated Promise* (Notre Dame, IN: University of Notre Dame Press, 1985).

[38] For Thiemann foundationalism is built upon the proposition that every coherent belief system rests upon certain convictions. These convictions are assumed to be true, often they are considered to be self-evident, and thus provide stability for the framework of belief. The coherence of many other beliefs depends on the acceptance of these beliefs as true. These foundational beliefs may be subject to revision; however, they do remain fixed, relatively. Ronald F. Thiemann, *Revelation and Theology: the Gospel as Narrated Promise*, see Ch. 1, The Modern Doctrine of Revelation: Faith Seeking Foundation, pp. 9–15, specifically, pp. 13–14.

footings on which a building is built. Ronald Thiemann comments how every coherent belief system rests upon certain convictions, which are assumed to be true and thus provide stability for the whole framework. These beliefs are basic because the coherence of many other beliefs depends on the acceptance of these beliefs as true. Now, he is almost quoting Aquinas when he says that. Actually Descartes may have claimed to be operating non-circular, but he was operating within a specific Catholic context; however Descartes does respond to a different situation than Thomas does.

Foundationalism, you see, can be defined as when a discipline claims that its rationality and truth are based on some generally accepted intellectual foundations. Thiemann is anti-foundationalist.[39] You see, Thiemann is saying that these three – John Locke, Friedrich Schleiermacher and T. F. Torrance – involve a Cartesian path, that is to say, they believe that they cannot have a doctrine of Revelation unless they base it on something prior. In other words they all depend upon modern evidentialism of some kind or other. What they are doing, or so Thiemann believes, is that they follow Descartes rather than the Reformers in constructing claims to knowledge of God as beliefs in need of justification. So these beliefs are dependent beliefs. They also use foundational epistemological theories to justify the possibility of Revelation. And they use the idea of intuition to claim that knowledge of God is in fact a gift of God's grace.

So they follow Descartes rather than the Reformers in construing claims to knowledge of God not as axiomatic background beliefs but as dependent beliefs in need of justification. This is the key; they have this modern anxiety, this Cartesian anxiety that unless things are, unless things are founded on something else, so to speak, then there is chaos. You see, they adopt a foundational epistemological theory to justify the possibility of Revelation; that is again quite clear. By foundational epistemology they mean that in some sense or other their doctrine of Revelation must be based on some universally established epistemology by either rationalistic or empirical means. Therefore, they employ the notion of intuition to justify the claim that the knowledge of God is a gift of God's grace. So given what foundationalism means you then by an intuitive leap, as it were, go from there to some kind of 'revelationalism'; in other words you can't, you cannot begin with Revelation as the Reformers did, or with some theory of grace, that is the assumption of these three, but neither can you justify Revelation directly inferentially because foundationalists don't need to. Therefore, you have to get your Revelation intuitively, you can move from there to a theory of Revelation. What Thiemann is suggesting is that you can't move from one to the other, except by an act of intuition. So this is 'faith seeking foundations'; not the Anselmian principle of 'faith seeking understanding'. Faith seeking foundations is an attempt to give a causal account of where Revelation comes from. Thiemann wants to pronounce that instead of saying, 'This *is* Revelation, *receive* it'; they want to say, 'We know this is Revelation because we have got *reasons* for believing that God

[39] Gunton, Colin E., 'Universal and Particular in Atonement Theology', in *Religious Studies* 28, December 1992, pp. 453–66.

causes it to be Revelation'. All three, as it were, are trying to justify Revelation as something caused by God. And they are trying to use their foundationalism to justify giving reasons why something is Revelation – again classic foundationalism.

ii. Locke, Schleiermacher and Torrance – Foundationalists?

Locke, Schleiermacher and Torrance think you can justify something if you can explain it causally, as coming from God.

Q: Doesn't Thiemann have something to say about the epistemological confusion between rational justification and causal explanation?

Yes, Thiemann somewhere writes about this,[40] that there is confusion between rational justification and causal explanation, in other words how do you justify something as Revelation. He sees this in Locke, Schleiermacher and Torrance. He says they think you can justify something if you can explain it causally, as coming from God – he thinks this is a confusion of categories. In other words some people today will say that if you can contribute a cause to something then that justifies it rationally. Thiemann is saying it doesn't necessarily; attributing a cause does not necessarily justify something rationally.

In fact Nicholas Wolterstorff tackles John Locke on foundationalism in *John Locke and the Ethics of Belief*, very good and well worth reading.[41] Wolterstorff on Locke: he argues that the unusual thing about modern conditions is that believers are expected to justify their beliefs on considerations taken from outside their religion. Normally if you justify something it is from reasons within it, so if you want to justify a discovery in physics, the reasons you give will be from physics, not from theology. The unusual situation about foundationalism is the demand that you justify your belief on something extrinsic to it. And I think Thiemann wants to suggest that all three of these are pretending to appeal to Revelation but are actually trying to found Revelation on something non-revelational.

Q: Do you think Torrance is actually trying to do that trap?

Oh yes! Torrance, you see, is, I believe, definitely falling into this trap! Interestingly enough this is the thing that people ask in this group year after year. When Torrance talks about intuition he doesn't mean a leap out of foundations to Revelation. It is intuitive in that sense. By intuition Torrance does mean, well, integrity, a kind of integration of data rather than leaping into another world. There is a very rationalistic side to Tom Torrance; he would use a foundationalist argument if he could.

Certainly Locke and Schleiermacher clearly are foundationalist. Schleiermacher is clearly a systematic theologian because he is building a system. Schleiermacher is certainly doing a foundationalist type of job; After all, what is it that he is appealing to? He is appealing to general, universal human experience and

40 Ronald F. Thiemann, *Revelation and Theology: the Gospel as Narrated Promise*, p. 14.

41 Nicholas Wolterstorff, *John Locke and the Ethics of Belief* (Cambridge: Cambridge University Press, 1996).

that is his foundation, and then he is trying to say that Christianity is one form of that universal experience, but he also wants to say that Christianity is the supreme form of this experience, so he wants to move from the general to the particular while using the general to defend the particular. That is classic foundationalism.

That is classic foundationalism: certainly with Locke, clearly with Locke. This is Locke's game, to try to defend in the light of his empiricism. Torrance is a more ambiguous character. Again this is a point made by Wolterstorff – we have to give reasons but are they ultimate reasons, and do they come from outside the system of belief? Thiemann is virtually saying that Aquinas is the first, or quintessential, foundationalist. I think some Catholic theologians would disagree with that.

Q: But what would you say causes the leap from causal chain to self-caused cause, from inferential beliefs to non-inferential reality?

This is a Kant–style question, because Kant argued that you couldn't move from one to the other. Yes, this is Kantian, it is at the heart of foundationalism: that is, that ultimately any justifying reason is the first cause. You see, then a belief is only justified when its origin – its source and therefore its cause – have been identified. But, we may ask, what causes the leap from causal chain to self-caused cause, that is, in effect, from inferential beliefs to a non-inferential reality? Yes, I think that is how it is. This is Kantian because Kant argued that you couldn't move from one to the other. The essence, the heart of Kant's objections to the proofs of the existence of God, is that they require a move outside the causal chain which he believes is intellectually invalid. But this is the sort of deconstructive game that Thiemann is playing; he is playing the sort of Kant game, showing that these ideas just won't deliver what they claim to deliver.

iii. Danger of Projectionalism

So, crudely speaking, one option after this is projectionalism, you are not actually discerning God, you are inventing God: so that is one option. If there is no foundation then it may be that you can't have theology at all – similarly you find this with Don Cupitt.[42] This is in many ways a quest for immediacy, attempting an unmediated apprehension of Revelation, which tends to avoid the question of epistemology. The logical development is then a turn to the self and the loss of any claim to objective truth.

Q: Is there scope for a common consensus?

42 Don Cupitt (b. 1934) is often classified as a radical theologian – Cupitt is an ordained Anglican priest, former Dean of Emmanuel College, Cambridge, where he was originally trained in science and theology. Cupitt describes himself in his works as a Christian non-realist, which is often defined as religious atheism. Therefore he is a writer and media celebrity of 'radical' theological ideas: in 1984 his television series, 'Sea of Faith', challenged orthodox Christian beliefs, advocating individualistic spiritual exploration. He has often asserted that he adheres to certain spiritual practices and attempts to live by the ethics that have usually been seen as Christian, but does not 'believe' in the actuality, the realism, of such entities as 'Christ' and 'God'.

Once you start doing that, creating a common consensus you are dangerously near to foundationalism again. The route is being taken away from foundationalism into narrative. Narrative is a particular; Thiemann uses Matthew's Gospel as an example of Revelation being given through the narrative. Once you particularize through narrative, the danger is why a Christian and not a Buddhist or a Hindu narrative and the only answer may be that I happen to be a Christian and you a Buddhist, and so on.

iv. Foundationalism as Externalism

Foundationalism then is pure 'Externalism'; it is the making of some external basis for criterion. Narrativism is a pure 'Internalism'. You are saying 'That's your narrative, you are sticking to it, but no appeal outside.' The question is can you begin to appeal outside without stepping back into foundationalism? This is obviously the question!

I think it is true that foundationalism has become insolvent. That is the chief argument against it, in some sense, as people like MacIntyre classically formulated: MacIntyre's great book *After Virtue* is based upon an argument that the project has failed, the Enlightenment project; the trying for universally agreeable foundations has simply failed.[43] These people always appeal to any common foundations any rational person can agree on. And of course no single example has been arrived at – anything you say somebody can disagree with, unless, of course, you come up with something boring like two plus two equals four which actually doesn't make any difference anyway. When you try to find something that is epistemologically foundational, then there simply has been no agreement.

Empirically speaking nobody can agree, so how can there be foundations? That is why postmodernism believes that everything is particular and that there are no relations between anything; hence we back onto our own subjectivity which is far worse in my view than the foundational crisis, because at least foundationalism tried to find something we all shared. Whereas the danger of postmodernism is that everyone's hand is against everyone else. So that's the kind of modern difficulty: 'Is there any way between external foundations and internal subjectivism?' That's the modern dilemma!

v. Biblical Epistemologists

Postmodernism, you see, works against the belief that there are universals.

Q: If Jesus is God incarnate does this not have universal meaning?

Yes. Yes, and many theologians are trying to find Christian forms of basic truths in the Reformed theologians, the foundationalists.

43 Alasdair C. MacIntyre, *After Virtue: a Study in Moral Theory* (Notre Dame, IN: University of Notre Dame Press, 1981).

Q: Is this like the Biblical epistemologists, that is, how do we know, we know from the Bible?

In a way it is, but it is more philosophical than that, like Plantinga's work.[44] In a way Thiemann is doing this because he is basing his proposal on a reading of Matthew's Gospel. But there is a lot of material in biblical studies at the moment, a lot of interesting material. In a way Francis Watson[45] is playing that sort of game (I mean 'game' in the Wittgensteinian sense of a serious pursuit) and I suppose that Tom Wright's quest, his proposal, is quite foundational.[46]

Tom Wright's quest is partly historical and therefore partly foundational as he puts trust in the historical–critical method to deliver things which are commonly apprehensible to be true. It's a great project, more Biblicist than many would subscribe to. But, you see, there are those who argue, who ask, why does Tom Wright have to go to all this historical Jesus material when all you need to do is read the Book of Isaiah if you want to know about the historical Jesus? In that sense his critics are trying to say to us that the Bible gives us Jesus. There are a lot of people in biblical studies who are trying to base everything on a biblical foundation. But are they fundamentalist because they see the Bible in some way as doing away with theology?

Once you have a theology you have the universal, that's the point you see, once you have a conception of God of some kind then you have something universal. The question then is 'How does it operate?' OK, 'How does this conception operate? 'Does it operate oppressively or does it operate passively?' This is where non-foundationalism began. They – the foundationalists – believed that ancient foundations were oppressive; the Christian God had to be replaced with a freely devised human foundation for science. In that sense, ideologically, science is an attempt to replace a divine foundation with a secular one: foundationalism is the tale of different attempts to find a secular basis for truth.

Once you bring in a concept of God, whether biblically or philosophically, God by definition is a foundation, the one through whom meaning and truth cohere and are to be found. Therefore, you will never get a resolution between the modernism/postmodernism view; you won't get a solution apart from a theological

44 Alvin Carl Plantinga (b. 1932), American philosopher who has focused on philosophy of religion, epistemology and metaphysics, and who is noted for his defence of an ontological argument using what is termed modal logic. See Alvin Plantinga (ed.), *Faith and Philosophy* (Grand Rapids, MI: Eerdmans, 1964); Alvin Plantinga (ed.), *The Ontological Argument* (Garden City, NY: Doubleday, 1965); Alvin Plantinga, *God and Other Minds* (rev. 2nd edn; Ithaca, NY: Cornell University Press, 1990 [1967]); Alvin Plantinga, *God, Freedom and Evil* (Grand Rapids, MI: Eerdmans, 1974). Of especial note considering Colin Gunton's emphasis on the work of Nicholas Wolterstorff is: Alvin Plantinga and Nicholas Wolterstorff (eds) *Faith and Rationality: Reason and Belief in God* (Notre Dame, IN: University of Notre Dame Press, 1983).

45 See, for example, Francis Watson, *Text, Church and World: Biblical Interpretation in Theological Perspective* (Edinburgh: T&T Clark, 1994).

46 N. T. Wright, New Testament scholar and theologian, Bishop of Durham (Church of England), widely published in New Testament studies, but noted in this context for his biblical theology, see the series, *Christian Origins and the Question of God*. Wright plans six volumes (three are published): N. T. Wright, *The New Testament and the People of God* (London: SPCK, 1992); N. T. Wright, *Jesus and the Victory of God* (London: SPCK, 1996); N. T. Wright, *The Resurrection of the Son of God* (London: SPCK, 2003).

solution because in the end the modernist/postmodernist view is purely secular, they have no true foundation: that's the issue, whether you can do a foundation without a theology.

Foundationalism is implicit in theology; the interesting book on this is by Edward Craig, *The Mind of God and the Works of Man*.[47] He shows how progressively the divine basis of knowledge and culture is displaced by the human mind. People like Rorty[48] are pragmatists; he wants to say that it is the works of man that have displaced God. It is human works that displace God. Edward Craig sees the history of modern philosophy as progressively displacing God for the human, first of all human thought and then human action. He has side-swipes at the end against certain liberal ecclesiastics, whom he clearly doesn't like.

6. Revelation and Foundationalism

So Revelation is a drawing out of the intellectual implications of the fact that there is a divine economy. The discussion of Revelation is unavoidable in the modern context. You can't avoid questions that are transmitted by the tradition. You can avoid being over dominated–by them, but it doesn't follow that you have to ask for them in the form in which they are conveyed. In other words the modern scepticism about God does require being taken seriously, you have to take this scepticism seriously; modern scepticism about the possibility of the knowledge of God can be faced with a doctrine of Revelation – God being known in some way. But you don't have to be dominated by the question. In some ways this is an over-discussed topic but it can be used to frame an enquiry; especially an enquiry about doctrine.

If God is one, then all theological truth is interrelated because it is related to God. Therefore, you can frame an enquiry into the nature of theology by beginning anywhere: Christology, Revelation, creation, you can start with any of these and use them as the basis of an enquiry. The advantage of Revelation is that it focuses on the question of knowledge: it is concerned with questions of epistemology. However, and this is I believe important, you have to ask, 'Is this knowledge? Does Revelation claim to be knowledge?' We have now existed for two or three centuries in which perhaps 90 per cent of the intellectuals, the leading intellectuals of our culture, have progressively argued that this isn't a form of knowledge – that actually it is 'opinion', or 'subjective'.

Therefore it seems to me that the topic of Revelation has advantages, but also disadvantages: it has the advantage that it focuses on the intellectual state of Christianity and what kind of discipline it is; the disadvantage is that it stresses too much the intellectual at the expense of the other side, the other claims of theology.

47 Edward Craig, *The Mind of God and the Works of Man* (Oxford: Oxford University Press, 1987).
48 Richard McKay Rorty (1931–2007), American philosopher, emeritus professor of comparative literature and philosophy at Stanford University. See Richard Rorty, *Philosophy and the Mirror of Nature* (Princeton, NJ: Princeton University Press, 1979).

You see, so many theologians since the Enlightenment are following a Cartesian path. Descartes was well aware that faith for many was only acceptable if proven through natural reason. Is that not so? So many theologians have followed Descartes rather than the Reformers. This is what Thiemann is saying, that theological method involves a Cartesian path; that is to say, they believe that they cannot have a doctrine of Revelation unless they base it on something prior. In other words they all depend upon modern evidentialism of some kind or other. So, as I have said before, this is faith seeking foundations.

Chapter 2

Subjectivity and Objectification

1. John Locke

So, John Locke.[1] John Locke wrote on the relationship of Revelation and reason. He stands at the beginning, in many ways, of modernity, the onset of the modern era in thought. He is behind our modern way of thinking. Locke's philosophy of religion, you see, is that Revelation is qualified by reason: reason places, or situates, Revelation. Locke argued that we could no longer allow the wisdom of the tradition to guide us; reason now must guide us. In a sense Descartes had done the almost identical thing on the continent.[2] There was no certainty in the teaching Descartes had received from his Jesuit teachers, and he, too, did exactly the same thing: he sought foundations, a ground. He sought foundations. There is quite a lot in Locke that comes out of Descartes. Descartes is only concerned with epistemology.

i. Epistemology

Locke is an empiricist: his *Essay Concerning Human Understanding* (1690)[3] is about human knowledge, its grounds, the origin of ideas that make up our knowledge. Locke writes that you don't perceive a snowball – you perceive, to put it crudely, a

1 John Locke (1632–1704), noted for his work in empirical philosophy and natural law, his writings focused on metaphysics and epistemology, particularly the interrelation of the two and therefore philosophy of mind (his theory of mind is considered the origin of modern conceptions of identity and self); he is also noted for political philosophy. Locke's influence was wide-ranging and he is considered one of the most influential early Enlightenment thinkers.

2 René Descartes (1596–1650), rated as the founder of modern philosophy and what is termed Cartesian Rationalism, was a philosopher, metaphysician and epistemologist, scientist and mathematician, and is noted for his axion, *cogito ergo sum*.

3 John Locke, *Essay Concerning Human Understanding* (ed. R. S. Woolhouse; Harmondsworth: Penguin Books, Penguin Classics, 1997).

convocation of ideas, like coldness, and then you infer that it is a snowball. So it is the ideas that count; in other words this is the image of the mind like a box into which these ideas come, and, in some way, out of which you have to go by inference rather than by any other way. So it is a turn inwards, which is usually associated with Descartes, but it is just the same with Locke.

So the mind is only aware of the mental. Do you see? That is what Locke is saying, and that is what has characterized modern philosophy. Certainly this model has dominated modern philosophy: ideas in our mind are mental representations of entities distinct from themselves – that's what is at the heart of Locke's epistemology, at least it is for many people. Rorty is in some ways tracing this back to Plato and the tradition of the mind as the mirror of nature.[4] Rorty does see Locke as one instance in a long tradition. Knowledge is, in some sense, taking up visual reflections of reality, taking up visual reflections of reality in the mind as in a mirror.

So by knowledge we mean – and this is Locke – to know is to perceive; but we can also know that we exist in the sense of Descartes' axiom, if you can call it an axiom. We can know that we exist because there exists something doing the thinking: *cogito ergo sum*. This is also straight out of Augustine: even if I am deceived I know there is something that is being deceived.[5] This is interesting because he is a very internal type of figure. He is the first to turn inwards in a major way, because he believed that in the mind was to be found the image of God, if we look into the mind we find the truth. In a sense all Western thought is a variation on Augustine in some way or other. Augustine is a 'modern': everything is different in different

4 Richard Rorty, *Philosophy and the Mirror of Nature* (Princeton, NJ: Princeton University Press, 1979). See also Richard Rorty, *Objectivity, Relativism, and Truth* (Cambridge: Cambridge University Press, 1991).

5 Augustine deals with the subject of sensory perception, truth and delusion and our self-consciousness in *The City of God*, in the context of refuting the Academicians: 'But, without any delusive representation of images or phantasms, I am most certain that I am, and that I know and delight in this. In respect of these truths, I am not at all afraid of the arguments of the Academicians, who say, What if you are deceived? For if I am deceived, I am. For he who is not, cannot be deceived; and if I am deceived, by this same token I am. And since I am if I am deceived, how am I deceived in believing that I am? for it is certain that I am if I am deceived. Since, therefore, I, the person deceived, should be, even if I were deceived, certainly I am not deceived in this knowledge that I am. And, consequently, neither am I deceived in knowing that I know. For, as I know that I am, so I know this also, that I know. And when I love these two things, I add to them a certain third thing, namely, my love, which is of equal moment. For neither am I deceived in this, that I love, since in those things which I love I am not deceived; though even if these were false, it would still be true that I loved false things. For how could I justly be blamed and prohibited from loving false things, if it were false that I loved them? But, since they are true and real, who doubts that when they are loved, the love of them is itself true and real? Further, as there is no one who does not wish to be happy, so there is no one who does not wish to be. For how can he be happy, if he is nothing?' Augustine, *City of God* (trans. Henry Bettenson; Harmondsworth: Penguin Books, 1972), pt. II, bk. XI, ch. 26, pp. 459–60. See also Augustine of Hippo, *De vera religione*, xxxix. 73. English trans. Augustine, *Of True Religion* (Washington, DC: Regnery Publishing, 1991).

contexts. In some sense there is in Augustine this confidence that by looking inwards you will find the divine or the truth.

Another interesting book here – again, we mentioned it earlier – is Craig's *The Mind of God and the Works of Man*.[6] Very interesting. What he does is show how the Augustinian idea that the image of God is in the mind is taken up by these rationalists in the early modern age and turned into a fundamental divinization of the human. So by the time you get to Richard Rorty and pragmatism it is the acts of man that are the works of God, as he puts it. And what you have is a kind of gradual shift whereby the real world becomes a human agent. It is a very interesting book.

ii. Faith and Reason

Faith and reason are covered in Book 4 of Locke's *Essay Concerning Human Understanding*.[7] Knowledge is different from assent or belief; to assent, to believe, to have faith, Locke argues, is different from knowledge. You see, all the time these people are seeking firm grounds for knowledge; he wanted to believe things in what he considered a responsible way, a way that respected reason. Yes, he thought revelation was possible, God might reveal directly to us, but it was unlikely, or so he thought. This meant he was sceptical about how to discern such revelation and how to communicate it. You see the problem, for him anyway – How do you convince someone you have a direct revelation from God? Enthusiasm is part of his problem; there is a chapter called On Enthusiasm. Enthusiasm for Locke means, of course, accepting beliefs on the grounds that one believes them enthusiastically. Sectarianism was another word for it, you see, sects were going their own way because of their claim for private divine revelation, the inner life tradition. That is the other thing, civil strife caused by religion: that was worrying him – remember he is writing in the wake of the English Civil War – which is partly theological and not simply philosophical or political. G. K. Chesterton said that the problem with the inner life is that it leads to outer darkness.[8]

So, for Locke, belief is held in accordance with reason: belief is grounded in reason. However, he did maintain that truths, certain truths are open to revelation. In other words God must be like the rational English philosopher who does nothing unreasonable, or ungentlemanly! Locke is also the classic broad church Anglican. He is very much the prophet of the liberal wing of Anglicanism. What we are interested in is the sources of the content of his thinking. He is at times a very

6 Edward Craig, *The Mind of God and the Works of Man* (Oxford: Oxford University Press, 1987).

7 John Locke, 'Essay Concerning Human Understanding' (1690). See John Locke, *An Essay Concerning Human Understanding* (edited by R. S. Woolhouse; Harmondsworth: Penguin Books, Penguin Classics, 1997).

8 G. K. Chesterton, *Orthodoxy* (Peabody, MA: Hendrickson Publishers, 2006 [London: John Lane, 1909]), see ch. V, The Flag of the World, pp. 41–49.

bland upper–class Englishman but at the same time this is very great thought. He is, or many would see him as such – Descartes is as well – in many ways the founder of a hermeneutic of suspicion.

Q: Can not a hermeneutic of suspicion be turned on these Enlightenment thinkers? Is their world view really so immutable?

Yes, it can. There are those who like to turn the tables on all these reason-led sceptics, but, and this is a serious but, there are limits in a hermeneutic of suspicion because if you have a hermeneutic of suspicion then Christians are in the end the ones who are going to lose out on it, beginning from Marx.

It would be interesting to put him and Kierkegaard in the same room together, that would be a very interesting experience, they could discuss the kind of reason that God subjects us to. To Locke, God would not expect unreasonable beliefs of us, yet as Kierkegaard would say a crucified criminal is the source of salvation. Is there anything reasonable in that!

You see, for Locke, reason situates Revelation, not Revelation situating reason. So, truth can't be revealed unless, in some way or other, reason judges it in some way to be rational. So you can't have a revelation in no matter what sense: Revelation must be concrete in its judgements, and the last word has to be had by reason.

Hume,[9] a generation on, says that the Indian Prince who refused to believe reports that there was a thing called ice reasoned rightly. The Indian Prince had never known freezing temperatures and had never known ice and therefore had never experienced ice and therefore Hume says that he is right to conclude that there cannot be such a thing as ice. Which is the exact point, the reasoning must be right even if the conclusion is wrong. It might follow from Locke's position but it certainly did from his successor Hume who did draw that conclusion which is very odd, very odd, and it suggests that we can never accept anything from anybody else however reliable they are as a person unless you can vouch for it yourself.

Q: Hume believed this position, Locke did not go this far but is this position of Hume's implicit in Locke's thinking? We can argue that if someone explained about freezing temperatures to him, and explained what happens then he might be persuaded. This is important because apostolic witness is based on such persuasion: testimony and witness. Law often revolves upon such signed testimony made under oath. Locke did believe in and accepted apostolic witness, did he not?

Yes, that's right; because Locke does believe apostolic witness in a rather limited way. Basically he believed in Christianity for two reasons: the fulfilment of prophecy, in other words he is checking the New Testament against the Old, and the other is miracles, in other words you can believe Revelation if it comes on the proposal of the founder as coming from the divine source. Jesus performs more mighty miracles than other religious figures, so then you can credit Jesus. This is a highly empiricist way of judging. And, of course, Hume shows that this doesn't work, and that is what Hume's theological significance is; he cuts out all of Locke's

[9] David Hume (1711–76), Scottish philosopher, economist and historian, a key figure in the Age of Reason and the development of the (so-called) Enlightenment.

remaining defences of the rationality of Christianity. But in the end what Locke is doing is trying to find something that is both empirical and theological.

You see, Aquinas' understanding is that reason is a capacity in us – this ability sets us apart from the rest of creation. Locke's idea of reason is functional. What is distinctive about the Thomist vision is the faith vision, so that the whole thing is a faith vision and reason and Revelation belong as two parts of the whole vision of the one truth of God. What you have here with Locke is that reason and Revelation become, well, reason is magnified at the expense of Revelation, because it is reason that is the fundamental faith object, the faith now is in reason as the source of truth – Revelation now has to justify itself at the path of reason.

But, yes, there is a point, which is a fair comment, that he is rarefying truth even more than Aquinas was; it becomes the God-like part of the human, really, and that instead of having one vision with two arms, so to speak, the vision is a rationalist one – it is a Christian rationalist one – so somehow or other he has got to find room for Revelation within it. A lot of people would argue, for example, Stephen Williams writes about Locke quite a lot. They would argue that there is much more of a religious vision going through Locke than his successors. That is because he wanted to defend the Christian vision in some way. In the end he chooses rather limited weapons to do it with. And by homing in on the fulfilment of prophecy and miracles as a defence he does leave himself thin, philosophically thin, his defence is very thin; you see he hasn't got the richness of the medieval understanding of Revelation.

iii. Foundationalism and Defence

The crucial thing, I think, and this is from Wolterstorff, is not only that you have to defend your beliefs by reason but you have to defend them by reasons from outside the religious world. That's foundationalism! This is what struck me in that preface, a telling preface of Wolterstorff's.[10] He says that twenty-five years ago he began to see the astonishing things that were expected of him if he was to defend religion – he was expected to defend it on an extra-religious basis.[11] In

[10] Nicholas Wolterstorff, *John Locke and the Ethics of Belief* (Cambridge: Cambridge University Press, 1996). See Preface, pp. ix–xxi.

[11] Wolterstorff, *John Locke and the Ethics of Belief* (1996): 'It is about twenty-five years ago now that I first became perplexed over the challenge so widely issued to religious people that they must have evidence for their religious beliefs – evidence consisting of other beliefs. It was insisted that at bottom a person might not reason from his or her religious beliefs but had to reason to them from other beliefs. Why was this? I asked. Nobody assumed, for example, that all our perceptual belief had to be based on other beliefs; what was it about one and all religious beliefs that made them different? Eventually I (along with colleagues of mine at Calvin College) concluded that the culprit in the matter was the assumption that foundationalism, specifically, "classically modern" foundationalism, states the truth of the matter concerning proper belief-formation.* So I reflected on the tenability of this epistemological position, eventually concluding that, when clearly formulated and then held up to the light, it is decisively mistaken – and it makes

other words you are expected to defend the thing by means coming from outside that overall vision, that is the crucial thing, and for Aquinas there would be nothing outside the overall Christian vision. In that sense he is not, in the classical sense, a natural theologian; I mean Locke is a natural theologian, there is no pretending he is not; no, I think it is the shift of the weight, the weight is shifted from being equally on the two – Revelation and reason – to being more strongly on reason. So I think it is more than simply a functional view of reason. You see, if you believe with Descartes, but then he doesn't believe everything Descartes wrote. Certainly for Descartes, reason is a kind of divine thing within us, a divine faculty within us. For Locke, I suppose, everything has to come in from outside: the mind begins as an empty box or a wax tablet that is as yet unmarked.

This is a functional view of reason. Yet he is also ascribing to reason God-like powers in the sense that everything must be judged at the bar of reason, in effect to say that reason is almost a transcendental capacity that we have by which we are called upon to decide between the truth, between competing claims of truth: What is the truth? The thing about Locke is that it is very experimental thinking; it is not a unified vision, the empiricist in Book 4 definitely becomes rationalist. Wolterstorff has said that Book 4 represents an empiricist with a rationalist criteria of knowledge. That is what is complicated about it; he is a rationalist with a supreme trust in reason so it is difficult to say that for him reason is simply a human function. It must be more than that or he couldn't claim so much for it: it is clearly something given to us by God.

iv. Subjectivism and Enthusiasm

Locke does want Revelation but it mustn't be something that relies on subjectivism because there lies enthusiasm. In that sense he is right, our belief in Revelation isn't a belief in our private vision, it is a belief that God has spoken to the human race, particularly through the human race and through Jesus: that is a communal belief. It is, in a sense, also an enthusiastic belief; a lot of people won't believe it and can't believe it, but even if you rationalize until you are blue in the face, in that sense, it is sectarian because it belongs only to those who buy into it. It is not sectarian in the sense that it isn't a series of private revelations, that is where you need an ecclesiology – which he hasn't got.

Once you have got an ecclesiology you have got the kind of authority and tradition that are precisely what was in question at the time of the Enlightenment;

no difference whether it is offered as a criterion for acceptance of scientific theories, as a criterion for entitlement to ordinary beliefs about the world and religious matters, or whatever' (pp. x–xi). Wolterstorff included a footnote on 'classic foundationalism' marked above by an asterix: * – 'By a classical foundationalist I mean one who holds that the only immediate (basic) belief which possesses whatever be the doxastic merit in question are those whose content is either a proposition self-evident to the person, or a proposition which is an incorrigible report of a mental act or object of the person', (pp. x).

authority and tradition were supposedly at the core of all the problems. People were fighting each other – the English Civil War, for instance, which was fought allegedly on the basis of religious differences. So, for these empiricists, these Lockian empiricists, it was the church institution on the basis of dogmatic differences that they thought they were getting rid of, and then they could make peace. Yet, of course, in the twentieth century it has been the proponents of reason who have been the most murderous and destructive, which is why so many people are saying that the whole Lockian thing has broken down irretrievably, it just hasn't worked, and that is why MacIntyre is such a great philosopher.[12] I think, he picked this up very early on – the need to go back to medieval type of philosophy. It does raise the question about the nature of Revelation; I mean, Locke has a very impoverished view of Revelation, doesn't he? – Revelation is for him just the fulfilment of prophecy and things like miracles.

Locke attempted to defend belief, religious belief, but the philosophers who came after him refute him. You see, there is a side of him that wants to be a genuinely Christian thinker but at the same time he has bought into all the arguments that find the specifically Christian things like dogma and tradition and authority deeply questionable. I suppose there is always going to be a tension, isn't there, a tension between someone who is a defender of the faith on the one hand and at the same time tries to be with good conscience a modern thinker as well, a modern thinker who swallows all that the Enlightenment has produced. Barth says this about so many of the nineteenth-century thinkers, theologians and philosophers who preceded him: they wanted to have a good conscience as a modern, and yet defend the faith at the same time. Now that is definitely one tension in him, in Locke. I suppose the other tension in him is a serious concern for Revelation and the fact that he has a concept of reason that doesn't leave much room for Revelation.

You see a foundationalist is someone who tries to seek foundations for faith not in faith itself, and in doing so he requires you to pass over, cross over, an epistemological bridge. In so doing a foundationalist is using the concept of Revelation to take you over an epistemological bridge, and that, he thinks, is not what the concept of Revelation is designed to do. For him it is a subsidiary part of the whole game of theology rather than being an attempt to get yourself out of a hole.

12 Alasdair C. MacIntyre (b. 1929), a philosopher who has also worked in the history of philosophy and theology. See, for example: Antony Flew and Alasdair C. MacIntyre, *New Essays in Philosophical Theology* (New York, Macmillan, 1964); Alasdair C. MacIntyre, *Marxism and Christianity* (New York, NY: Schocken Books, 1968); Alasdair C. MacIntyre, *Hegel: a Collection of Critical Essays* (Garden City, NY: Anchor Books, 1972); and Alasdair C. MacIntyre, *After Virtue: a Study in Moral Theory* (Notre Dame, IN: University of Notre Dame Press, 1981).

v. Christ and Reason

Q: 'What specifically does Locke have to say about the Revelation of God in Christ? It does not seem to be very Christocentric?

In *The Reasonableness of Christianity* it is Christ, he wrote, who is fulfilling prophecy.[13] This, for Locke, makes Christianity reasonable. I don't think you can look at this back through modern views of Revelation, like Barth's for instance, and so on. It is Christ who is fulfilling prophecy; he is not making anything of the propositional view of Revelation. In principle it could be applicable to any other religion except for the miracles. Why? Because, yes, I think he has got this view that by miracles you defend certain truths or claimed truths. That is what is meant by Revelation and tradition. And that is why the fulfilment of prophecy is so important to him. Prophets say that this will happen and it does, then you have got some kind of revelatory correspondence, or correlation between that which was predicted and that which happened. That is why I said that it is a rather thin, impoverished view of Revelation.

LOCKE'S THREE CONCEPTS OF REASON

RATIONAL	CONTRARY	HIGHER
The first concept is the rational concept: this is where you can prove something.	The second concept of reason is contrary to reason: an absurdity like a square circle.	The third concept of reason is above reason, but is seen as defensible

Figure 5

There is very little of the idea of a personal God making himself known, that is almost non-existent. You can put a certain proposition 'That God exists', by reason; other propositions 'That Jesus is the Son of God' have to be defended in other ways, that is to say, by miracle. These are above reason for him. He has three concepts of reason, one is rational, when you can prove it, another is contrary to reason, meaning it is absurd like a square circle, the third is above reason but defensible (figure 5). So he is really almost entirely propositional, defensible, but only by some special means, proved by God as proved by miracle. It is not surprising that he doesn't have much of a view of Revelation with that sort of view. That is part of the problem; the idea of a personal God revealing himself just doesn't seem to be part of the game.

[13] See John Locke, *The Reasonableness of Christianity, as Delivered in the Scriptures* (1695), also, *A Vindication of the Reasonableness of Christianity* (1695). John Locke, *The Reasonableness of Christianity: as Delivered in the Scriptures* (Clarendon Edition of the Works of John Locke, ed. John C. Higgins-Biddle; Oxford: Oxford University Press, Clarendon Press; 2000).

And for Baillie, yes, Baillie he is right, his idea in that book on Revelation and reason, is that in recent centuries the idea of propositional Revelation has been replaced by an idea of a self-revealing, personal God who reveals himself. [14]

2. T. F. Torrance

i. Theological Science

T. F. Torrance established the concept, or what he is attributed with, of theological science. Now what is science? – and how does it relate to what we've been talking about, the use of reason over Revelation. Barth uses the German word for science, *Wissenschaft*, in his discussion in *The Christian Dogmatics*, [15] which actually means an ordered form of knowledge.[16] To Torrance science was the activity in which we look into, we scrutinize, we investigate things – often a scientist interrogates, but that is something else I suppose, well, it's similar – science investigates things and events for their regularity, their order, which they manifest. That is all to do with observing – they observe their order in their interconnections, their relationships one with another. Why? For Torrance, this is because it is an effort to reduce the manifold, yes, even the diversity, of relations in the world, if not the world then at least in some field of experience. You see, reductionism, that's in one way what science is about; and this is to reduce to some kind of uniformity and if possible to penetrate down into – and this could almost be Torrance's own words. He says this somewhere, I think – their unitary logical basis in the understanding of them through which the whole field of our experience can be illuminated.[17]

ii. God as the Object?

Now, can you do that with God? Can you reduce God to an object? Some would say Torrance believes you can, though I think he would have been more subtle and

14 John Baillie, *The Idea of Revelation in Recent Thought* (New York, Columbia University Press, 1956). See also John Baillie, *Our knowledge of God* (New York: Scribner, 1959).

John Baillie (1886–1960), Scottish theologian, Church of Scotland minister was Professor at the University of Edinburgh and Moderator of the General Assembly of the Church of Scotland. Baillie explored the relationship between the epistemology (knowledge of God) and the spiritual/moral life.

15 Karl Barth, *Die Christliche Dogmatik im Entwurf – Erste Band Die Lehre vom Worte Gottes, Prolegomena zur christlichen Dogmatik 1927* (Gesamtausgabe 14; Zürich: Theologischer Verlag Zürich, 1982).

16 *Wissenschaft, die*, specifically, science, but also generally to be scholarly; *wissenschaftlich*, in a scholarly manner, *Wissenschaftlichkeit, die*, scholarliness, scientific rigour, academic rigour, research conducted in a proper manner.

17 T. F. Torrance, *Theological Science* (Oxford: Oxford University Press, 1969).

nuanced that that. You see, if theology is the intellectual side of the Christian faith showing it as a unified body of truth then he has got to be right somehow, certainly to a degree. Though science really is specializing in the material realm – and there are many scientists who only believe in the material realm (figure 6).

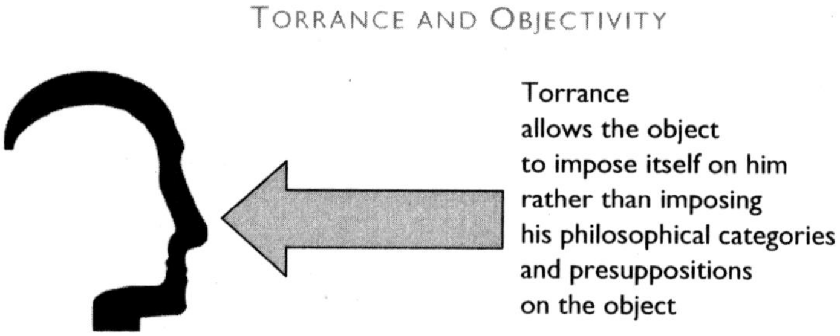

Figure 6

There is the influence here of Torrance's teacher A. E. Taylor from the 1920s. Taylor called for the locating of authority neither in individualism nor in institutionalism, but in a reality that is wholly given and trans-subjective and is simply and absolutely authoritative. If knowledge is to be more than personal opinion then there must be limits placed on our personal intellectual constructs by something that is not constructed but received. This is a typical objective view. Now, by intuition Torrance means not a leap but a Polanyian integration.[18] What a scientist does according to Polanyi is to bring together all the various clues in a problem and integrate them by an act of bringing them together, seeing them make sense.

This is what Torrance is doing with theology, using these tools for Revelation, integrating them intuitively, as it were, into a whole. Torrance comes after Kant; Locke is before Kant; that seems to me to be important, crucially important as we shall see.

[18] Michael Polanyi (born Mihály Polányi, 1891–1976), Hungarian–British polymath whose work transcended physics, chemistry, economics and philosophy; Polanyi was Fellow of Merton College, Oxford. In the 1930s he began to argue against the dominant logical positivism in science, claiming that such an approach failed to identify the importance of what he termed tacit knowledge and the creative role played by the imagination. See Michael Polanyi, *Science, Faith, and Society* (Chicago, IL: University of Chicago Press, 1966 [1946]); Michael Polanyi, *The Logic of Liberty: Reflections and Rejoinders* (Chicago, IL: University of Chicago Press, 1951); Michael Polanyi, *Personal Knowledge: Towards a Post-Critical Philosophy* (Chicago, IL: University of Chicago Press, 1958); Michael Polanyi, *The Tacit Dimension* (Gloucester, MA: Peter Smith, [1967]); and Michael Polanyi, *Knowing and Being* (Chicago, IL: University of Chicago Press,1969).

3. Hans Urs von Balthasar and Theological Aesthetics

And then of course there is Hans Urs von Balthasar.[19] He takes a different line though not unrelated. He too is concerned with this subject–object relationship.

i. The Third Transcendental

Balthasar talks of aesthetics, beauty, theological aesthetics – Do they provide a method for us? Very different, some would say, very different from Torrance and theological science – Is that right? Others would say not. You see, Balthasar talked of the third transcendental, that is to say, to contemplate the vision of the true and good with that of the beautiful (figure 7).[20]

HANS URS VON BALTHASAR - THE THREE TRANSCENDENTALS

The First Transcendental	The Second Transcendental	The Third Transcendental
THE GOOD	THE TRUE	THE BEAUTIFUL

Figure 7

Balthasar saw Luther's aesthetic as the root of the, yes, gradual elimination of the third transcendental. This is not to say that Luther did not have an aesthetic of course; he is quite wrong about Luther in general, Luther had an aesthetic – especially music, he wrote hymns. What Luther objects to, I think, is a medieval kind of aesthetic, which in some sense excludes rather than includes the Word. That would be a Lutheran type of reply. But anyway this is polemics.

[19] Hans Urs von Balthasar (1905–88), Swiss Roman Catholic theologian, studied in Vienna, Berlin and Zurich, and was awarded a doctorate in German literature. He became a Jesuit in 1928. However, he left the Jesuits in 1950 to found a secular institute that sought to work for the sanctification of the world. He worked for a time with Karl Barth, publishing what is still regarded as a seminal study of the Swiss Reformed theologian. John Paul II appointed him a cardinal in 1988, however he died before the ceremony. Balthasar is regarded as one of the most important though controversial twentieth-century Roman Catholic theologians; his response to modernism was to resist reductionism, and to oppose the focus on the human, arguing that Christianity should challenge and stand against modernity and its philosophical assumptions. Many see the influence of Karl Barth in this stance.

[20] Balthasar, Hans Urs von, *The Glory of the Lord* (*Herrlichkeit*, trans. Andrew Louth, Francis McDonagh and Brian McNeil 1982–91; 7 vols; the first part of his 16–volume trilogy of systematics: *Herrlichkeit*, 1961–9, *Theodramatik*, 1973–83 and *Theologik*, 1985; London: Continuum International Publishing Group, T&T Clark, 2003).

But then Balthasar does consider the Roman Catholic Church a more acceptable home for theological aesthetics, you see, he considered his heritage in Anselm and Aquinas though for him Rome is not without criticism, he criticized Rome as well. What I think worries him is this turn away from the object of theological reflection, that's how he puts it, a turn away into subjectivity and he criticizes both churches for that.

For Balthasar form is the real presence and gives us the depth of reality: you see, form is not something that we need to get behind first in order to reach reality, it is part of reality. This is quite important. The way a thing presents itself to be seen is important and of value. This is not Platonic form, which does mean getting behind appearances. This is the giving of the shape, the form, of the thing in itself, as it presents itself.

A lot of this he does learn from Barth as he might admit because he was one of the first commentators on Barth's dogmatics; he was one of the first major commentators on Barth.[21] He picks up from Barth this notion of the beauty of God. Barth's principle in theology is that content must cohere with form. This is written against Bultmann; the Bultmannians are in effect trying to get behind the form to get to, in this case, some sort of anthropological response to the form. And I think that Balthasar here wanted to go from the way things actually are, as they present themselves to the enquiring mind. And obviously this is a very Catholic way in which he does it.

So, the concept of beauty is important to him, and Jesus Christ is the form of Revelation, and we should not abstract or try to get behind him, it's no good trying to deconstruct Jesus Christ! What you see is what you get.

In a way this is objective because it arouses the delight – that is the point he is stressing about the objective. He is arguing against the view that beauty is in the eye of the beholder: it is not; it is in the form. And as such, to a degree, it imposes itself on us, I think. When you see a beautiful thing the first thing you see is its beauty and not your response to it. He's right, isn't he? Beauty is in the form, it is not in our subjective response.

ii. The Priority of the Objective over the Subjective

This is right because he says that the objective has priority over the subjective. There is a sense in which the beauty conveys its beauty to us so in that respect we are passive, in an odd way it is active, in some ways it almost wants to impose itself on us. Bestowed is the key word, very active (figure 8).

So he is in a way drawing an analogy between the way in which some natural beauty or artistic beauty imposes itself upon us, and an analogy between that and the shape of the Incarnation imposing itself upon us. That is, I think, the point he

[21] Balthasar, Hans Urs von, *Karl Barth, Darstellung und Deutung seiner Theologie* (Köln: Verlag Jakob Hegner, 1951), English trans. *The Theology of Karl Barth – Exposition and Interpretation* (trans. John Drury; New York: Holt, Rinehart & Winston, 1971).

is trying to make. The whole notion of form enables us to understand what is going on. Inevitably there is an Incarnational theology underlying everything that he says.

Figure 8

Q: Is there a distinction between hearing the word and seeing beauty?

Of course there is, then there is the question of the relationship between *hearing* and *seeing*, and comprehending, is there not? There is, for him, a parallel between the hearing and the seeing. Obviously invisibility is a seeing metaphor, you see the invisible through the visible Christ; but he talks about hearing the word as well. He is operating on both of those images, he mainly talks of seeing the form, but that doesn't exclude hearing the form the word takes; you see, all the time this is moving towards love: man loving God, the love of God by man. This is our proper response to Revelation: we love God.

iii. Abstract Isolation

What concerns him so much is what I think he calls 'abstract isolation'. He talks about this as disengaging and disincarnating. Disengagement is interesting because that is one of the crucial concepts that Charles Taylor took up in his book *Sources of the Self* to characterize the modern enlightened approach to reality.[22] This is a very important book. Taylor argues that disengagement is what characterizes the modern attempt to rationalize. In attempting to grasp rationally a thing, do we not abstract from our engagement with it? You can't do this with ethics, well you can try, but it fails because the whole notion of ethics involves engagement of some kind.

22 Charles Taylor, *Sources of the Self: the Making of the Modern Identity* (Cambridge, MA: Harvard University Press, 1989).

You see there is disengagement; well it does suggest that what Balthasar is doing is what lots and lots of theologians are trying to do and that is trying to get away from this disengaged rationality of modernity and trying to relate this object and subject in a meaningful way rather than by developing an abstract objectivism.

Michael Polanyi's polemics are exactly the same – you can't have a rationality without some measure of being involved in some way in that which you are attempting to analyse. So for him there is a subject–object engagement which is a precondition of rationality: if rationality isn't engaged it isn't rational; rationality must be engaged with the real world. Balthasar is batting on the same sort of wicket, travelling the same sort of route. This is the common factor; it is a feature of so many modern theological attempts to engage with the aridity of modern rationalism.

iv. Beauty Is True and Good

Balthasar does place much importance on beauty, he is I suppose quite different in some ways to other twentieth-century theologians in doing that; Barth does, of course, but I don't think he has a doctrine of beauty, I don't know.

Q: Is he trying to value beauty over truth and goodness?

No. Well, no, I don't think that's what he is doing – you see all he is trying to do, in concentrating on the third transcendental, is to give it equal status. When he talks about beauty he seems to be talking about something that we can take positive pleasure in. It is interesting, of course, that Barth writing on Anselm writes how Anselm wants understanding because he wants joy. Barth picks up from Anselm the very aesthetic note that Balthasar says, that in some sense the truth should increase your pleasure in it. I think that is what he is driving at. I am sure he is right.

I am sure Balthasar is right that unless the beautiful bears in some way upon the good and the true you haven't got it. Unless the good and the true are in some way bound up with beauty then you probably haven't got them. This raises the whole question of aesthetic truth: A thing can't be beautiful and yet immoral, can it? Or can it? That is the interesting question theologically speaking, if a thing is truly beautiful it won't also destroy one's ethical grasp upon reality.

It is a very un-modern, very unfashionable thing to say: Can the ugly define the eschatologically good or true? Modern novels which glory in, or which express the sordidness of life, have their place because they teach us something about Original Sin. A certain kind of modern novel that is pessimistic and brutal is true in the sense that it shows us something about the human fight so that in its depiction of ugliness it is depicting some truth.

Another question is 'Is Original Sin the truth about us?' You have to allow for the fact that works of art may tell us the truth about us through their ugliness, yet ultimately you may still want to say that beauty is truth, and truth is beauty.

Q: Is the Cross ugly?

Tragedy is an expression of suffering, Greek tragedy that is, not Shakespeare, because that has been Christianized in some sense. Greek tragedy is suffering of rather a horrible kind – and that on the whole is the final message we are left with from reading them. But it isn't the final message, Christianly speaking. If something has an overall meaning it can't be entirely bad.

But, be careful that you don't justify sin and evil; because if you turn the Cross into a tragedy as some people do, if you look at the Cross in literal terms, if you look at these things in literary terms you are in danger of reducing their horror, you are reducing them to some kind of order. They haven't got order, only in so far as God uses them to overcome evil. You see, you can beautify that which ought not to be beautified.

Q: The relationship between compassion and pathos – Where does sentimentality come in? People may feel a sense of beauty or pathos when they see the error of their ways, can they not?

We are dealing with a dangerous area. One thing we have not thought of is how far is beauty in its own way redemptive, how far does beauty in some way redeem by transmuting the ordinary and the ugly – or is such a transformation eschatological? That is the other side of it. Art can be redemptive: we can go in, weep tears and come out better people. It can be redemptive. But if you aestheticize everything you somehow lose the bite, you sentimentalize.

I think it is important for us to remember that Balthasar is not talking about, no, he's not promoting an aesthetic theology, this is still proper systematics; he is simply re-addressing the third transcendental.

4. Karl Rahner: Revelation and Transcendentality

Hans Urs Von Balthasar is not alone. He's a modern Catholic theologian, influenced by Vatican II, but so is his – to many – polar opposite: Karl Rahner. Though for that matter they both influenced Vatican II – as did Barth, but that is another story. Maybe they are not that opposite, it's just that their supporters and detractors tend to gather in groups supporting one and denying the other. But they both have written much from a Catholic perspective on Revelation and reason which is relevant to our discussions. It is appropriate here to consider Karl Rahner's *Foundations of the Christian Faith*.[23] Rahner talks of two forms of Revelation: transcendental Revelation and categorical Revelation. Why transcendence?

[23] Karl Rahner SJ (1904–84), one of the most influential Roman Catholic theologians of the twentieth century, his theology was important for the development of the modern understanding of Catholicism, and was influential on the Second Vatican Council. Written near the end of his life, Rahner's *Grundkurs des Glaubens* (*Foundations of Christian Faith*) is probably the most systematic of his works. The basis of Rahner's work is that all human beings have a latent awareness of God in their freedom as finite subjects. He regarded this experience as transcendental.

See Karl Rahner, *Grundkurs des Glaubens: Einführung in den Begriff des Christentums* (Freiburg: Herder, 1976). English trans. *Foundations of Christian Faith: an Introduction to the Idea of Christianity* (London: Darton Longman & Todd, 1978).

For Rahner transcendence is a mode of being. Humanity is in closeness and immediacy with God. This is – as Rahner puts it – the event of the free unmerited and forgiven self-communication of God. So, man is the event of the self-communication of God for Rahner. History then is the history of man's transcendentality, history is not a spectacle – that's the word he uses I think, spectacle – it is not a case of history just happening and man being involved at the end. History is humanity's history, and it is of foundation and Revelation. So, this marks Rahner as the characteristically modern theologian in that he begins with some form of reflection on the human condition (that's one definition of modernity, I suppose, it's one symptom of the modern world this preoccupation with the human condition): therefore his theology is grounded in an analysis of what it is to be human, to be a human being in the world.

i. Transcendence

So where is Revelation in this? For Rahner Revelation is in God's self-communication to humanity. Transcendence then is the key here. He moves from his fundamentally anthropological starting point to what is for him an implicit theological message. Individuals can then accept this self-communication of God – or not. For Rahner, the history of salvation is the history of Revelation: the two sit hand-in-hand.

This is rather like Barth's position, though their understanding of Revelation is different; for both of then salvation and Revelation are two sides of the same historical process or event, both are theologians of Revelation and salvation at the same time – you can't evacuate either side without misunderstanding what they are about.

For Rahner the encounter of transcendental Revelation is a conception of God breaking into our personal world, entering our consciousness, but this is not objective, it is God breaking into our consciousness through our deepest restlessness. This is simply there. So this is Revelation as God entering into the person. In some ways this is a version, a variation, on a basic Augustinian theme – God has made us for himself and our hearts are restless until we find rest in him.[24] So Rahner's transcendentality is a version of the heart's restlessness, or need, or orientation, to God, though it is not necessarily thematic. It's a modern thing to do with consciousness, it is below the threshold of consciousness, as it were, but it's there: a classic Western thesis! It is a level beyond anything we do or feel.

Q: Is this comparable with Schleiermacher's use of 'feeling' as a theological basis?

This is not feeling. It is not the same as Schleiermacher's use of feeling, though it is undoubtedly like Schleiermacher in one sense. It is not about feeling –

[24] 'You stir man to take pleasure in you, because you have made us for yourself, and our heart is restless until it finds you.' Augustine, *Saint Augustine: Confessions* (Oxford: World Classics; trans. Henry Chadwick; Oxford: Oxford University Press, 1991), see bk 1 Early Years, p. 3.

but it is parallel, it's attempting to identify the basic human religiousness. The structure of the theology here in *Foundations of the Christian Faith* is rather like Schleiermacher's because Rahner first analyses general religiousness and then a specifically Christian religiousness. He is in parallel to Schleiermacher in the sense that this transcendentality is not limited to Jews or Christians; he is trying to characterize the universal human condition – it is in many ways Augustinian, what is it that makes the human being religious, that directs him or her God-wards.

ii. John Hick and Universal Religiosity

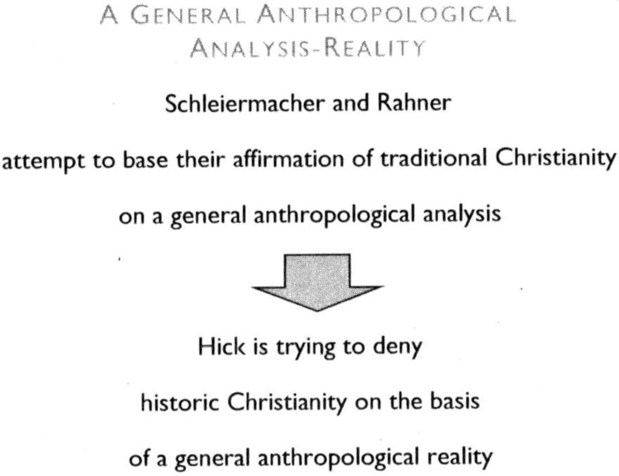

Figure 9

Q: Is this what John Hick is about? – seeing the religious in all.

In the way he assesses and interprets religion Hick is trying to do something like this but Hick is much more Kantian: there is much more of God in Rahner than in Hick![25] But in terms of the universality, that is right: what Hick wants to do is a much more sceptical Kantian job. What he is saying is that there is this kind of religiousness which is a sort of drive towards reality, he wants to talk about God as the ultimately real, or the ultimate some-thing, and that therefore all religions are variations on this one quest for ultimate reality, and I think that Schleiermacher and Rahner are also doing something like that in the sense that they want to say that there is something universal, but it takes a specifically Christian form. And that is where Hick leaves; he doesn't want or need anything specifically Christian, he wants to say that all these religions are equally unsuccessful attempts to characterize the ultimate. Hick is much more, well – you see, both Schleiermacher and Rahner attempt to base their affirmation of traditional Christianity on a general

[25] John Hick, *An Interpretation of Religion: Human Responses to the Transcendent* (Basingstoke: Macmillan, 1989).

anthropological analysis. Hick by comparison, by contrast, is trying to deny historic Christianity on the basis of an anthropological reality (figure 9). Hick wants to say that all these religions are routes to the same reality; Rahner certainly would deny that. For Rahner they are all routes, but only Christianity is the true and satisfying way.

Q: But what about Rahner's concept of 'Anonymous Christian'?

Yes, but, to acknowledge anonymous Christians presupposes that Christianity is the criterion, right? To say there are anonymous Christians is to say that there are conscious Christians and that they as it were affirm the truth of Christian Revelation, but also that there are people who appear to behave in a Christian way and we have to say that although they are not, although they don't accept Christ or even know about Christ, they are in their own way Christ-like: that is definitely hierarchical. Right, OK? Hick is against all forms of hierarchy, you see, really – except Hick's own theory of the ultimately real, which, of course, he knows about, and others are ignorant of. But seriously – seriously – there is no such thing as pluralism. Gavin D'Costa has rightly been concerned with this; there was a paper given here a few years ago, at a conference, a paper that annoyed a number of Hickians, which said that there is no such thing as pluralism, because pluralism is itself a particular position, a particular viewpoint.[26] And that's right; Hick is taking up a position, a particular position, and therefore it is not pluralistic because Hick's position is just one among several competing supposedly equally valid positions. D'Costa's was a very interesting paper; having used this phenomenology of exclusivism–inclusivism and pluralism, D'Costa then realizes he cannot use it anymore – because every position is exclusive. Every position is exclusive, and that's right, logically it's right: if to say that 'A' is true, it logically requires you to deny the truth of 'not A', then you are being selective, you are excluding. So any thesis in that sense is exclusive.

Rahner is prepared to use this universal basis but to say that the Trinity is the criterion: he's not a general religionist in the way that Hick is. Rahner argues for a form of Revelation that is within the church's tradition – but this is not necessarily natural theology. Humanity must, you see, have for Rahner some a priori knowledge so as to be able to respond to the word of God. Rahner is in effect arguing that Revelation needs a point of contact – Revelation must need something ready for it, prepared for it. The reason why human beings accept divine Revelation is that there is an intrinsic directedness to it, a preparedness to it, in their basic – to use Rahner's term – 'transcendentality': human beings open up towards God's inbreaking.

iii. The Nature–Grace Dichotomy

A more traditional way of putting this would be to say that there is a grace in creation, you are created and there is objective divine grace, and that this appears in

[26] Gavin D'Costa, 'The Impossibility of a Pluralist View of Religion', *Religious Studies* 32 (1996).

the fundamental structure of your being. Rahner is, like so many modern Catholic theologians, trying to get away from a rigid nature–grace dichotomy, where there is a world of nature to which grace is then applied. Aquinas's conception of this had been hardened in late nineteenth-century scholasticism into a rather rigid form in which the two worlds tended to be closed-off from one another. It is against this that certain Catholic modernists try to develop questions like Rahner's question about the readiness, the openness, of the human being to Revelation. So it is an attempt to integrate the worlds of nature and grace rather than putting them alongside one another. This is the whole essence of much modern Catholic theologians: Balthasar is similar but in a different sort of way, though it is important to remember that Rahner and Balthasar are presented as opposites, they are set off against each other, rightly or wrongly, in the same way that Barth and Tillich are set off against each other in Protestant circles.

There is an interesting book by Ralph del Colle, a Catholic theologian, it's mainly on Christology, but it is interesting here because he explores the way by which Christology is affected in the neo-Scholastics in the nineteenth century. Christology, you see, is affected by this nature–grace model.[27]

iv. Categorical Revelation

The innate a priori basis for Revelation in humanity does not exist in and for itself: it exists to be open to mediation, to categorical revelation. Revelation must be grounded in the historical: Jesus Christ is the highest point of God's self-revelation; Rahner goes on to explain that Jesus Christ is likewise the only tangible point in salvation history.

Categorical Revelation is something like particular Revelation in many ways. So the question is raised between the categorical Revelation that is also salvation on the one hand and the general Revelation that provides its basis. The problem here is that transcendental Revelation may appear pure and untouched by human sin, while categorical Revelation can appear corruptible. This in some ways reflects Aquinas's assertion that the will is fallen but not the intellect. There is, it is fair to say, much of Aquinas's Scholasticism in Rahner's work, but this approach had become rigidified in the neo-Scholasticism: Scholasticism was largely Thomist but the First Vatican Council ruled that Aquinas's system was *the* Catholic theology. In the twentieth century there is this attempt to make it less rigid, this is where Rahner belongs, I think.

Rahner is asserting that transcendental Revelation is a necessary background to categorical Revelation: transcendental Revelation and categorical Revelation must be taken hand-in-hand. Does this mean that one supplements the other? If categorical Revelation cannot exist without transcendental Revelation then he is in

27 Ralph del Colle, *Christ and the Spirit: Spirit-Christology in Trinitarian Perspective* (Oxford: Oxford University Press, 1994).

effect, I believe, saying that grace perfects nature. Therefore salvation cannot be found outside the church, but – and this is important – certainly for Rahner, there is the possibility of salvation for those outside the church. The question raised by this is whether it denies *extra ecclesiam nulla salus* or simply broadens it?[28]

Q: But this still leaves the question of other religions, does it not?

Rahner sees God's self-revelation as on offer to all: Is not God working in other religions, Christ working in other religions? He writes about all peoples being open to God's grace, but these other religions must be seen as fragmentary attempts to explain God's truth, they are not therefore necessarily false; you get this in Barth as well – though Barth takes it beyond religion, which is why he so loves Mozart, doesn't he? As I have said before, and will continue to say, Revelation's ultimate form is in Jesus Christ. I think it is fair to say that for Rahner everyone has transcendental Revelation; only if you are in the church do you have access to categorical Revelation. Only in Jesus will you find final and total Revelation. But then we are in history and history moves, you need to have a sufficient doctrine of the telos here do you not? – you need to have some understanding of teleology, the way everything is moving towards completion in Christ.

v. Vatican II: Revelation and other Religions

This is in some ways acknowledging the Second Vatican Council's attempts to make the Catholic attitude to other religions – and other Christian groups (they don't call them churches) – less exclusive. But, you may ask, what lies behind it? It is this, that the Roman Church is the only true ark of salvation. Rahner rightly cannot deny that without denying its being; but at the same time he does want to qualify some of the more exclusive claims that appear to follow from it. So, it is an attempt to say that although the church does mediate salvation, nonetheless there is the openness of God to be found everywhere, and that openness of God may bear all kinds of fruits.

The Second Vatican Council did want to express the greater possibility of conversation between the churches. The Rahner approach is mainly orientated towards other religions, because he doesn't want to be too exclusive towards them. And that is exactly the balance: they may not be true, they are not necessarily false, they very likely are, but they are nonetheless in their own way a response to grace. You see, everything in its own way is a response to grace. It is not a question of prevenient grace – is it? It's a doctrine of universal grace really. It's the grace of creation: because the gracious God has created the world, then the world, the universe, simply reflects the marks of *His* creating grace. This is particularly seen in

[28] Cyprian of Carthage (d. 258) is credited with the phrase, *extra ecclesiam nulla salus* (outside the church there is no salvation). See St Cyprian of Carthage, *On the Church* (Vol. I. *Select Letters*, Vol. II. *Select Treatises*) (trans. with intro. and commentary, Allen Brent; Popular Patristics Series, No 32 and 33; Crestwood, NY: St Vladimir's Seminary Press, 2007).

human transcendentality, human openness to that which is beyond the immediate reality. This is the grace of creation.

vi. Incarnation and Language: adaequatio

REVELATION IS INCARNATION, INCARNATION IS REVELATION

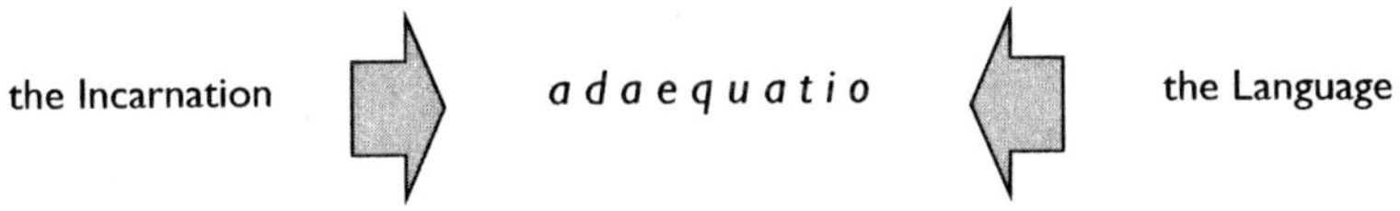

Adaequatio **brings together the Incarnation**

and the language in which the Incarnation is described

and mediated by the Church:

To bring into positive relation
the mind and the thing.

Figure 10

Although statements about Revelation are important, they must be seen as inadequate, simply because they do not compare with the Incarnation. This must be seen as another Vatican II advance in the sense that Revelation is to be seen as more than the statement in which faith is mediated, communicated: there is the move towards a much more biblical or open concept of Revelation, which is basically the Incarnation. This is, I think it is fair to say (and most theologians would acknowledge this), is the influence of Barth on Roman Catholic theology. So Rahner is opening up space between the Incarnation and the language in which the Incarnation is described and mediated by the church. He describes these things as being *adaequatio* – that is a sort of correspondence.[29] He is interested in bringing the two alongside: the Incarnation and the language (figure 10). This is classic Thomist epistemology: to know is to 'adaequate'; well it's more than that, it is to bring into positive relation the mind and the thing. You can say that you know something, a thing, the object, if you describe it rightly. So again, this is a classic scholastic thesis. But it is not a classic concept of Revelation; it is much more biblical, much more incarnational. But Rahner has learnt from his interaction with the moderns.

These statements we have of categorical Revelation are therefore finite, they are historically set, this historical setting does condition to a degree the form of the statements, does it not? Trying to deduce all the logical consequences of this

[29] *Adaequatio*: approximation, or bringing alongside one another, that is the intellect and the thing, the mind and the object. From the Latin (seventeenth–century): *adaequat-*, *adaequare*, 'to make equal to', from *ad-* 'to' with *aequus* 'equal'; *adaeque* 'in like manner'.

Revelation is not the be-all and end-all: I think this again is Rahner attacking a sort of neo-scholasticism. We are talking about a living contact with the thing itself, but categorical Revelation must be seen as contextual.

vii. The Problem with Transcendentality as Revelation

Q: Why is transcendental Revelation, Revelation? The way Rahner sets it out makes it sound like a capacity, a capacity to *receive* Revelation, rather than Revelation *in itself*: Is it in itself Revelation?

Well, yes, Rahner does see the ability put in us by God to receive Revelation as Revelation in itself: Is he right? For Rahner the transcendental nature of the human is bound up with Revelation itself. Is this the weakness in Rahner's doctrine of Revelation? It's not really the transcendentalism that is the problem, it is the concept of Revelation: the question is 'In what sense is it Revelation?' If it is not natural theology then what is it if it is not Revelation? There are questions here: If grace is God acting then can we say that grace is Revelation? Grace is not Revelation, it is a divine act; it is another step to say it is Revelation. If transcendental Revelation is so complete, if – by being given – it completes the human, then why do we need categorical Revelation?

Q: It sounds as though transcendental Revelation is the hole in itself in the human not something that is put in the hole, the space, is this not so?

Yes, that is maybe the problem, because if you say that this hole, as you put it, is full, then why do you need categorical Revelation. Is categorical Revelation more than transcendental Revelation? There is something of a distinction between content and method here: Rahner wants to get a content out of a method – I think that is what is happening.

Q: I was wondering about Calvin, didn't he have the idea of the noetic impulse of the eternal that was put in everybody?

Well, *sensus divinitatis* or *sensus deitatis*,[30] yes that is a classic Augustinian pattern which we see recurring in Schleiermacher and Rahner but in a different form. I think that's right, that there is innate in every human being a kind of God-ward drive in some way, that's right, that's Calvin, but this is fundamentally different from Calvin.

Q: Is this salvation? Is this transcendental Revelation a form of salvation?

But is this salvation? Well, that is an important question: Is this transcendental Revelation salvation? And is this within the church? The only real salvation surely for a Catholic lies within the church, well not only for a Catholic but that's another question. You cannot say that transcendental Revelation is salvation. Definitely not; it is, it can be a preparation for salvation: it's universal, but it is a preparation.

30 *Sensus divinitatis*, the sense of the divine which is an intuitive fundamental perception or consciousness of divine existence, which is to be found throughout all religions; often termed, *sensus deitatis*, the sense of God

There is an important difference here between Calvin and Rahner's thesis – for Calvin the sense of sin almost completely obscures the sense of divinity; as the Apostle Paul says, it is only enough to make you without excuse, right?[31] Karl Rahner is much more optimistic about the universal possibilities of this transcendental Revelation. That's the difference between the Augustinian Calvin and Rahner, you see. Augustine is really like Calvin in that respect, for Augustine basically sin has not completely removed the sense of the divine but sin has obscured it in such a way that grace will only save you. Rahner belongs on the Thomist rather than the Augustinian side, because Rahner is more optimistic about the fact that sin diseases the will but not the intellect. For Thomas the intellect is relatively unscathed, whereas for Calvin it is scathed, highly. And that is why the Reformers rejected the scholastic tradition: it was too optimistic about human possibilities. Rightly or wrongly Rahner is still in the line of Thomas. The interesting thing about Balthasar is that he still tries to operate within the same framework but he is much less optimistic than Rahner, in fact the interesting thing about his own struggle with the nature and grace question is that it almost leads him to contortions: he wants to remain true to the tradition and yet at the same time to have a much stronger doctrine of Revelation as an answer to sin. That is where those two really are interesting polar opposites – Rahner and Balthasar – they are interesting polar Catholics in that respect.

viii. The Concrete Reality of Revelation

There is something here which is relevant, which I shall read to you, it was spoken by Barth to people who were just coming out of Nazi Germany in 1946 and it is about Revelation, indeed it is about the concrete nature of Revelation as distinct from whatever transcendental Revelation may be. Barth says *'He was of necessity a Jew.'* Right! *'We cannot be blind to this fact. He belongs to this concrete reality of God's Word, and His revelation.'* And he ends this paragraph *'The man who is ashamed of Israel is ashamed of Jesus Christ and therefore of his own existence.'*[32] So the problem over transcendental Revelation is in the problem of specificity: Revelation is in the person of Jesus Christ who was from God's chosen people. So the problem over Israel is the problem of existence itself: deny Israel, you deny yourself as made in the image of God. So Barth is much stronger on the concrete reality of Revelation than Rahner is.

31 'Ever since the creation of the world his eternal power and divine nature, invisible though they are, have been understood and seen through the things he has made. So they are without excuse' (Romans 1.20).

32 Karl Barth, *Dogmatik im Grundriß* (München: Christian Kaiser Verlag, 1947). English trans. *Dogmatics in Outline – Lectures on the Creed* (trans. G.T. Thomson; London: SCM Press, 2001 [1949]). See ch 11, The Saviour and Servant of God, pp. 63–72; the passage quoted by Colin Gunton can be found on p. 67.

Chapter 3

REVELATION, MEDIATION AND SCRIPTURE

1. Concepts of Revelation

Let's turn now to concepts of Revelation; this as a matter of course has a lot to do with scripture. We can ask 'Is the Bible to be understood as Revelation?' Or 'Is the Bible the witness to Revelation?' Or, if it is neither of these, how should the Bible be understood in connection with Revelation? This is an important question, very important. What is the link between the Bible and Revelation? In fact, we can identify seven concepts of Revelation:

Scriptural as an Eschatological Concept
Revelation in General
Revelation as a Religious Category
Revelation as a Theological Category
The Problem of Mediation
Scriptural Examples
Revelation and Relationship

These are not exhaustive; these categories are not complete, though they are pretty comprehensive; you may come up with more; you may subdivide, but they are workable, we can work with them. Using these categories we can outline some of the ways in which the word 'Revelation' is used.

2. Scripture as an Eschatological Concept

i. Eschatology

Scripture as an eschatological concept: it is tempting to say that all words are, or can be seen in an eschatological context. However, scripture is definitely to be seen as such. For example, 'The Book of Revelation'; also Paul's 'First Letter to the Corinthians' and Peter's 'First Epistle'. You see, listen to this:

> *So that the genuineness of your faith – being more precious than gold that, though perishable, is tested by fire – may be found to result in praise and glory and honour when Jesus Christ is revealed.*
>
> 1 Peter 1.7
>
> *So that you are not lacking in any spiritual gift as you wait for the revealing of our Lord Jesus Christ*
>
> 1 Corinthians 1.7

It was argued that eschatology was misunderstood by everyone until the nineteenth century in the sense that Liberal Protestantism had changed the Gospel; the rediscovery of eschatology showed that there was more to be said. Therefore, in the late nineteenth and early twentieth centuries eschatology was, you see, rediscovered.

Franz Overbeck,[1] the church historian, regarded eschatology as a death warrant: eschatology meant that if Christianity was eschatological, we can be no more; therefore there can't be any Christianity. Overbeck said in so many words that Christianity was not really a religion, it was eschatological or it was nothing. Barth read this, saw this, and took it. Barth took eschatology as Christianity's life warrant.

Barth, in the early twentieth century, attempts to reintroduce an eschatological concept of Revelation. His *Commentary on Romans* is important.[2] Very important, it establishes Barth as a theologian, in fact as a rebel. His teacher's did not like it, it seemed to them to contradict everything they held, but, yes, it is important: Barth's *Commentary on Romans* reflects a doctrine that is an eschatology of event, you see. It is more Kantian-two-world eschatology than a biblical eschatology, that's a fair way, I think, to describe it. In Barth's *Commentary on Romans* you have the concept of a God that breaks in from outside with a timeless realized eschatology. God breaks into this world, God hits this world at a point, but this is a timeless point, it

1 Franz Camille Overbeck (1837–1905), German Protestant theologian, born in St Petersburg to German–French–Russian parentage; from 1870 he was Professor of New Testament Exegesis and Old Church History at the University of Basel, from which time he became friends with the German philosopher Friedrich Nietzsche, the two sharing many ideas. In 1873 he published his key work, *Über die Christlichkeit unserer heutigen Theologie* (*How Christian is Our Present-Day Theology?*), which established the principle that Christianity was eschatological or it was nothing, which greatly impressed Barth. See Franz Overbeck, *On the Christianity of Theology* (trans. John Elbert Wilson; San Jose, CA: Pickwick Publications, 2002) and Franz Overbeck, *How Christian is Our Present-Day Theology?* (trans. by Martin Henry; London: Continuum, T&T Clark, 2005).

2 Karl Barth, *Der Römerbrief* (Erste Fassung; Zürich: Theologischer Verlag Zürich, 1985 [1919]). Karl Barth, *Der Römerbrief* (Zweite Fassung; Zürich: Theologischer Verlag Zürich, 1999 [1922]); English trans. *The Epistle to the Romans* (trans. Edwyn Hoskyns; Oxford: Oxford University Press, 1933).

is not to be treated like the rest of history – he's talking about the Incarnation, you see, Barth's God breaking in.

Pannenberg's[3] objection to all this is that it is not biblical, it Platonizes eschatology – it puts into the present what belongs in the future. Both Pannenberg and Jenson have concentrated on seeing eschatology in the future. For Pannenberg, it is what is to happen that is important, even creation is seen as happening in the future. You see, to say that something is created is to say that it is on its way to being made; full knowledge will be granted at the end – this will be full Revelation. Anything before is only an indirect anticipation. Paul seems to reflect this in 1 Corinthians 13:

> *For we know only in part, and we prophesy only in part; but when the complete comes, the partial will come to an end. For now we see in a mirror, dimly, but then we will see face to face. Now I know only in part; then I will know fully, even as I have been fully known.*
>
> 1 Cor. 13.9-10, 12

We can only at present say that we are known: eschatologically we will know. But as for the present is it truer to say that we are known by God more than we know God? Pannenberg would ask the question – How much are we known? – rather than – How much can we know through Revelation?

ii. Pannenberg

Let's look at Pannenberg a little closer. Now, Pannenberg of course is operating in a world that is hostile to God and God's existence; he sees theology as tackling this world view, operating against this *Weltanschauung* even though it is now a postmodern world view – or so we are told. Pannenberg said somewhere that after Feuerbach theology can no longer speak of God without offering explanation.[4] This is typical of the approach of Pannenberg; he is essentially going back to before Barth to an Enlightenment type demand for rational justification – very rationalist. Barth, by contrast, begins with Revelation. So, for Pannenberg, there is no God without explanation.[5]

[3] Wolfhart Pannenberg (b. 1928 Szczecin, Poland), theologian, who has sought to establish/defend theology as a rigorous academic discipline (*Wissenschaft*), proficient to stand/interact with philosophy, history and the natural sciences.

[4] Wolfhart Pannenberg (ed.), *Revelation as History* (trans. E. Quinn; London: Macmillan, 1968).

[5] For example, there is Pannenberg's concept of eschatological ontology where the essence of something, its being, is determined by its future. The future therefore exercises a retroactive (*rückwirkend*) causality on the present; therefore something that is created can possess its essence here and now only by anticipating what it will be in the future. See Wolfhart Pannenberg, *Metaphysik und Gottesgedanke* (Göttingen: Vandenhoeck & Ruprecht, 1988); English trans. *Metaphysics and the Idea of God* (trans. Philip Clayton; Grand Rapids, MI: Eerdmans, 1990).

Pannenberg is very aware of how theological statements can be seen as subjective judgements. As with Ritschl, you see, Ritschl believed that one came to believe in the significance of Christ by a value judgement. His was a theology of value judgements; you see, you learn about Christ from the historical–critical kind of project and then you come to value him as God.[6]

Q: How close is this to T. F. Torrance's idea that it is intuitive how you come to faith?

No, intuition is a rational risk for Torrance, a rational response to something already given. Ritschl is a Kantian, in that sense it is the opposite; for Torrance you are recognizing something, for Ritschl you are on the whole reading something into it, rather than recognizing it. The value judgement is something you make – well that seems to be the picture. No Ritschl and Torrance are the opposite. Ritschl doesn't really have a theology of Revelation, I think it's true to say, or at the least it is a very weak one if he has one, it is a weak theology of Revelation. But then again he is a Kantian who believes that our knowledge is largely by imposition of our, in this case, value judgements, rather than by discovery or reading out. For Ritschl you read in rather than you read out.

For Torrance and Barth you read out, in other words you read from the object (God) to the subject (the enquiring mind), whereas for Ritschl that tends to be from the subject to the object, and that is exactly why Barth rejected the nineteenth century. One of the many reasons why he rejected the nineteenth century is because it is anthropocentric (figure 11, overleaf). So, you see, God discloses his own being rather than a lot of propositions: so it is a modern personal concept of divine self-revelation. What is different is what he understands by it – that is where he differs from Barth. They are similar, yes, I'll grant you that, but there again there are important differences between Barth and Pannenberg.

You see, almost all of Barth's theology is based around this concept of veiling–unveiling or revealedness–hiddenness – these are dialectics. It is almost a Father–Son, or Son–Father dialectic where God reveals himself in the Son, but the Father remains hidden, so to speak. But nonetheless it is a dialectic, for God reveals himself as the one who remains hidden. So a veiling is also an unveiling. Barth would say something like 'God reveals himself as the one who cannot be unveiled.'

6 See, for instance: Albrecht Ritschl, *Rechtfertigung und Versöhnung*, published in English as *The Christian Doctrine of Justification and Reconciliation* (trans. J. Sutherland Black; Edinburgh, 1872). A contemporary edition is, Albrecht Ritschl, *The Christian Doctrine of Justification and Reconciliation* (Kila, MT: Kessinger Publishing, 2006). See also the recently published edition of Ritschl's lectures on ethics: Albrecht Ritschl, *Vorlesung Theologische Ethik* (Rolf Schäfer; Berlin: De Gruyter, 2007). For a general study of Ritschl, see David L. Mueller, *An Introduction to the theology of Albrecht Ritschl* (Philadelphia, PA: Westminster Press, 1969); see also Gerald W. McCollah, *Christ's Person and Life-Work in the Theology of Albrecht Ritschl: With Special Attention to Munus Triplex* (Lanham, MD: University Press of America, 1990); and, Clive Marsh, *Albrecht Ritschl and the Problem of the Historical Jesus* (Lewiston, NY: Edwin Mellen Press, 1992).

So, all Revelation is also a veiling: to say that it has to be absolutely the whole lot or nothing is a kind of literalism. Pannenberg, of course, is wary of paradox. Barth isn't. However, that is if Barth did mean a full self-disclosure. What I think he means is a real self-disclosure: if revelation is also a veiling then it can't be a full self-disclosure. But Barth seems to say on the one hand that it is a full self-disclosure, and on the other hand it is a full veiling.

Barth would then say that what his concept of Revelation is doing, what it is attempting, is to characterize what is true in general from biblical Revelation. However it may be that Barth tries too hard to try to make scripture reveal a certain kind of triune God. This is so important because it is enabling you all to think about in what sense Revelation is revealing. OK? Is it personal self-manifestation? Or is it a personal unveiling of God? In what sense is it complete and full, and in what sense is it personal and how is it to be understood in terms of the Trinity? It is a sort of Son–Father dialectic that I think shapes the revealed–hidden: one remains hidden, the Father remains hidden while revealing himself in Jesus.

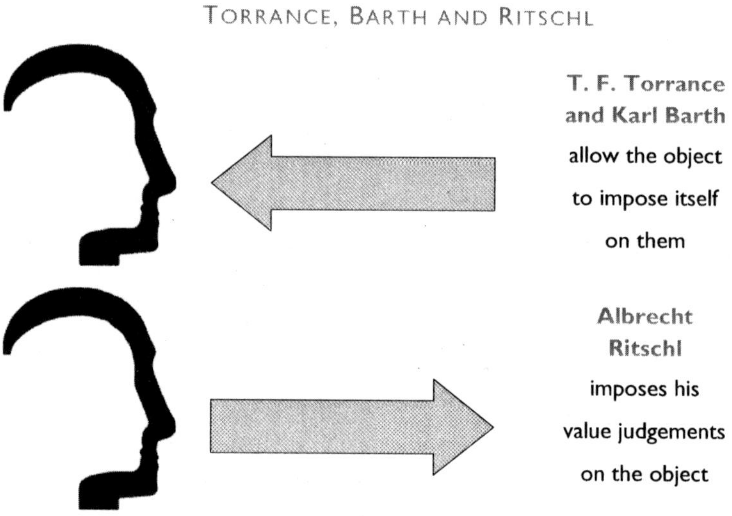

Figure 11

'Indirect', that's the word, that's the crucial word here, Revelation is indirect. For Barth you see, it would be direct, if you were to bump into Jesus Christ, as you wandered around Israel in the first century. You would actually be bumping into God. In that sense it is direct: to see Jesus is to see God. For Barth, Jesus is God's self-revelation. Pannenberg will not go that far, it has to be indirect. You see, for Pannenberg, full Revelation happens, is disclosed, in the fullness of time. This is where I believe he differs from Barth and where the accusation that Barth is over-realized comes in.

For Pannenberg, full Revelation is disclosed in the fullness of time: that means the whole of history. So there is only Revelation at the end. Therefore, Pannenberg is pushing for Revelation as an eschatological concept, so only at the end will God be revealed. Therefore, what he is accusing Barth of, to put it in different language, is an over-realized eschatology. You see, for Pannenberg, a knowledge of the historic event, the fact of Jesus of Nazareth is the basis of our faith in the future.

It is historical reason that concerns Pannenberg much more than cosmological reason in terms of proof. By 'historical reason' he means the 'historical–critical method'. Basically Pannenberg believes that by the historical–critical method you can actually find out quite a lot about Jesus' story. In *Jesus – God and Man*, he actually argues that the resurrection narratives are historically quite respectable.[7] That you can establish beyond reasonable doubt that Jesus rose from the dead. And that is the key, it is the eschatological event.

For Pannenberg, our job is not to proclaim Jesus as Revelation as Barth does. No, for Pannenberg, our job is to follow the career of Jesus through his ministry and through to his death and resurrection by historical investigation – in other words follow the same track as the disciples had to follow – on the basis of which, we can establish that an eschatological event has happened in the middle of history. Revelation belongs at the end. Revelation – note 'Revelation' with a capital 'R' – will only be when the whole of history has ended and God is known fully.

There is an anticipation of all of this in the resurrection: resurrection is something that belongs to the end. So it is an end event happening in time. Therefore, for him it is a clue to the meaning of the whole of history. I suppose what we can say is that it is revelatory rather than Revelation for him, for Pannenberg.

3. Revelation in General

Samuel Taylor Coleridge had much to say about Revelation in general which is significant to our concerns. He said 'All Truth is a Species of Revelation'.[8] All truth, all that is true, is in some form or other revelation; in other words whenever someone says something that is true, it is revelation. Coleridge is a very unsystematic thinker, but he produced systematic theology because he knew the implication of what he said. He is the most unsystematic systematician there is, it

7 Wolfhart Pannenberg, *Jesus – God and Man* (trans. Lewis L. Wilkins and Duane A. Priebe; Philadelphia, PA: Westminster Press, 1968).

8 Samuel Taylor Coleridge, *Collected Letters of Samuel Taylor Coleridge*, Vol. II: *1801–1806* (ed. by E. L. Griggs; Oxford: Clarendon Press, 1956), p. 388.

Samuel Taylor Coleridge (1772–1834) was a leading Romantic English poet, critic, philosopher and theologian, close associate of William Wordsworth and co-founder of the Romantic Movement in England. Probably his most famous work was *The Rime of the Ancient Mariner.*

has to be said. Despite his failures, inadequacies and the medicinal drugs he took that he was addicted to, he was searching for truth and freedom and God. You see, that's what drove him, this search, with passion, but the question is – Is this drive for truth and freedom and God, systematic theology?'

What he is saying, I think, is that Revelation is ongoing and continual, especially in a general sense. Music is a good example of this – music objectively reveals aspects of the structure of the universe. There are dimensions of the music which science can't uncover, especially the nature of time. The scientific approach reveals time as decay and end – the universe is slowly ending, we are slowly dying. Music reveals the opposite; the completeness of a symphony is at its conclusion. Music is a temporal art, but it is also a building – it constructs. This is a different concept from Newtonian physics. This relates to the question, where is a note of music? Many believe a thing is either here or there, but when you sound a note, it exists in many places, or does it only exist in our perception, and either way it exists in many places at once.

Mozart, you see, was disreputable, disorganized and considered by many to be an obscene, crude-talking man, yet he was the mouthpiece for revelation, was he not! Barth believed so, certainly Barth believed so. You see – 'revelation' is not necessarily explicitly religious. Scientists, take scientists, many of them are not immune to revelation – the famous line of Archimedes where he found and realized. Many scientists speak of discovering as though they were meant to find something. So we are almost in the area of inspiration here. Revelation is the gift of the spirit wherever it comes: OK, revelation is a gift of the spirit.

So revelation in general is a sort of success word where truth breaks through to the human knower in some way. But we have to deal here with a question of relativity. There is here an epistemological question of how we know – which is too vast to be covered here. It can be argued that grace and truth came through Jesus Christ: therefore we *must* bring to bear the full armoury of systematic theology. But we still have the question – How do we know? Science presents itself as empirical but often there is no way of testing absolutely. There is no way of actually constructing a test for the theory of evolution. Formulating cast–iron tests is very difficult.

4. Revelation as a Religious Category

Keith Ward in *Religion and Revelation*[9] argues that there is a universal, primal, religious sense, which answers to this 'revelation' that can be found deep down in all cultures and religions. He is here moving towards an experiential definition of revelation. Then there is Paul Tillich also, he has this sense of a notion of ultimate concern, which is really an experiential, revelatory core at the heart of each human

[9] Keith Ward, *Religion and Revelation* (Oxford: Oxford University Press, 1994).

character or human nature. It is really Niebuhr who has worked on this, explored this.[10] This is, however, more of a philosophical than a theological concept.

This view of Ward's can be considered subjective in the sense that it is to do with an individual human being's response to the world. General revelation refers essentially to the way the world reveals the deity generally. Classically, Paul writes in Romans on the notion of 'general revelation', about how the creator is known through the created world.[11]

So there is everywhere a trace of the creator's presence. That's important; it can some–times be forgotten or overlooked, we can easily ignore it as theologians, we can I suppose, get carried away and ignore it, but it is true, there must be a trace of the creator in the world. Whatever scientists want to believe, or sceptics want to say, there is a trace of the creator's presence in the world.

Calvin developed this view of Paul; Calvin though was more dubious, he developed the view that most of the human race could not read these signs in the natural world. Many would argue that the Bible and/or the Holy Spirit are needed to enable an individual to perceive God in this way. Barth, by comparison, almost takes the position that there isn't a revelation in the natural world.

5. Revelation as a Theological Category

Is it true to say that today we rarely hear revealed truths? We rarely hear today the phrase 'revealed religion', we are rarely confident at using the concept. Are people uncomfortable with the idea? Are theologians today uncomfortable with the idea? Those who want to find some sort of consensus within the world's religions; perhaps they are uncomfortable with such a concept. Certainly such a concept is unfashionable.

i. Medieval Notions of Revealed Truth

But it was not always so. In the Middle Ages there was a highly developed concept of revealed truth. The general position in the Middle Ages was that what the church passed on was revealed truth. The church has received these truths, handed on by Christ to the apostles, and the current generation now inherits them: therefore, the church teaches this material as received truth. Most medieval theologians accepted this, or regarded it as the position from which they spoke. I think this is certainly so with Anselm, who of course was important to Barth.

10 H. R. Niebuhr, *The Meaning of Revelation* (New York, NY: The Macmillan Company, 1941).

11 'Ever since the creation of the world his eternal power and divine nature, invisible though they are, have been understood and seen through the things he has made. So they are without excuse' (Rom. 1.20).

ii. The Bible as Revealed Truth

The Protestant equivalent of this would be to treat the Bible as revealed truth. This was one of the problems that Coleridge agonized over towards the end of his life; however, it is important to remember that Coleridge lived before Darwin, so the problems over Genesis did not arise for him. Though, yes, in Coleridge's time there was a reaction against rationalism, a reaction that led towards a sort of biblical literalism.

Coleridge wrestles with this. Coleridge wrestled with this because he wasn't prepared to accept it. His view was that on the one hand every truth he thought worth knowing came from the Bible, yet he wasn't prepared to lie for God by defending the indefensible.[12] Coleridge's solution was to distinguish between inspiration and Revelation. This was an important distinction to make – it is one thing to say that something is revelatory, it is another to say that it is inspired by the Spirit. A literalist view would equate the two, asserting that these words are true because the spirit inspired them. Coleridge makes an important conceptual point here using the story of Baalam's ass.[13] God makes Balaam's ass say certain words, therefore the ass speaks Revelation, but they are not inspired words. What Coleridge wants to argue for is the view that inspiration is compatible with the humanity of the writers of scripture – thus we can distinguish between inspiration and Revelation. So, the crucial point is that Revelation is a personal act of God in some way or other. Hence the concept of revealed truth, or revealed proposition, tends to avoid this point.[14]

6. The Problem of Mediation

If the words themselves are not the Revelation, though they may be, then they are secondary. If Jesus Christ is the Revelation then are his words secondary? If not the words, then what mediates Revelation? This is Pannenberg's point, that the only true Revelation will be when all is done and we see face to face. Anything short of final Revelation is not Revelation.

[12] For his understanding of Scripture, see Samuel Taylor Coleridge, *Biographia Literaria: or, Biographical Sketches of My Literary Life and Opinions* (ed. and intro. George Watson, Everyman's library 11; London: Dent, 1956). See also, Charles I. Armstrong, 'The Absolute Implied: Coleridge on Wordsworth and the Bible', in *Literature and Theology*, 14.4 (2000), pp. 363–72.

[13] Num. 22.21-34.

[14] See David Jasper, *Coleridge as Poet and Religious Thinker: Inspiration and Revelation* (London: Macmillan, 1985); also, Anthony John Harding, *Coleridge and the Inspired Word* (Kingston, ON: McGill-Queen's University Press, 1985).

Is it possible for God to mediate so that he can be known in the present? This is an important question. How can God be known incomplete in the present? Doesn't Revelation mean God making himself known now in some way or other? Therefore we must face the question, 'How?' You see, the question becomes 'How, and by what means?'

For example, what place do the words of scripture have, or those of theologians – or preachers? Barth's view was that Jesus Christ was the Word of God; scripture is the word of God in so far as it witnesses to Jesus. The preacher's words are the word of God in so far as they realize the words of scripture in the present. So we have a pattern of dependence. This doctrine, though, needs a theology of mediation: the truth of God is to be mediated through human words or human language or human actions. Therefore, we can't escape in all of this the question 'What is mediation?' Essentially in the end this is a Christological question, especially if God has made himself known through Jesus Christ: 'How does Christ mediate truth, revealed truth?'

7. Scriptural Examples

Pannenberg complained that scripture is only eschatological. Is scripture only eschatological or does it show, or more pertinently teach, more than this about Revelation? Many would argue against Pannenberg, that although full Revelation is in the future (therefore it is eschatological), this future Revelation could be made present by the spirit today. So now the question becomes pneumatological, does it not?

There are scriptural examples of future Revelation taking place in the present are there not? In Exodus 3, the burning bush, which was not consumed, was linked with the word of God. To many this is quintessential Revelation: God's Revelation – 'I am who I am'. There are, of course, many examples of prophets standing in the council and hearing what God said; these are recorded all through the Old Testament. In Deuteronomy we find the criteria for Revelation: Is it given in any other name than 'Yahweh'? Second, does it become true?[15] Brian Haymes in *The Concept of the Knowledge of God* asserts that whenever the story of the Exodus is retold then we are doing Revelation.[16] When we tell the acts of God, we are revealing what he is; we are revealing something about God – Are we not?

In the New Testament, for example, the Letter to the Ephesians is almost revelatory throughout; yes, I think that is correct, it is revelatory from beginning to end. You see, in chapter 3, Paul talks about the Revelation of a mystery, a mystery revealed: that is, that Jews and Gentiles belong together in the House of God. What does he say? Listen –

15 'If a prophet speaks in the name of the Lord but the thing does not take place or prove true, it is a word that the Lord has not spoken. The prophet has spoken it presumptuously; do not be frightened by it' (Deut. 18.22).

16 Brian Haymes, *The Concept of the Knowledge of God* (New York, NY: St Martin's Press, 1988).

In former generations this mystery was not made known to humankind, as it has now been revealed to his holy apostles and prophets by the Spirit: that is, the Gentiles have become fellow-heirs, members of the same body, and sharers in the promise in Christ Jesus through the Gospel.

Eph. 3.5-6

By 'mystery' Paul is not talking about something mysterious; no, he is talking about something made known, you see — something either discovered or revealed, hence the Greek μυστήριον (*musterion*).[17] You see, what was once unknown is now made known, revealed. This, of course, is Paul writing in Galatians.
Listen –

For I want you to know, brothers and sisters, that the Gospel that was proclaimed by me is not of human origin; for I did not receive it from a human source, nor was I taught it, but I received it through a revelation of Jesus Christ.

Gal. 1.11

Here the Greek word ἀποκάλυψις (*apocalupsis*)[18] is very important: apocalypse is Revelation. Pannenberg is avoiding direct revelatory/apocalyptic language in scripture. For example, Paul's conversion experience on the road to Damascus: Paul comments *'I did not receive it from man, nor was I taught it, but it came through a revelation of Jesus Christ.'*[19] In 2 Corinthians 12 we have Paul experiencing revelations – in the plural, the only example in scripture – Paul lifted up into the third heaven and knowing things others did not know. Truths are revealed to him.[20] It is important for us to remember that Paul also talks about prophetic utterance as Revelation in 1 Corinthians 14. In the synoptic Gospels we have Revelation from the point of view of the recipients – the disciples received Revelation, but did not understand. After the resurrection they did understand. The baptism in Mark's Gospel is a classic example of this. Listen –

17 μυστήριον, ου (n.) secret, mystery, of something formerly unknown but now revealed.

18 ἀποκάλυψις, εως (f.) Revelation.

19 Gal. 1.12

20 'It is necessary to boast; nothing is to be gained by it, but I will go on to visions and revelations of the Lord. I know a person in Christ who fourteen years ago was caught up to the third heaven – whether in the body or out of the body I do not know; God knows. And I know that such a person – whether in the body or out of the body I do not know; God knows – was caught up into Paradise and heard things that are not to be told, that no mortal is permitted to repeat. On behalf of such a one I will boast, but on my own behalf I will not boast, except of my weaknesses. But if I wish to boast, I will not be a fool, for I will be speaking the truth. But I refrain from it, so that no one may think better of me than what is seen in me or heard from me, even considering the exceptional character of the revelations. Therefore, to keep me from being too elated, a thorn was given to me in the flesh, a messenger of Satan to torment me, to keep me from being too elated. Three times I appealed to the Lord about this, that it would leave me, but he said to me "My grace is sufficient for you, for power is made perfect in weakness." So, I will boast all the more gladly of my weaknesses, so that the power of Christ may dwell in me' (2 Cor. 12.1-9).

> *And just as he was coming up out of the water, he saw the heavens torn apart and the Spirit descending like a dove on him. And a voice came from heaven 'You are my Son, the Beloved; with you I am well pleased.' And the Spirit immediately drove him out into the wilderness.*
>
> Mk 1.10

The Eastern Orthodox Church regards the baptism of Jesus as a Revelation of the Trinity. Though I think primarily the baptism is a Revelation of the Son by the Father. This is repeated at the transfiguration:

> *Then a cloud overshadowed them, and from the cloud there came a voice 'This is my Son, the Beloved; listen to him!'*
>
> Mk 9.7

This is all confirmed in the incident with the disciples at Caesar Philippi, you know, where Jesus says *'Blessed are you, Simon son of Jonah! For flesh and blood has not revealed this to you, but my Father in heaven'* (Matthew 16.17). Once again, you see, the Father reveals the truth to the disciples. Many commentators have regarded this scene as Revelation, that is, the transfiguration as anticipated eschatology – glory in anticipation. However, in the Fourth Gospel, Revelation is from the point of view of the early church. What is distinctive here, in the Fourth Gospel, is that it reflects 'Jesus the Incarnation' from the experience of the church. It is the fruit of profound reflection on the Incarnation by the church; profound reflection on what has happened in Revelation, what has been revealed. Many of the expressions in John's Gospel are in the words of the church. For example the prologue to John's Gospel:

> *And the Word became flesh and lived among us, and we have seen his glory, the glory as of a father's only son, full of grace and truth.*
>
> Jn 1.14

We have 'seen' his Revelation we might say.

> *No one has ever seen God. It is God the only Son, who is close to the Father's heart, who has made him known.*
>
> Jn 1.18

How has God made him known? – as the Lamb who takes away the sins of the world. This follows; you see, immediately, it says, when they see him they know –

> *The next day he saw Jesus coming towards him and declared 'Here is the Lamb of God who takes away the sin of the world!'*
>
> Jn 1.29

This is one answer to Pannenberg – the picture is simply much richer than a merely eschatological approach would give. Revelation is of course bound up with salvation. That's important, that's something we must consider; Revelation is bound up with salvation. And salvation is bound up with Christ. Therefore, it can be concluded from the Fourth Gospel that it is not so much the Father revealing the Son, but the Son revealing the Father. Those passages are so important – where Jesus talks about having revealed the Father. Listen –

> *Not that anyone has seen the Father except the one who is from God; he has seen the Father.*
>
> Jn 6.46
>
> *Jesus said to him, 'Have I been with you all this time, Philip, and you still do not know me? Whoever has seen me has seen the Father. How can you say, 'Show us the Father'?*
>
> Jn 14.9 [21]

The synoptic gospels reflect an earlier tradition where they wanted to project Jesus as the Son; by the time John's Gospel was written this has been accepted – it is the relation of the Father to the Son, and what the Son reveals of the Father that is important.

There is also a pneumatology here as well. The Holy Spirit leads into all truth. There is much on how the Spirit works to reveal in the central chapters of John's Gospel – around chapters 15, 16 and 17.[22] This pneumatological material shows that Jesus is the Revelation of the Father; the self-effacing Spirit reveals the true nature of the self-effacing Son. You see, Jesus leads beyond himself to the Father. In Acts of the Apostles we have other examples. There are many stories about prophets revealing truths. This is a form of Revelation; this is also a form of Revelation.

8. Revelation and Relationship

i. Varieties of Mediation

The key to understanding all of this and to see how it all interrelates is to perceive varieties of mediation, to acknowledge varieties of mediation: Revelation is mediated in a number of ways: each way is a different way of revealing something of God and the truth, whether prophetic, Christological or pneumatological (figure 12). You see, whether it is through prophecy, or whether it is Christological or

[21] See also Jn 1.14b; 3.35; 5.18-19; 6.46 and 10.4. Also, most of chapter 5 deals with the relationship between the Son and the Father and how the Son reveals the Father (Editor).

[22] 'When the Spirit of truth comes, he will guide you into all the truth; for he will not speak on his own, but will speak whatever he hears, and he will declare to you the things that are to come' (Jn 16.13).

pneumatological there are a variety of means through which we can gain Revelation. It is not only future; it is not only something that will happen in the future, at the end of time. Barth may have over stressed the present nature of Revelation in response to scholars reflecting the view that Pannenberg does, but it is important to see the variety of forms of Revelation. It is important to focus on the question of how various revelations may be given.

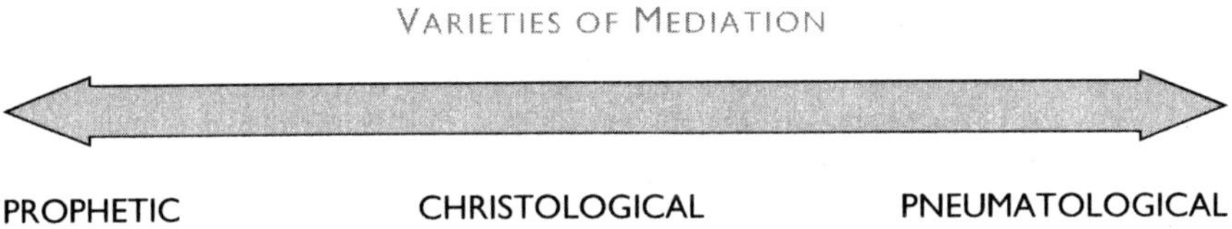

Figure 12

Inspiration, narrative, all have a role to play in Revelation. Inspiration is a measure of how God works. This is an especially pneumatological issue: the Holy Spirit inspires the prophet, the theologian or the preacher. It is the same Holy Spirit that inspires the musician, the writer, the artist, as Barth would say. Mediation: that's what I want us to talk about, mediation. How is Revelation mediated to us?

ii. Revelation, Mediation and Relationship

Mediation leads us to consider Revelation and relationship. We have not spoken about Revelation and relationship, which is sometimes thought unique to twentieth-century theology, but it has always been there. Anselm's great prayer is because of his relationship with the Lord: you see, theology is revealed through a relationship with God as Lord. Revelation and relationship is about a question. That question is 'How does God communicate to us today?' The answer is, for many, through a text – the Bible – through the church, and through the Holy Spirit? Mediation, you see, God's truth, that's what's mediated is it not? *His* Revelation is mediated, is it not?

You see, our primary relation to God is one of faith and trust, not of propositional knowledge or information. This is important because much recent theology that calls itself post-liberal talks about mediation and relationship, and some post-liberals are sceptical about first–order propositional statements resulting from Revelation, but that's to get ahead of ourselves. So, our primary relation to God is one of faith and trust – this is not so much Revelation as a form of present personal relationship. This is a saving relationship. That's what Christ is about. It is a saving relationship before it is knowledge. John Baillie has written on this.[23] But, and this is the question, but 'Just how does God communicate with us today?' OK, how does God communicate today? – the Holy Spirit? – Or, is it the Church, through the Church? Catholics would say so. Or, is it through the text, through the Bible? Or, is it a case of all three? Then it becomes a question of weighting.

iii. Mediation: the Text

There's a danger, as you probably know – in fact as you should know – there's a danger of reducing the Gospel to narrative, to a realistic narrative, almost to the genre of a realistic novel. Hans Frei is important here, because he is very influential. His book *The Eclipse of Biblical Narrative*, is very important, a very, very important book.[24] What Frei is saying is that in the eighteenth and nineteenth centuries the hermeneutical tradition focused upon two things in its search of the scriptures: scripture is either a historical particular event, or it is a generalized moral teaching, one or the other; so they tried to save scripture, as it were, they tried to save scripture's message by looking for either teaching or facts.[25]

[23] John Baillie, *The Idea of Revelation in Recent Thought* (New York, Columbia University Press, 1956). See also, John Baillie, *Our knowledge of God* (New York: Scribner, 1959).

[24] Hans Wilhelm Frei (1922–88), one of a group of theologians identified with post-liberal or narrative theology, which was seen as a reaction to liberal theology; others included George Lindbeck and Stanley Hauerwas (part of a movement known as the 'Yale school'); Frei worked on biblical hermeneutics. See Hans Wilhelm Frei, *The Eclipse of Biblical Narrative: A Study in Eighteenth and Nineteenth Century Hermeneutics* (New Haven, CT: Yale University Press, 1974); Hans Wilhelm Frei, *The Identity of Jesus Christ: the Hermeneutical Bases of Dogmatic Theology* (Philadelphia, PA: Fortress Press, 1975); Hans Wilhelm Frei, George Hunsinger and William C. Placher, *Theology and Narrative: Selected Essays* (Oxford: Oxford University Press, 1993); and Hans Wilhelm Frei, George Hunsinger and William C. Placher, *Types of Christian Theology* (New Haven, CT: Yale University Press, 1994).

[25] Colin Gunton is here referring to the German Liberal Protestant tradition starting in the eighteenth century with Reimarius and Lessing and culminating with the work of Strauss, at the end of the nineteenth century: the so-called 'Quest for the Historical Jesus'. The 'Quest for the Historical Jesus' was/is an attempt to use historical–critical methodology, driven often by a hermeneutic of suspicion to construct an accurate biography of Jesus (faith and Revelation do not, it would appear, come into the study). The term, the 'Quest for the Historical Jesus', was coined by Albert Schweitzer in the early twentieth century to refer to this first quest. There have been other quests in the twentieth century culminating in the so-called 'Jesus Seminar' comprising white liberal American scholars who attempted to classify from the gospels what were the genuine words of Jesus and what had been added/altered afterwards. Many exponents of the 'Quest' are using a hermeneutic of suspicion, driven by a concept of rationalism usually associated with the Age of the Enlightenment, but all appear to be unaware of their cultural conditioning, their prejudices and believe themselves to be writing universal truths when – certainly with the late twentieth-century 'Quest' – they operate within a cultural *Zeitgeist* of postmodernist relativity (Editor).

Frei argues that this was on the presumption that the texts didn't mean what they said. In other words, he accuses eighteenth- and nineteenth-century hermeneuticists of beginning with the assumption that the Bible was wrong, so to speak, and trying to find under the text some meaning that was hidden in it that could only be found by the critic. What scripture means, according to this, is hidden, something beneath the actual text.

What Frei is trying to do is to say that the text does actually communicate by its narrative. There's no hidden meaning: what it says is what it is meant to say. But it is pretty commonplace to say this. In fact, it was quite a fashionable thing thirty years ago. Frei's appeal to narrative is to say – we saw this with Thiemann's book as well, he is into this narrative model or mode – what Frei tries to argue is that narrative is different from history and it gives up its meaning by a combination of things: character, circumstance, the way the plot moves. And to abstract from that is to falsify: Frei argues that to analyse and claim whether Jesus did or did not do 'x' or whether Jesus did or did not teach 'y', is to falsify the text because you can only understand the text – the gospels – in and through its narrative which is, he says, history-like.[26] So what Frei is trying to do is to say that you find what scripture has to say by reading it as a whole rather than by cutting it up into little bits and by seeing if these bits are credible.

What Francis Watson is saying, on the other hand, is that this isn't enough; it is not enough to say simply that the narrative is the meaning.[27] Hence Frei is critical of those who would attempt to read the gospel only as realistic narrative, those who would attempt to assimilate the gospels to the genre of a realistic novel. Though Frei doesn't assimilate it, he says it is in certain ways *like* a realistic novel. Watson does argue that the 'Quest for the Historical Jesus' is trying to strive to penetrate and break open the text, it's trying to search for fragments of what he calls an extra-textual reality that have been preserved, hidden, behind the text, and of course the assumption with the 'Quest' is that everyone else has missed this extra-textual reality – everyone over 2000 years has missed it. That is where Watson is, I think, agreeing with Frei: the 'Quest for the Historical Jesus' has failed to recognize that the reality of Jesus is only accessible through the mediation of an irreducible textuality. You see, as Watson would say, the Bible is not the same as other texts.

That's it, you see, it is so important to make a distinction between the reality of Christ and the textual mediation of it – the textual mediation through scripture. Watson therefore, I think, accuses Frei of being tied to textuality. He wants scripture to be read as scripture but not in the sense that that is all you have got. That is what Watson, I think, suspects Frei of saying; but if it is the narrative that

26 Influenced by Karl Barth and the linguistic philosophy of Ludwig Wittgenstein, 'Narrative theology' was a late twentieth century movement supporting the church's use of the Bible as a narrative presentation of the faith; often termed 'Postliberal theology', narrative theology was centred on a group of theologians in the 1970s and 1980s at Yale Divinity School and the work of George Lindbeck, Hans Wilhelm Frei and Stanley Hauerwas.

27 Francis Watson, *Text, Church and World: Biblical Interpretation in Theological Perspective* (Edinburgh: T&T Clark, 1994)

has the meaning then you identify the narrative with the message. So Watson is saying that you have to distinguish between the Christ as an ontological reality on the one hand and the Christ that the text mediates. You cannot say 'All you need is the text and that's that.' That is what he suspects Frei – and Lindbeck – of doing. That is why he doesn't like the idea that the Bible is like a realistic novel: in a realistic novel nothing has really happened, it is just a story. Francis Watson wants to be a firmly theological realist against any suggestion of idealism or mere textuality.

Q: Can you give us an example of this? Doesn't Watson write a lot on creation from the Bible in a new way?

Let's see, Watson on Genesis, on the creation story, well, he says essentially three things. First, there is the 'speech–act' conception of creation: God speaks and things happen. Second, the second model of divine action is what he calls the 'fabrication model', where the objects of creation do not immediately spring into being but have to be constructed. The third is the 'mediation model'; God creates immediately by command and by fabrication, but he also and simultaneously creates in employing one of his creatures as the womb out of which the others proceed.[28]

God says in Genesis, let the earth bring forth: Francis Watson's point there is that Genesis 1 isn't simply creation by word. In effect he is going after the postmodernists who say words are all there is. God doesn't only create by word, he also forms; he also enables part of the earth to form something new. So, Genesis says let the earth bring forth creatures. And he is right. I found it very illuminating; he shows how Genesis 1 has a very complex pattern of mediation. It isn't just simply 'let there be'. This is the point; Genesis 1 has this theology of mediation, which shows God acting in various ways, in a range of ways towards the world – both to create and to form.

Q: What does Barth have to say?

What does Barth have to say? Well, Barth sees the text communicating divine and human history – content and form cannot then be separated. He comments on this somewhere, how the Bible demonstrates itself as Holy Scripture as the *form* of the content.[29]

However, Barth tends to put the weight not so much on the process by which the writers were inspired to write what they did, but how their writing, by inspiration, becomes Revelation here and now. This has led to Barth being

28 Francis Watson, *Text, Church and World: Biblical Interpretation in Theological Perspective*, ch. 8, Language, God and Creation, pp. 137–53, specifically, pp. 140–3

29 'As the witness of divine revelation the Bible also attests to the institution and function of prophets and apostles. And in so doing it attests itself as Holy Scripture, as the indispensable form of that content. But because this is the case, in the case in question of divine revelation the church, and in and with it theology has to hold fast to this unity of content and form. In this question of revelation we cannot, therefore, free ourselves from the texts in which its expectation and recollection attest to us. We are tied to these texts.' Karl Barth, *The Church Dogmatics* (eds G. W. Bromiley and T. F. Torrance; Edinburgh: T&T Clark, 1957), vol. I/2, §.19 The Word of God for the Church, p. 492.

criticized for an excessively actualistic view of the Bible. His critics say he is conceding too much to the doctrine of humanity and not enough to the intrinsic inspiredness of the text.[30]

Can you see where this is driving? The text is scripture because it witnesses to Revelation, this is a narrow way in which God is related to the text. And therefore for the Watson–type model you have a richer and an almost more interactionist view of the relation between God and us in responding to the text.

Q: What exactly is a Barthian view of scripture and how does it differ from Barth himself? Is there a difference?

A Barthian-type view? Well, the Spirit enables the text to be written as an inspired text: that's Barth. I think it's fair to say that is Barth. However, the Barthian view is not paramount for Vanhoozer among others. Illumination is, well, a doctrine of illumination rather than inspiration. This is the classic difference. A doctrine of inspiration is usually to do with how the text came to be sacred or an inspired text. A doctrine of illumination is the doctrine of how the Spirit illumines our minds and hence the text with understanding. Vanhoozer is concerned with the latter, and how the Spirit enables us to accept the text for what it claims to be.[31]

Technically mediation has to do with how something mediates the *Word* or *Act* of God. This is not so much the subjective reception of it: for Watson, mediation has to do with God's engagement with the world or the text in such a way that the world or text obeys the divine reality at its own level, or as an instrument of God's action which conforms to our understanding. That is why it has to be mediated: for God is God and we are the world. Obviously, if we are to know God there has to be mediation, unless we are going to know God immediately. Christianity has always been a religion of mediation rather than of immediacy – you don't know God immediately. Schleiermacher says you do, but that is another matter. Classically the doctrine is that you don't know God immediately unless you are some mystic or something. Therefore, God has to be mediated to you, classically through Christ.

iv. How Does Scripture Mediate?

But the secondary question arises of 'How does scripture mediate given that in effect Jesus is absent?' He is in one sense absent, though in another sense he is present. Given that *He* who mediates also requires mediation then you come to scripture. OK? – that is when you come to scripture. It all depends on how you believe *He* is mediated. And that is why scripture is so central: so 'Text, Church and the Spirit'. Text, the Bible, church, the tradition and the Holy Spirit: but the

30 These critics are often from an Evangelical perspective. See, for example, Sung Chung (ed.), *Karl Barth and Evangelical Theology: Convergences and Divergences* (Milton Keynes: Paternoster Press, 2006).

31 Kevin J. Vanhoozer, *Is There Meaning in This Text? The Bible, the Reader and the Morality of Literary Knowledge* (Leicester: Apollos, 1998), p. 413.

balance between the three will vary – in various weights of understanding. They are not symmetrical. The Spirit is God and so we have the text and the church. The question now becomes how do these exegeses – text and church – become used by the Spirit to realize divine truth or action at the human level? That is the sort of question we are now concerned with.

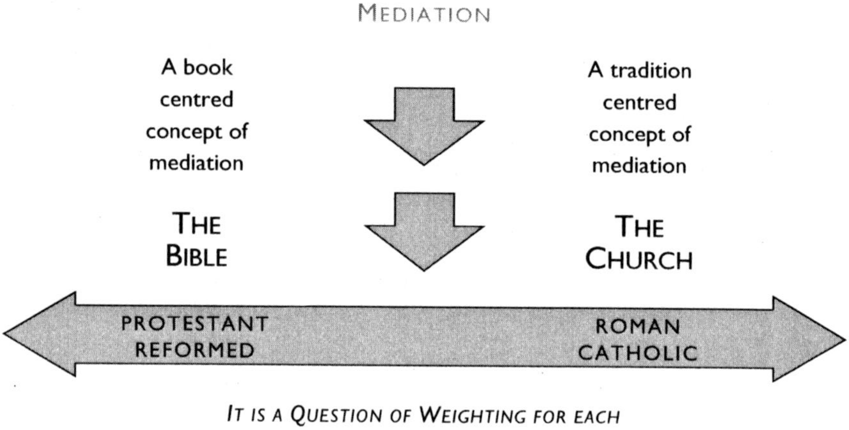

Figure 13

In a sense all the major theologians have either had a greatly or slightly different concept of mediation: you could say that all theology boils down to differences of mediation. And therefore, on the Protestant side it is much more strongly a book-centred conception; on the Catholic side it is much more of a tradition-centred, church-centred conception (figure 13). Not that either would want to reject the other completely, not realistically, that is important to note; it is in the end a matter of weighting. A theology of mediation really is a matter of how one who appears to be a past historical figure is mediated as some kind of present realization of God today.

Q: Do Baillie and Watson see all existence as a medium of Revelation?

Baillie I think yes, yes – cautiously; but Watson, well, Watson would be more nuanced; you see, for Watson it is God's turn to us that's important. This is the God who reveals *Himself*, he reveals *Himself* in exceptional circumstances, it is in an event of salvation. That is why he reveals himself; it is not primarily knowledge – I've said that before, haven't I.

Q: Can we therefore say that God is sovereign if he does not reveal in all occurrences? – Involvement always reveals doesn't it?

So, can we say that God is sovereign? Well, yes. The question is this 'Can we say that God is sovereign?' Does this mean that every event reveals Him – does it? It means that every single event is in *His* control. That is not the same thing as some events concealing God.

So the question is 'Are sovereignty and Revelation equivalent?' How do you recognize God if everything is Revelation? At the same time you wouldn't want to say that if God is, so to speak, in charge of things, then sovereignty is everywhere. Would you? Does Revelation have to be more particular?

Let's take a case, that you were presenting a paper, and that you hadn't understood a thing of what you were writing, but you wanted it to appear that you did. For then you would be concealing yourself. It might be that you revealed yourself in a way that you didn't want to. You can conceal yourself if you want to – can't you? We often do. You see – a revealing can also be a concealing.

Sovereignty is total and therefore everything that God does is an expression of his sovereignty. But it doesn't follow that everything reveals. Some people will say that 'I don't believe that God is in charge because why do all these nasty things happen?' Does God appear to hide?

Q: Can it be said that the Christian church is the primary reading community for the texts of The Old and New Testaments?

This brings us back to scripture; we mustn't lose sight of scripture in this. Scripture has to be our primary reading, and the church surely must be seen as the primary reading community if you want to put it in those words. Scripture is capable of certain interpretations; it is not a direct mediator of God but in some way or other it is indirect.

It is not the words that carry Revelation in themselves – Or, do they carry a possibility of revelation? Or, do the connections need to be made? Their revelatory character needs to be indicated. Otherwise, you have to say that Revelation is the actual words of scripture. And that seems to be problematic because the Revelation we are concerned with is the Revelation of God.

I think Watson is behind your question. Watson is trying to say that there is a space between the text and the theological interpretation – otherwise theology would have no point at all.

He says something like, the concept of scripture implies authoritative normative status and yet this authority is encountered through the mediation of preaching – quite Barthian that. This is compatible with a degree of interpretative freedom, but, and this is what Watson *and* Barth think, I believe, this freedom has limits set by the Creed, does it not?[32]

In Islam they seek to deny the role of mediation: the vision of the Prophet was immediate; he saw the actual pre-existing words. In Islam, the Qur'an is the actual words of God; in Christianity there is mediation through the humanity of the writers; then there is mediation by the Spirit through the text to an individual reading. Comparison with the Qur'an is instructive, although we still do not have an immediate voice of God: the Prophet is in some sense a visionary or a medium – he sees, and writes.

The authority of scripture does not depend on the fact that you can show that there are no contradictions in it; that is not the problem. The problem is not the contradictions; the positive side is 'How does God deal with us?' He deals with us as human beings, therefore, there can be contradictions; I don't think this is hostile to the authority of scripture. In so far as God deals with us humanly then there has

32 Francis Watson, *Text, Church and World. Biblical Interpretation in Theological Perspective*, p. 224.

to be space between the words and God. In one sense you will want to hold to the infallibility of scripture which is a broad sense, but there has to be space between the words and the *Word* as Barth would see it, between the words and *God.*

v. Relationship and Community

The text, the Bible, communicates God's saving action and God's desire for a covenant relationship with *His* people. I say again, if we fall into incorporating scripture into the genre of a realistic novel we reduce Christ, the whole Trinity in fact, to a story, an image.

Q: Does this reduce our capacity for relationship with *Him*?

Yes. Yes, if all you have got is the text you lose the personal relationship with God. You have to be aware of the distinction between the reality of Christ and its textual mediation.

Q: Though God can communicate through the faithful rendering of the history of mankind in relation to God, the word is living and active, we cannot break up its surface or separate its content and form. Is this fair?

That's interesting because it is almost a modernizing of the traditional Reformed tag: scripture as interpreter of itself. Where scripture gives us the guides, this frees us from any suggestion that we interpret scripture, as we happen to want. If you interpret scripture it must be on the grounds laid down by scripture. Interpretation must be intrinsic to the text and not something that you bring to it.

Q: Where is the community in this? Surely it is the community of faith, the community that owns the narrative and manifests relationship with Christ through faith. I think a believer needs to participate in the interpretative community, the body of Christ, because that is where God communicates.

You can say that a lot of interpretation is a sort of prophecy in that it has to do with making concrete the word of God: classical Reformed theology would say that that is what interpretation is about.

I do think that pneumatology has a lot to do with particularity, making particular things happen. You can say that the Spirit is a function of God's omnipresence but that doesn't mean that it will be uniformly omnipresent. It is quite clear that some things are not done by the Spirit but against the Spirit. If you do something against the Spirit, do you presuppose that the Spirit is there but you are grieving the Spirit or resisting? Can you say that you can resist the Spirit? You could say that the Spirit is omnipresent – but the point is that a lot of people ignore his promptings.

Both the Father and the Spirit are omnipresent, they are both God but they are active in different ways. The activity of the Spirit is very difficult to pin down. It is mysterious how it works. But we must allow for particularity – the Spirit seems to inspire some people and not others.

But surely we are concerned with how the Spirit enables the text to mediate the Word, are we not? It is simply a book with words printed in it – How can that mediate the act of God and not just the knowledge of God? Once you build in a space between the text and God in some way or other, then these questions arise: 'How is God mediated?' If he is not, so to speak, dictating the word, as some people claim he is, then you need to have a theology of mediation.

9. Propositional and Non-Propositional Revelation?

Scripture involves propositional statements. We formulate propositional statements from scripture, do we not? Also from the creeds: the creeds and scripture, they provide a basis, a ground, for our statements of belief, which inevitably are propositional – They correspond do they not to an ontological reality? We've mentioned 'Narrative Theology, and yes we've considered Hans Frei, but we should consider how post-liberalism has tried to rid us of the propositional certainty of orthodox statements, of orthodoxy.

i. Lindbeck and the Nature of Doctrinal Statements

Lindbeck's work on the nature of doctrine has been popular in recent years;[33] I'm not sure it deserves to be so, but there we are. In the end it is a lot to do with trying to reconcile religious differences and he does this by reducing the status of propositional theological statements. He effectively relativizes them. But you are left wondering if there is anything of Revelation left afterwards. Serious question: that is a serious question!

Lindbeck's *The Nature of Doctrine: Religion and Theology in a Postliberal Age*, is a theoretical reflection on doctrine, primarily for ecumenical reasons.[34] Lindbeck is often classified as post-liberal. What does he want? He wants to leave behind theological conservatism, which is often caricatured as propositionalism, but he also wants to leave behind what I think he labels experiential–expressive liberalism. This is just the sort of thing that Francis Watson is going at in his attacks on those who liken scripture to a realistic novel. What Lindbeck wants, what the post-liberal theory of religion that Lindbeck among others proposes, what he is aiming at is a cultural–linguistic approach, together with a rule or regulative theory of doctrine.

So, he is not looking at the Schleiermachian view that religious propositions are simply expressions of some non-cognitive prior experience – Schleiermacher's

33 The son of American Lutheran missionaries of Swedish descent, George A. Lindbeck (b. 1923, China) received his PhD from Yale University. He was invited as an observer to the Second Vatican Council, as a representative of the Lutheran World Federation; his subsequent work therefore focused on ecumenical dialogue. This resulted over many years in his seminal work, *The Nature of Doctrine: Religion and Theology in a Postliberal Age*, which established Lindbeck as an exponent of Post-liberalism – often referred to as 'New Yale School of theology' – which for Lindbeck is characterized by a cultural–linguistic approach. See George A.. Lindbeck, *The Nature of Doctrne: Religion and Theology in a Postliberal Age* (London: SPCK, 1984).

34 George A. Lindbeck, *The Nature of Doctrine.*

view was that theology is the rational explication of an essentially supra-rational experience. What Lindbeck is concerned with is what might be called a cognitivist view, that is to say we are basically concerned with the same truths that other people believe. How then do you develop a broader framework of meaning in religion?[35]

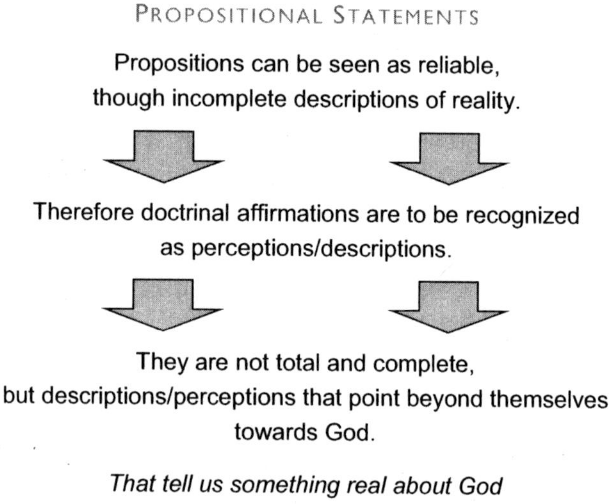

Figure 14

Lindbeck defines a cognitive–propositionalist approach as the way church doctrines function as what he calls informative propositions – truth claims – about reality.[36] His rejection of a cognitive–propositionalist approach is questionable: he claims it is not possible to state the objective truth about God in definitive propositional form.[37]

In expressions like, made known in two natures, one hypostasis made known in two natures, that would be the Chalcedonian definition of Christ: the suggestion is that the Chalcedon view is that there is one Christ made known in two natures. This is then seen as the heart of Christology and it is informative, it tells you something about Christ, and in a sense, as Robert Jenson would say, it is irreversible, it is just there. This is what Lindbeck calls the cognitive propositional view that these things are there to tell you the way things are.

Lindbeck actually suggests that those who – and I think it is worth quoting Lindbeck here – he argues that those who perceive or experience religion in

[35] For Schleiermacher and a Schleiermachian approach, see George A. Lindbeck, *The Nature of Doctrine*. Chapter 1, Christian Doctrine and Systemization, section 4. Foundationalism, sub-section ii. For Locke, Schleiermacher and Torrance in more depth, see Chapter 6, A Historical Perspective 2: The Triumph of Reason?, section 3, The Nineteenth Century.

[36] George A. Lindbeck, *The Nature of Doctrine*, p. 16.

[37] George A. Lindbeck, *The Nature of Doctrine*, p. 78.

cognitivist fashion combine insecurity with naivety.[38] That's it – those who don't subscribe to his non-propositional cultural–linguistic theory and insist on propositional Revelation, he accuses them of psychological insecurity and almost a childlike naivety. I think this Freudianizing of one's opponents is disgraceful, quite disgraceful. The question is 'I may be insecure but is it true?' It may be true as well, despite the sort of neuroses that we *all* suffer from, including those who accuse us of being insecure!

OK, so if we say that Jesus Christ is one person but two natures, what we are saying is that Christ corresponds with something that actually is in reality. If we say that Christ is green, we may be wrong, but our words in some way correspond to the world.

Lindbeck thus evades the question of whether our language refers, or attempts to refer, to realities, which, however elusive, lie beyond it. In other words there is a much more subtle way in which you can understand correspondence than simply on a naive one-to-one basis. Propositions can be seen as reliable because they will be incomplete descriptions of reality (figure 14). And, yes, often, there will be a givenness about them. Lindbeck fails to see that propositional Revelation attempts to achieve clarity. Clarity of what? Clarity of concepts and modes of discourse *in the recognition* that doctrinal affirmations are to be recognized as perceptions, not total perceptions, but descriptions, perceptions that point beyond themselves towards God.

ii. Revelation as a Non-Propositional Cultural–Linguistic Theory

Lindbeck's non-propositional cultural–linguistic theory claims that the function of doctrine is not to convey first-order propositional truth, or truths, that correspond to reality. No, that's not how he sees doctrine, but as Michalson has asserted in his criticism, Lindbeck's non-propositional cultural–linguistic theory is about intra-systemic truths that indicate consistency within a given story, within a given religion.[39]

Q: Doesn't Lindbeck say something about them being like a grammatical rule?

Yes. You see, what Michalson asserts – and I think he is right – is that for Lindbeck you are being obedient to the grammatical rules inherent in a religion. OK? Then, you see, being faithful to these non-propositional cultural–linguistic statements is more like following a grammatical rule than believing a first–order claim about objective truth, about reality.

[38] George A. Lindbeck, *The Nature of Doctrine*, p. 21.

[39] Gordon E. Michalson Jr. 'The Response to Lindbeck', in *Modern Theology* 4.2 (January 1988), pp. 107–20. Michalson notes how Lindbeck's non-propositional cultural–linguistic theory *'fulfil the second-order function of stating intrasystemic truths that signal the coherence of the "story" or form of life making up the religion. In other words, doctrines are the "grammar of a religion", and faithfulness to them is more like following a rule (such a grammatical rule) than believing a first–order claim about ultimate reality'* (p. 118).

The name of Wittgenstein can be placed somewhere around this view: that a system of belief is in some sense its grammar. Wittgenstein appeared to believe that you can't get outside the rules to check them over against a transcendent reality. The grammar of religion is provided by the words from which it is expressed: the moment the word 'grammar' comes up, I see Wittgenstein.

This is more about conformity to a religious tradition: this is right, of course, absolutely right, one can concede to Lindbeck that this is how you learn to become members of a faith, by practising and by getting inside its ways of worship and so on, but he confuses that, of course, with the question of the creedal confessions that might be part of the worship. These creedal confessions are independent to a degree from the acts of worship.

I think it's fair to say that for Lindbeck the primary knowledge is how to be religious: so he is claiming knowledge by acquaintance as against knowledge of facts, or whatever. So you have knowledge of religion by acquaintance, by learning its ways, its grammar. You see, you may say that you know your friend. This is knowledge by acquaintance: you know that your friend can be trusted. Lindbeck is playing on this; what counts is knowledge of the set-up rather than any factual claims that may even be thought to be intrinsic to it. But I think that all this talk about non-propositional cultural–linguistic statements, is just a way of getting a direct proposition. Why? Because the problem with a non-propositionalist position is that you actually write a lot of propositions trying to prove to people that they are not propositionalists. In doing this Lindbeck and his supporters are stating a proposition!

What Lindbeck is saying is that where there are discussions within churches on, say, the Eucharist, or bishops, these issues remain church–dividing. They divide the churches – so he argues – because they involve an appeal to ontological realities. The nature of these ontological realities cannot be agreed upon or decided with agreement. So, and this is the crux of his argument, what he is saying is that instead of dealing with these things on the level of facts, we look at them as systems of rules, so then it might be possible in some sense or other to solve the differences, the problems (if the differences are problems), by treating them as systems of rules. That is the proposal that arises out of the apparent failure of ecumenical conversations, meetings and conversations that don't really get anywhere.

The interesting thing is that Robert Jenson also wrote a book called *The Unbaptized God* on the same thing.[40] This argument is predicated on a similar thing: he says, why is it that when these conversations between churches come up with some kind of solution to something it is only apparently solved, because next week they come up with something else. They can't agree that they have become reconciled. And the reason is that they are not actually coming to grips with the prior question and that is the 'nature of God'. Jenson pushes it towards an even

[40] Robert W. Jenson, *Unbaptized God: The Basic Flaw in Ecumenical Theology* (Minneapolis, MN: Fortress Press, 1992).

more ontological direction that in the end there is only one way you can solve this problem and that is to engage with the question of God.

What Lindbeck is saying is what he is doing, where he is going is in another direction; you see Jenson is saying, don't deal with the differences at the level of formulations, deal with them at the level of God. Lindbeck is saying don't deal with the differences at the level of formulations regarded as ontological or cognitive; no, says Lindbeck, rather deal with the differences as sets of rules: that might relativize them and enable people to come together.

These two approaches are going in opposite directions – they are both Lutheran – but they are addressing the same problem.

iii. Propositional Language and Revelation

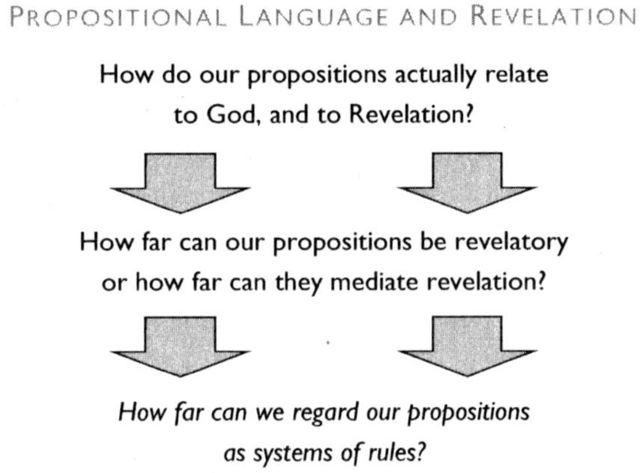

Figure 15

There are several questions here, all related to propositional language and Revelation. You see, the issue is about how our propositions actually relate to God, and to God's Revelation. But then you must ask about how far can our propositions be revelatory or how far can they mediate Revelation in themselves? But then we can also ask how far can we regard our propositions as systems of rules? If they are regarded as systems of rules then it is easier to change them. But then I believe that Lindbeck doesn't want to change them; he wants to say that these creedal things remain rock hard (figure 15). This relates to Barth's view that in the patristic era, say, you could have two people saying the say thing, but the very same words might mean something different. We have to accept that words do change their meaning. Therefore, Barth says that to say the same thing you might use different words.

This relates to the Yale School: it does have a tendency to remain at the level of the narrative or the linguistic systems, it remains a bit light and that is why Francis Watson accuses them of not really believing in God but believing in the language (Francis Watson, of course, is an Anglo-Saxon realist!).

Q: Isn't Lindbeck just side-stepping the issue, the challenge? Is he hiding in relativity, which is really quite a liberal thing when he claims to be post-liberal, putting liberalism behind him?

Well, yes, I'm not sure that Lindbeck's supporters would like that. They don't believe they are liberal because they want to ground all the time in language, and the grammar of these religious statements. But, I do think that this can empty the words of their meaning and their reference and to say that their meaning is not concerned with reference beyond themselves: the meaning is what they convey within themselves. And there is something to be said for that position – this is, after all, how we learn language. But a lot of the language of praise and worship does work in this way.

Language isn't just about stating facts. A lot of the language we use in Christian worship is not about factual claims. They, the words in Christian worship, are to do with involving ourselves in a certain way of life. They do different kinds of things rather than simply stating facts.

Q: But don't the words actually imply factual realities, or ontological realities?

Yes, you are right, your point is rock hard, you are right; you cannot get away from the fact that they imply factual realities or ontological realities. And to say that they don't is to evade what they actually mean.

Q: Is this about cultural conditioning?

No. No! He is not in that game at all. He is saying that religion is a culture and that you can learn it. You can move from one culture to another. Like becoming a Christian and joining in the Christian language game. He is not saying anything at all simple, and that is why it is a difficult book. It is a different game to say that someone is culturally conditioned. He is not saying how you happen to believe these things; he is saying how you insert yourself in a religious system, which is by sharing in it in worship and work.

Linguistic systems are how we live in the world. Lindbeck is saying that all these linguistic systems are different ways of living in the world and are not necessarily superior to each other. First of all they have to be understood as equals as they are all ways of living in the world, but this leads to relativism, and he is a relativist: you can't get out of your cultural–linguistic skin; or you can either by adding to it or getting into another one – like moving from a Marxist view to a Christian view.

This is another thing in support of the Schleiermacher–type view of religion, that religions are social systems that people share and experience, but the language for it and the experience can't be unpacked. It is very difficult to unpack an experience and describe it. You can transcend this culture, this is what prophets do: prophets stand outside it and see what is corrupt about it.

There isn't an easy way of testing how our theological language corresponds to the being of God, or the acts of God. That is why theology is so difficult. That is the way it is.

Part Two: The Modern Problem in a Historical Context

Chapter 4

REVELATION AND REASON, THEOLOGY AND INSPIRATION

1. The Problem of Revelation

What do we do with the problem of Revelation? – if there is a problem. What do we do with Revelation? What do we do with reason? Are there differing concepts of Revelation and reason? These are important questions that won't go away and need to be addressed. There are a huge number of concepts and definitions of Revelation; likewise, there are a huge number of and definitions of reason. Different generations seem to interpret these concepts differently.

i. Categories of Revelation

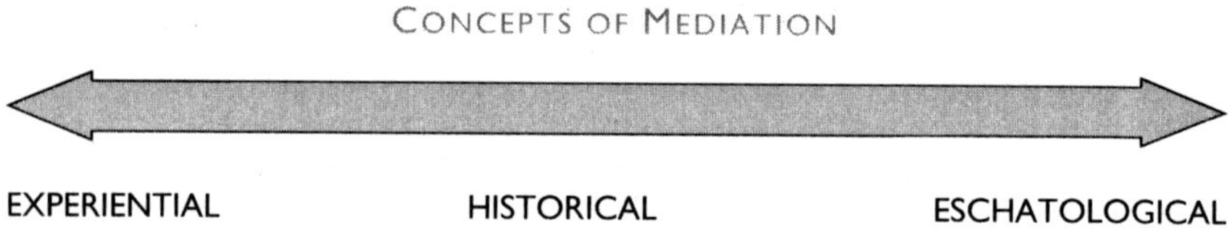

Figure 16

The question then arises, you see, can we chart most theologians within this range of definitions? We can, I believe, chart concepts of Revelation from the experiential through the historical to the eschatological; these three categories do, I think, allow us to place most theologians' definitions of Revelation and reason (figure 16).

First, the experiential: this is individual experience of a personal Revelation. Paul, I suppose, is a classic example of this, you know, about being caught up into the third heaven – 2 Corinthians 12 – this is seen as the experiential. This is a classic example of personal Revelation, which can seem self-centred and egocentric but it must be remembered that such Revelation is to be seen in a communal context. The Old and New Testaments are littered with such examples, as is the history of Christianity down the centuries but they are always, or should be, in a communal context. This is individual spirituality.

Second, the historical: historical Revelation is clearly in the centre with both Israel and the Incarnation as examples. These examples are probably the most important; again, such examples, as the Bible bears witness occur in a communal context and the contribution to the history of the people is crucial, the contribution to the salvation of the people of Israel, for example, is crucial.

Third, the eschatological: Revelation here is Jesus Christ at the end of the era. There are touches of Pannenberg here, of course, because of the completeness of eschatological Revelation; also of Barth because of his insistence that the Incarnation was a full and final Revelation. Revelation is seen here as 'completion'. Therefore, the question arises as to how 'full' is the eschatology of individual theologians? Or, how realized is this eschatology, their eschatology?

ii. A Realized Eschatology?

REVELATION AND TIME

DIACHRONIC:	SYNCHRONIC:
concerned with the historical development of a subject	describing a subject as it exists at one point in time

Figure 17

If Revelation is an eschatological concept then it is primarily to do with that which will be made universal and clear at the end. And then you want to say that there will be Revelation within time and history. You see, you are saying that eschatology is 'realized'. In Jesus of Nazareth it is realized. But in what sense and in what way? The differences between individual theologies are often centred around this question – What is the sense and definition of the realized eschatology in Jesus of Nazareth? To Pannenberg, Revelation was essentially an end of time event; by contrast Barth placed more emphasis on the temporal. Pannenberg accused Barth of an over-realized eschatology. Barth talked about Revelation as a final all complete event in Jesus. This raises a serious question, it raises much to consider. For example, you see, there's the following question to consider: 'How much can be taught?' How much can we learn of, know of, this eschatology, this final Revelation? Then we have to ask how final is the Revelation in Jesus? This is, of course, a Barthian question, a Barthian issue, is it not? This means we must then ask how final is Revelation at the end of time? To Barth the *eschaton* is when Jesus is: Pannenberg rejects this. You see, if Revelation is eschatological how much can be anticipated now, today, here and now? This is a diachronic approach, as distinct from synchronic (figure 17).

A synchronic account would be looking at the different possibilities of Revelation given at any different time, different moments in time. Revelation has a history in that concepts of Revelation have changed. For Barth, Jesus Christ is the Revelation of God; for Pannenberg the resurrection of Jesus is an anticipation of final Revelation. Pannenberg regards Barth as subjective because theology relies upon accepting that the end is present in Christ. For Barth, Revelation means God being actually present and demonstrating his presence in Jesus Christ. That is what Revelation is for Barth; it is God's self-demonstration of *His* being and act – in Jesus. For Pannenberg this is hopelessly subjective.

There must be room left for historical enquiry – Revelation will be at the end of history, but there will be anticipations. This can be achieved by following the pattern of the disciples from relative unbelief to belief. Mark's Gospel is a good example of this. You have to trace the historical development of belief in Jesus' oneness with the Father, you can't simply assert that this is the eternal Son around history. There is here a huge theological difference. You see, both regard the significance of the resurrection differently (figure 18).

RESURRECTION FOR PANNENBERG AND BARTH

WOLFHART PANNENBERG:	KARL BARTH:
resurrection	resurrection
is	is
retroactive	*retrospective*

Figure 18

So we have differences in conception, differences that give rise to different concepts of what theology is about. If Revelation has a history in so far as the concepts of Revelation have changed, then we need to examine briefly this history. We can, yes, I think that's right, we can almost say that historically speaking the movement is from the personal to the propositional; from the personal to the propositional, even legal. Revelation begins in some of the earlier Fathers as being concerned primarily with God's personal action in history.

Ignatius of Antioch uses the expression 'God revealed himself'. We have a self-presentation of God in history. Pannenberg takes exception to this; he associates this with theophany (that God appears in time). But this is an early view of Ignatius. However, this approach is attested to in the early creedal statements. The early creedal statements were responses to an act of divine Revelation: early Christian history is revelatory, it is a creedal faith. For example, 1 Corinthians 15.3. You see, listen –

> *For I handed on to you as of first importance what I in turn had received: that Christ died for our sins in accordance with the scriptures,*
>
> 1 Cor. 15.3

The response to Revelation is confession. Scripture is full of creedal statements, which are responses to Revelation. This is what Dodd is about; he's very good at showing this.[1] Dodd asserts that there is great variety in the way these early creedal statements are put but there is a broadly unified group of expressions, particularly about Christ, and about salvation through him, and about the fact that this is in fulfilment of the Old Testament. This is how people summed up their response to Revelation. These responses, you see, they are very kerygmatic and very soteriological. This work of Dodd's was based on lectures given at King's College London in the 1930s. You have in the New Testament a series of proto-creedal expressions, which presents the early Christian response to Revelation, to Christ, for Christ is Revelation. These proto-creeds are then open to development into systematic theology by the early Patristic Fathers, they become doctrinal statements. By the time of Irenaeus you have these creedal formulas regarded as a rule of faith.

2. The Second Vatican Council

The question then arises 'How reliable are the early Fathers?' How often do they assume that something is? For example, Irenaeus champions the presence of a bishop over each congregation/church. But is this merely wishful thinking on his part?

i. A Rule of Faith

Irenaeus uses the rule of faith as his chief response/weapon against the Gnostics. However, Irenaeus quotes the rule of faith on several occasions, but he never uses the same words. Here, the form of the rule of faith, according to Irenaeus, is:

> **God the Father, creator of heaven and earth**
> **The incarnate Son**
> **The Holy Spirit**

The rule of faith is an open structure, but its content is fixed. We can compare this with certain documents relating to Revelation, for example, from the Second Vatican Council. In Vatican II we find the statement that tradition transmits in its

1 C. H. Dodd, *The Apostolic Preaching and its Developments: Three Lectures with an Appendix on Eschatology and History* (London: Hodder and Stoughton, 1936). Charles Harold Dodd (1884–1973), Welsh New Testament scholar and Protestant theologian adopted a realized eschatology in the form of Jesus' preaching (the Kingdom of God) rather than an emphasis on a future apocalypse.

entirety the word of God which has been entrusted to the apostles.[2] What is important here is the idea of entirety – you have a move towards the idea that Revelation is the entirety of the church's teaching. It is not the church's response to Revelation; it almost becomes Revelation, legally formulated.

ii. Dei verbum

The First Vatican Council was essentially Thomist in structure; however, biblical criticism was important to the Second Vatican Council, especially the historical–critical approach. Therefore, we have a running argument between the modernizers and the traditionalists. Vatican II as a document is open to differing concepts of Revelation, rather than a closed view where Revelation is formulated in words, which are then transmitted down the years, unchanged. However, the Vatican II document on Revelation – *dei verbum* – claims that the last word on interpretation is with the *magisterium*.

iii. Tradition

Tradition is seen universally, quite universally, as two-fold: content and process. The content is often referred to as the deposit of the faith, though this doesn't always stay constant; then there is the process of how the content is passed on. Rome comes to mind, doesn't it, the Roman Catholic Church's tradition of handing on the deposit of faith from the apostles. On the other hand the Second Vatican Council has proposed that tradition is a single source of truth flowing forth in both scripture and church tradition.

This is all to do with questions of authority, as my colleague here who teaches the ecclesiology course would say, it is all about, the question is, 'By what authority do you say and do these things?' You may also ask 'To what extent is the church the body of Christ?' Then there is the question of scripture: the question of authority is often seen in the relationship between scripture and the historic church. Also, 'Do we accept what Rome says about the continuation of the apostolic succession?'

This is the key to the Catholic position, that the bishops are in some sense continuous with the apostles, bearing their authority. Many Protestants see this continuity between the apostles and the bishops as broken at best, false at worst. You see, it is because of this apostolic tradition that the Church of England will find it difficult to ordain women as bishops. Ordaining as priests is OK, but ordaining as bishops is a problem if you believe that the bishops are in some way

2 *Dogmatic Constitution on Divine Revelation – Dei Verbum Solemnly Promulgated by his Holiness Pope Paul VI on November 18, 1965*, ch. 2, §§. 7–10. See Walter Abbott, *The Documents of Vatican II* (New York, NY: Guild Press, 1966), pp. 114–18.

the same or a continuation of the apostles – that they must do everything that the apostles did. It is a deep-set tradition that women are not ordained. In my own church we ordained women in 1918, in terms of two millennia – that is a very short time. You can say by what right do we overturn centuries of tradition, and the answer is by better theology not by quoting proof texts.

Another thing that underlies this is the sinfulness of the church, the inherent sinfulness of the church, which again Orthodox and Roman Catholic theologians have difficulty accepting but Protestants wouldn't. Protestants would not find it difficult to believe that the church is sinful. The less directly continuous with the apostles we are the more difference there is between the church now and the apostles, and there is a greater chance for the church to make a mess of things. And we will have to say that historically there is a good deal of evidence for the fact that the church is less than perfect.

Then there is the canon of scripture. It is a very important question – To what extent does the church decide that scripture is authoritative, or accept that scripture is authoritative? Because the church has to accept the canon, it made a decision and certain books were in. A very strong Catholic position would say that it created the canon or constituted the canon.

Protestants value tradition but for them priority must be given to the witness recorded in scripture, but of course these scriptures are produced, verified, are they not, by the church. And so we have the concept of *sola scriptura*, 'by the Bible alone'. But there is more to the Reformers than simply the rallying cry of *sola scriptura*.

Q: Is Canon Law another form of *sola*?

Good question. Well, it depends who you are talking about. Certainly there still are some Anglican bishops who would regard, who would definitely say, that Canon Law is more important than scripture. A canon lawyer is someone whose function it is to interpret the canons of church law, so fundamentally a form of lawyer rather than a theologian. What is happening here is an attempt at a contemporary or present–day articulation of Christian belief, and the laws by which the church organizes its business.

By comparison, we have the interesting sociological phenomenon in modern Roman Catholicism where we find theologians who think they are above the church – Hans Küng, for example. He quite clearly believes that he is able to speak down from a great height to the benighted church below him. Is that so? Well, is that how he comes across?

Once you undermine the traditional view that it is the canon lawyer who is the one who rules, that it is the theologian who rules in his stead, then you get the danger of what Barth would call the virtuoso theologian. This raises the question of how far the theologian is a servant of the church and in what sense.

Q: Do Roman Catholics see the church as an equal authority to scripture?

Well, again, it depends which Roman Catholics you are thinking of, certainly some might have thought of the authority of the church in that way. If that is right then you have a metaphysic in Roman Catholic theology that says that the church is bound to do the work of the Spirit, whereas the Protestant position would be that the church has done the Spirit's work and continues to but may not always –

the church might not always be faithful. It would take a very extreme Catholic position to say that the church can never do wrong, just as it would take an extremely literalist position to say that no word of scripture can ever be other than totally true.

Vatican II, it was at Vatican II that the Catholic Church reformulated her understanding of tradition. Yes, I think it is clear from *dei verbum* that they are moving away from a two-source doctrine of Revelation and towards a single source of truth flowing forth in both scripture and tradition.[3]

There is always the danger that, in other words, the doctrines become Revelation rather than Christ being the Revelation. And that is a danger that is open to all the churches, all of them.

Q: It is here that tradition is put into perspective, and the finitude of the church is seen in contrast to the final full Revelation of Christ to come – Is that how you see it?

REVELATION AS AN ACT AND AN EVENT

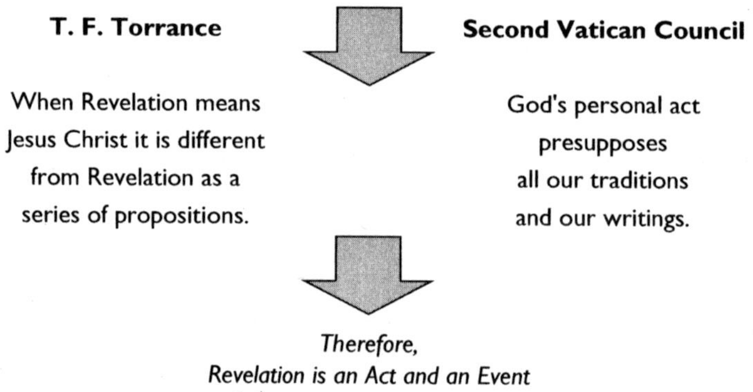

Figure 19

Well, sort of, you see – so obviously if tradition is founded by a human being doing something, or something happening to that human being which is conceived as Revelation, this is rather different from tradition as conceived as a body of teaching handed over from one body of men to the next. That is the pole of the argument. Obviously, you can't escape the fact that the teaching has to be handed on by bodies of people, but this is what Torrance is saying that, when Revelation means 'Jesus Christ', it is rather different from when Revelation means a 'series of propositions': Catholics meaning creedal propositions or Protestants meaning biblical propositions. So Torrance is arguing, and so is the Second Vatican Council, that God's personal act presupposes all our traditions and our writings (figure 19).

3 *'Sacred Tradition and Sacred Scripture make up a single sacred deposit of the Word of God, which is entrusted to the Church'* (Dei Verbum, ch. III, §§, 11–13; ch. IV, §§. 14–16; ch. V, §§. 17–20; and ch. VI, §§ 21–25).

3. Personal or Propositional

T. F. Torrance has written a very important article criticizing the approach to Revelation that has been adopted by the Roman Catholic Church.[4] The work is, yes, polemical, but there are some important observations in it. Torrance asserts that for Irenaeus the canon of truth is in fact the truth, the rule of faith, it is a response to Jesus. Then, later, among the Fathers we have Tertullian. Tertullian is a lawyer, he formulates things carefully; as a lawyer he likes to make things rigid. For Tertullian the rule of faith was to be consistently regarded as a fixed form of truth and belief: this had been instituted by Christ and handed down entire and unchanged. This is exactly what the Roman Catholic Church is saying, for Torrance. So, is Christ the truth? Or, is the truth tied down in a set of sentences? Torrance roots his view in the patristic writers.

i. A Deposit of Faith?

This raises an important question: Is Revelation personal or propositional? This is very important; you see, Torrance's view is that when Tertullian talks about irrefutable truths they are in danger of a legalized, extrinsic view of Revelation. Torrance is critical of the fixed system of interpretation that the Roman Catholic Church adopts. It came to be held that the faith is a set of timeless propositions, and that these are handed on from one generation to another by the church's teaching, or if you are a Protestant, in the actual words of scripture: the modern world is essentially in revolt against this.

Robert Jenson in his systematic theology comments that dogma is irreversible.[5] Once the church has decided that something is true then it is irreversible. For example, once the church has decided that Jesus Christ is both God and man it's now lodged in history as an irreversible fact. You see, there is something about the way Christian claims are formulated that embeds them in the past; if there is a problem then the problem in the modern world is caused by the awareness of the relativity of language. The way a word was used in ancient times will be different to today. The way a word is used from one generation to the next will be different.

Barth, you see, is conscious of this relativity of language. This raises several questions:

> **Is God revealed?**
> **Is God revealed in Christ?**

4 T. F. Torrance, 'The Deposit of Faith', *Scottish Journal of Theology* 36.1, 1983.

5 Robert Jenson, *Systematic Theology*, Vol. 1 (Oxford: Oxford University Press, 1997). See generally pp. 17, 22, 25–6, 34–9; specifically, ch. 2 The Norms of Theological Judgement, section VI, pp. 35f.

Is Revelation a personal thing?
Is Revelation a series of statements?
Is there revealed truth?
Is the propositional form secondary to revealed truth?
Is God personally present in history?
Is God self-presented in history?

When Paul says he trusts in scripture, this is a view of Revelation. Using words is propositional. So, is Revelation in the propositions of scripture? Is the Revelation of scripture, in scripture, as fixed and as propositional as the dogmas of the Roman Catholic Church? You see, we're talking about the irreversibility of dogma. If we are talking about the fixed nature of doctrine, then is the question of the irreversibility of dogma only limited to the Roman Catholic Church? And if the irreversibility of dogma is a problem in Rome, is it caused by their belief in papal infallibility? Is this question of the irreversibility of dogma only limited to Rome? Not necessarily so, after all many Protestant churches regard the Bible as literally infallible: Does not the Bible constitute an irreversible dogma for many Protestant Churches? One general dogma, which is irreversible could be the canon of scripture: Is the ordering and contents of the sacred text available for analysis and question? The canon has remained pretty stable, fixed, since the patristic era. John Baillie's book on the idea of Revelation is – it's important here to this discussion – *The Idea of Revelation in Recent Thought.*[6]

ii. Creeds and Coumcils?

You see there are other considerations in this. Are the decisions of the Council of Nicaea reversible, or the creeds and canons from other councils? You need to think about these questions. Can the decisions of various church councils although accepted as irreversible dogma, be rejected if on consideration they conflict with scripture? Can Nicaea be rejected on biblical grounds? It can be accepted as an implicit dogma of Protestantism that the canon of scripture is accepted as Revelation, that it is fixed. Some may consider that the writers of scripture are above, or outside the church. This is wrong; the scriptures are a product of the church. Certainly the New Testament and the place of the Old Testament. So, and this is crucial, we need to decide what we understand by Revelation and by inspiration, this can seem to be what is at the heart of the distinction between propositional and personal Revelation. You see, you need to decide – this really is important, it is something that is fundamental to this course – you need to decide what we understand by Revelation and what we understand by inspiration. Your

[6] John Baillie, *The Idea of Revelation in Recent Thought* (New York: Columbia University Press, 1956).

decision will be at the heart of how you distinguish between propositional and personal Revelation.[7]

4. Inspiration

Inspiration underpins Revelation. OK, inspiration reveals. How can we look at inspiration? Not all inspiration is the same; that seems obvious on the one hand, on the other hand it is so often overlooked.

i. Inspiration and Humanity

Figure 20

We can look at the inspiration behind Revelation on a scale (figure 20). On the one hand inspiration can be seen as a human filter. The writers of the Gospels can be seen as being inspired by the Spirit, but something of their humanity affects what is written. Revelation here consists in being inspired. On the other hand, the writers of scripture can be seen merely as a channel – the dove whispers in the ear, effectively dictating the words.

How do we avoid a dry propositionalism? We need to decide what precisely the word of God is today; the ground rules for interpretation need to be decided. The writing of scripture is one issue; the interpretation is another. The Holy Spirit must have a role in interpreting scripture; this needs to be defined. However, we must be acutely aware of the modern dogma, which asserts that there is a great gulf between us reading them today and the scriptures. We are still affected by the Enlightenment dogma that anything as old as scripture must be suspect. In Calvin's day anything as old as scripture would be considered good: ancient meant good.

7 Colin Gunton placed great value on the work of the, primarily, Romantic English poet Samuel Taylor Coleridge who formulated an important understanding of the distinction between Revelation and inspiration, and systematically categorized imagination (in relation to the infinite 'I AM'). See Samuel Taylor Coleridge, *Biographia Literaria: or, Biographical Sketches of my Literary Life and Opinions* (ed. and intro. George Watson, Everyman's library 11; London: Dent, 1956), p. 175, see also p. 77. For an understanding and placing of Coleridge on inspiration and imagination see P. H. Brazier, 'C. S. Lewis and Christological Prefigurement', in *The Heythrop Journal*, 48.5 (September 2007), pp. 742–75 (Editor).

What did Barth do? Barth rooted the inspiration not in the words of scripture but in the way they inspire us today.

So, historically and diachronically there are a number of definitions of Revelation. We can't distinguish in a clear-cut manner between the personal and the propositional but this distinction has to be made. This returns us to the question, 'What precisely is Revelation?' Which in turn returns us to the question, 'What is the relationship between Revelation and reason?' Propositional Revelation must have a different standing to personal Revelation. Propositional revelations are already proposed and established, therefore they exist in reason to some degree. We can look at the relation between Revelation and reason by looking at key examples in history.

ii. 'Word' and 'word'

God's personal self-revelation is in rational form in the sense that it is the 'Word': Jesus. You must know this, the Barthian principle: Jesus is the 'Word of God' – note the capital 'W'. Jesus is the focus of Revelation. And yet, of course, in some sense reason has to find words to describe this, and yet in a way it doesn't have to find them if the words, the verbal forms, are already given. OK? In Jesus Christ the words/verbal forms are already given: Is that right? You see, Jesus Christ – and I suppose this is pure Barthian – Jesus Christ is the self-revelation of God, he is a person and an event. Though we have to be careful how we use the word event.

The other approach is that which is clear from Tertullian and Kierkegaard, where Tertullian says I believe it because it is absurd.[8] Tertullian does not mean that Christianity is absurd but that the form of the faith is resistant to rational expression. Therefore, there are limits to how much you can do with rationality. That's important: rationality is not going to give you everything. This is also the case with Kierkegaard: the rationality at the heart of the Christian faith means that our rationality is limited. God and man are given together and reason cannot understand this. Kierkegaard commented, did he not, that against this reason beats its brow until the blood comes.[9] Kierkegaard does not deny that certain of these

8 *'I believe because it is absurd'*, is a translation of Tertullian's statement, *'Credibile est, quia ineptum est'*: Tetullian, *De carne Christi*. The phrase *'Credibile est, quia ineptum est'* essentially implies that something might be absurd or illogical, ridiculous or strange, even preposterous, that although it is inconsistent with experience, yet there is truth. Quintus Septimius Florens Tertullianus, Tertullian (c.155–230), a church leader and theologian, early Christian apologist, was a Romanized African from Carthage. See Tertullian, *De carne Christi liber. Tertullian's Treatise on the Incarnation*, The Text edited with an Introduction, Translation, and Commentary (ed. Ernest Evans; London: SPCK, 1956).

9 See Søren Kierkegaard, *Concluding Unscientific Postscript to Philosophical Fragments* (ed. and trans. Howard V. Hong and Edna H. Kong; New York, NY: Princeton University Press, 1992); Søren Kierkegaard, *Philosophical Fragments: Johannes Climacus* (ed. and trans. Howard V. Hong and Edna H. Kong; Princeton, NJ: Princeton University Press, 1985); Søren Kierkegaard, *Purity of Heart is to Will One Thing* (New York, NY: Harper and Row, 1938); Søren

fundamental claims are rational because they are true, but they are not rational in the sense that they can be encompassed in our words. We must be careful not to attempt to encompass all in words: you see, we have to face, we must face the limits of the human intellect. But this does not open up a mystical vacuum.

5. Reason and Theology

Figure 21

So, we need to look at some of the different concepts of reason, which have been used by theology. This focuses again on the distinction between the synchronic and the diachronic. Synchronically there are two extremes – Tillich brings this out well.[10] Tillich distinguishes between a range of different possibilities of reason, there are two poles: on one hand there is a functional concept of reason and on the other hand there is ontological reason (figure 21).

i. A Functional Concept of Reason

So, what is the functional concept of reason: the functional concept of reason is where reason is the function of the human response to the world. Tillich is saying, and I think this is right, he's asserting that we must avoid thinking of reason as a distinct faculty; we must see it simply as human beings responding in a certain way to what is before them, what they are comprehending.

Reason here has a function, it doesn't particularly characterize a thing within us; the rational needs to be defined but here we can simply describe it as the ability to reason. Barth sees three meanings to reason in Anselm. This includes the subjective capacity to make judgements, for example, the ability to say two objects are green, or that rationality is God himself. So, what are we talking about here?

Kierkegaard, *The Sickness Unto Death* (trans. Alistair Hannay; Harmondsworth: Penguin Books, 1989); Søren Kierkegaard, *Training in Christianity* (trans. Walter Lowrie; Oxford: Oxford University Press, 1941).

10 Paul Tillich, *Systematic Theology*, Volume 1, *Reason and Revelation: Being and God* (Chicago, IL: University of Chicago Press, 1951), see Part 1 Reason and Revelation, ch. III The Structure of Reason, pp. 79–118.

We are talking about the human capacity to generalize, make judgements, to universalize and to make truth claims. That's important – to make truth claims.

For Barth there are two higher senses of the term. One of them is the rationality inherent in the object. To Kierkegaard we are talking about what kind of rationality is inherent in Christology. We need to consider the status of the human reasoning faculty, that is I believe what all these people are saying, what they are asking. They are asking 'What status, what value, do we give to the human capacity, the faculty to reason?' This is, of course, tied up with the ability to use words; it is inevitably to do with language. That is I suppose one concession to modernity, particularly the philosophy of language.

ii. An Ontological Concept of Reason

Tillich also identifies ontological reason. By ontological reason Tillich means something like that part of us that is in some sense or other continuous with, or responsive, to the deep structures of reality. He is saying that our rational faculty in some sense or other answers to the being of things, the 'beingness' of things that we comprehend.

We have a mind or a reason, and this mind is in some sense or other qualified to, or is directly continuous with, the rationality that shapes or permeates reality. In other words there is some sort of continuity between the human mind, which is the spark of the divine, there is continuity between the mind and reason. This is essentially a Greek concept. The Greeks essentially believed that the human being was made up of two elements: the material, which was the irrational, and the intellectual, which was the rational. This intellectual part is in some way a part of the divine – this is why the mind can discern the forms.

The Greek myths express this in many ways: the myth of the Titans recounts how a group of Titans came across an infant god, cooked and ate him, and were subsequently charred to a cinder by Zeus' thunderbolt. From the charred remains of the giants the human race was made. The doctrine underlying this myth is that the human being is rubbish with a bit of divinity within in it, a spark of divinity. To be a human being is to be a material being that is inferior with a spark of the divine in you. This spark of the divine is knowledge as reason – it is the god-like within you. We can know God because we have reason. Natural theology would assert that in some way or other, even without scripture or Revelation, that reason can glimpse God.

This assumption that reason is a source of truth is deep in the theological tradition. For example, Richard Hooker,[11] the Anglican theologian, author in many ways of the Anglican *via media*, asserted that there were three sources in theology:

[11] Richard Hooker (1554–1600), an Anglican priest and theologian who is attributed with the form of the Anglican *via media*, and along with Thomas Cranmer and Matthew Parker for the basis or ground of the Church of England after the Henrician Reformation. Hooker was born in the village of Heavitree, Devon; he became a fellow of Corpus Christi College, Oxford,

scriptural
reason
tradition

But are they all the same kind of thing? Is there really any difference between the three? And how do they relate to Revelation? Are they all equally revelatory or is there a hierarchy at work here? Scripture is clearly a source of theology. You can't have a theology that is not in some way or other grounded in scripture. Reason is a source of theology in some sense – Does this mean that the divine is already there and has to be teased out? From Anselm on, God is seen as reason itself. Earlier, Augustine commented that the divine likeness is memory – memory of the understanding in the world.[12]

It seems to me that there is a range of conceptions from the purely functional – say reason as simply a function, something we do – to saying that it is ontological, saying that it characterizes our being and is that which links us to the world that is known.

6. Romans

Natural reason: we've been talking, almost, about natural reason, our innate capacity to *reason*, have we not? Paul's comments in the first chapter of Romans are crucial to our understanding of natural reason – or the capacity for natural theological reason. So what does Paul say? Listen to this –

> *For what can be known about God is plain to them, because God has shown it to them. Ever since the creation of the world his eternal power and divine nature, invisible though they are, have been understood and seen through the things he has made. So they are without excuse.* [13]
>
> Rom. 1.19-20

1577. He was ordained priest in 1584, and later served as Sub-dean of Salisbury Cathedral. Hooker's *Of the Laws of Ecclesiastical Polity* was highly influential on the development of the Church of England and was essentially a treatise on church–state relations, focusing on issues of biblical interpretation, soteriology, ethics and sanctification. Like Anselm, Hooker asserted that theology must be grounded in prayer.

12 See Augustine, *Saint Augustine Confessions* (Oxford World Classics; trans. Henry Chadwick; Oxford: Oxford University Press, 1991), see bk X Memory, pp. 179–220.

13 V.19 διότι τὸ γνωστὸν τοῦ θεοῦ φανερόν ἐστιν ἐν αὐτοῖς ὁ θεὸς γὰρ αὐτοῖς ἐφανέρωσεν. V.20 τὰ γὰρ ἀόρατα αὐτοῦ ἀπὸ κτίσεως κόσμου τοῖς ποιήμασιν νοούμενα καθορᾶται, ἥ τε ἀΐδιος αὐτοῦ δύναμις καὶ θειότης, εἰς τὸ εἶναι αὐτοὺς ἀναπολογήτους. Rom. 1.19-20; Barbara Aland, Kurt Aland, Johannes Karavidopoulos (eds.), *Nestle-Aland Novum Testamentum Graece* (Stuttgart: Deutsche Bibelgesellschaft, 1995 [1979]), p. 410.

So, what does this tell us? Well, here we find that God's invisible power and deity is revealed in the things he has made. However, since the beginning of the world attributes of God have been known, perceivable, *'seen through the things he has made'*. This is extremely interesting. Some translators have interpreted *'seen through the things he has made'* as *'are known to the eye of reason in the things that he has made'*. But this is eisegesis, this is reading too much into the text.[14] All Paul is saying is that the heavens and in some sense the earth declare God's being, or his invisible power and deity. We tend to assume that this means we can reason from the natural world to the existence of God, but is Paul saying that here we need to make a central distinction that is very, very, rarely made? Paul may be talking about general Revelation. As I have said many times before, you can't necessarily read the God of Revelation from nature: if you look at nature you can easily come up with the idea that there is no God, certainly not the God in Jesus Christ.[15]

What does general Revelation mean; well it means, roughly speaking, the Revelation that is everywhere real. If it is true that the *heavens* declare the glory of God, or the earth his handiwork, what you are making is a claim about what reality is and what it reveals. You are not making any claim about the human mind's capacity to see this because that is a different concept from natural theology. Natural theology is about human capacity: it is about the human capacity to know something of the being of God apart from any special Revelation from God.

So, is Paul saying that the creation reveals God's deity? I think he may be saying that simply from the created order we can come to some knowledge of God – some idea, or knowledge, of God from the created order. It may be that he then denies this – saying that we are without excuse. You see, although the heavens do reveal the creator, all this does is render us without excuse. So, God is knowable in the world but because of human incapacity and sin we cannot know him from the world. This seems to be Paul's overall message in this passage.

This has given rise to two opposing poles in theology, one pessimistic and one optimistic. These two positions are analogous with Aquinas and Calvin (figure 22). It is important to try to come to some understanding of where these different views come from. This is really, I believe, tied up with one central question: 'To what extent is it possible for a human to know of God apart from special Revelation?'

14 The phrase τοῖς ποιήμασιν νοούμενα καθορᾶται (literally, *'by the things made being understood are perceived'*), translated by Colin Gunton as *'seen through the things he has made'*, is variously translated thus:
'have been understood and seen through the things he has made' (NRSV); *'being understood by the things that are made'* (AV/KJV); *'have been visible to the eye of reason, in the things he has made'* (REB); *'have been clearly seen by the mind's understanding of created things'* (NJB); *'have been clearly seen, being understood from what has been made'* (NIV); *'have been clearly seen; they are perceived in the things that God has made'* (GNB); *'are clearly seen, being perceived through the things that are made'* (ASV); *'has been clearly perceived in the things that have been made'* (RSV).

15 Five years on since Colin Gunton's death one only has to consider the militant evangelical atheism of many celebrity media scientists (Richard Dawkins, Steve Jones, etc.) who look at nature and read an atheistic doctrine of creation from the natural world, which they then project into a full systematic theology of a no-god (Editor).

Knowledge of God: The Opposing Poles

POSITIVE: AQUINAS	**CALVIN: NEGATIVE**
Aquinas' view is that there is a limited knowledge of God, which can be obtained quite apart from the authoritative teaching of the Church: Aquinas derives this process of argument particularly from the Bible, but especially from Aristotelian causality. *This is a relative optimism – it is important to try to understand where this optimism comes from.*	*Calvin's position is essentially negative. The Reformation's position was, to a degree, a reaction against Catholic optimism. Calvin's view is that there are indeed two sources of the knowledge of God apart from scripture – the natural world and the human religious capacity. But we are so sinful and blind that scarce one in a hundred brings the seed of the knowledge of God to fruition: without scripture you can't even recognize God from the natural world. Hence many cannot even see the world as creation.* *We are like a short-sighted old man who can't see: scripture provides the essential spectacles.*

Figure 22

Chapter 5

A Historical Perspective 1: *Apocalypsis et Ratio*

1. Early Medieval

i. Introduction

It's time we looked at the development of Revelation and reason. Now, when looking at an assessment of the development of Revelation and reason – in a historical context – I think we have to regard the Reformation as a defining moment, a turning point. The Reformation must be regarded as a watershed.

ii. The Medieval Mindset

The Middle Ages, or the medieval period, really extended from around the year 500 to 1500. This was the period of the great flowering of Christendom. This period was very much the result of the work of one figure: Augustine, especially in his combination of Greek and Hebrew traditions. However, by the late fifteenth century the system was beginning to collapse, even implode, under its own weight. This system resulted from the fusing, by Augustine, of two traditions: Revelation from the Hebrew tradition, from the Jews, from the Old Testament, which was fused with Greek logic. So you have, you see, Hebraic Revelation, the Revelation of the Jews and Greek reason (figure 23).

It is this synthesis, this Graeco–Hebrew synthesis, which in many ways creates the world order that we now call medieval. The great historical era of Christianity was a success, you may say; it resulted from Augustine combining these Greek and Hebrew legacies. The Middle Ages are when you have the medieval synthesis. This system broke down in the late Middle Ages through its own inadequacies, its own logic – it fell apart.

So we have a combination of Hebrew Revelation and Greek reason. This is a difficult 'marriage' because in Revelation you are taught, whereas in reason you find

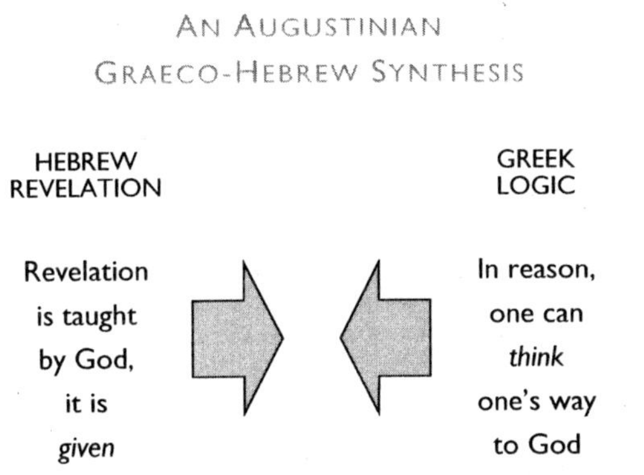

Augustine brought together Hebraic Revelation and Greek reason-logic

Figure 23

out for yourself. Yes, that's a generalization, and although we should avoid generalizations I think it is one that is fair and it is one that most people would, could, agree with, don't you think? Augustine fused them, combined them, and he combines what we might call the rational quest for God and the situation where God meets us halfway. That's really what the medieval synthesis is about. Reason is not useless, but we can't think ourselves all the way to God: Revelation will complete the task. That's how the medieval synthesis worked, though what reason has to do with salvation is another question, but we won't go into that now!

iii. Philo

Philo[1] is important in this development. He works on a doctrine of creation: God reveals; the mind discovers. Philo gives us an account of Genesis in which he synthesized the Greek and the Hebrew. He does this by adopting a Platonic view in which he argued that when God creates he first creates the forms and then, only then, does he create the material world. You see, what Philo does is shift Plato's forms from the world outside to the mind of God. To the mind of God: that is important.

1 Philo (20 BC – AD 50), Philo of Alexandria or Philo Judeaus, a Hellenized Jewish philosopher born in Alexandria, Egypt employed allegory to combine Judaic theology and philosophy with Hellenistic ideas and philosophy, particularly in his use of the Stoics. His writings were appreciated by the early Christians, for example, his idea of the Logos as the creative principle of Yahweh. See Philo of Alexandria, *The Works of Philo: Complete and Unabridged* (trans. Charles Duke Yonge; foreword, David M. Scholer; Peabody, MA: Hendrickson, 1993)

Plato asserted that the deep forms, which are behind material objects and the world, are discoverable by the mind. Reason therefore has its role: the forms are discoverable, perceived, by the mind. However, you see, no biblical commentator could really go along with this because the Platonic system is that these forms are created, they are part of creation – according the Hebrew system they are eternal, they are uncreated. However, because Philo moves the forms to inside the mind of God, they can be seen as possibly eternal, at least, eternally created.

However, what is important, certainly from the historical perspective, is that Philo began this merging of the two great traditions: Greek and Hebrew. Furthermore, Philo uses the idea of an architect. God as the architect creates the form and then puts this into practice in the way an architect draws plans. This in many ways can be thought of, or seen – but we need to be cautious – as the ontological side of medieval philosophy. You see, ontology – the nature of being – becomes important in understanding the relation between Revelation and reason.

iv. Boethius

THE EPISTEMOLOGICAL FRAMEWORK

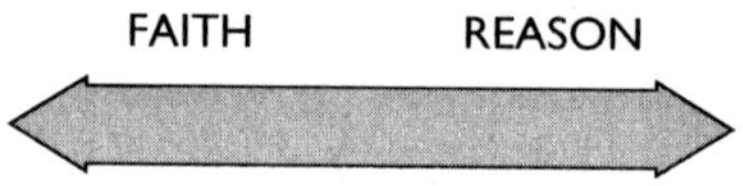

The Two-Source Theory of Truth: Faith (Revelation) and Reason

Figure 24

Boethius[2] was the last of the ancients and the first of the 'Medievalists'; that's certainly how I see him – the last, so to speak, of the ancients in the sense of classical thought and the first of what we can term the Medievalists. Boethius was working in the sixth century; and he laid down the epistemological boundaries or framework in the same way that Philo laid down the ontological framework. Epistemologically there are two sources for truth: faith and reason (figure 24). Faith comes from the church and from belief – all right. Faith comes from what the church teaches. Reason is the intrinsic capacity to know; that is, to know rationally. Boethius asserted that if you can, combine faith and reason. OK; this is important to our thinking. We have the two – Revelation and reason – we have them set together. Faith – which here is linked with Revelation (though some

2 Anicius Manlius Severinus Boethius (c.480–524/525), a Christian philosopher of the Roman aristocracy and a leading political family; a leading politician himself, while in prison awaiting execution for supposed treason, he wrote *The Consolation of Philosophy*, and continued his project to preserve the ancient classical philosophy by translating it into Latin. See Boethius, *The Consolation of Philosophy* (trans. V. E. Watts; Harmondsworth: Penguin Books, Penguin Classics, 1999); also Henry Chadwick, *Boethius, The Consolations of Music, Logic, Theology and Philosophy* (Oxford: Oxford University Press, Clarendon Press, 1981).

would dispute the link), is here together with reason. But it is important to remember that they are not the same.

Josef Pieper in a short work called *Scholasticism* promoted the importance of combining the Greek and Hebrew worlds and their mindsets.[3] This is in a way what is happening here. Boethius' *Consolations of Philosophy* is an important work even though it is non-Christian.[4] This pattern dominates the medieval period, the balancing of Greek rationality and philosophy and the Hebrew revelatory spiritual tradition. This is I believe fairly attributed to Boethius; well worth reading, because, you see, it sets the pattern for the medieval world, the medieval mind. It sets the scene for scholasticism.

This balancing act between faith and reason, Revelation and reason, is not the same throughout the medieval period, and it is not consistent throughout the period c.500–1500. The earlier period tends to be more Platonic in its view of the knowledge of God, more intuitive; the latter Middle Ages tend to be more Aristotelian. Boethius is essentially Aristotelian; yes, he is certainly more Aristotelian. Then in the later period the faith and reason balance tends to merge in Thomas' work, in the *Summa*.[5] Aquinas seems to run with this Boethian pattern of having faith and reason running in parallel; we will look at that later.

2. Anselm: *fides quaerens intellectum*

Then we come to Anselm, for Barth the great Anselm.[6] Anselm, of course, is much more Platonic; much more Platonic that Boethius or Philo or any from the early medieval period. He does successfully combine the Platonic and Christian worlds. He combines the Platonic world and the Christian world – successfully, many believe successfully. Anselm's Platonism comes in a number of ways. One of them is in his belief that words simply as words are fit to be theological. In fact, according to him God creates words so that we may theologize. God has created language in us so that we may praise God: as simple as that. And theology is a form of praise. Anselm continues this synthesis of the ancient world and the Hebrew–Christian world. Wherever you look in the Middle Ages you have this synthesizing of the two fold heritage of the ancient world. And it was a great civilization – the ancient. There is quite a Platonic doctrine in Anselm. Mind you, many of the problems we are still wrestling with today were created by the medieval system,

3 Josef Pieper, *Scholasticism; Personalities and Problems of Medieval Philosophy* (trans. Richard and Clara Winston; London: Faber & Faber, 1960).

4 Boethius, *The Consolation of Philosophy* (trans. V. E. Watts; Harmondsworth: Penguin Books, Penguin Classics, 1999).

5 Thomas Aquinas, *Summa Theologiae* (the complete paperback set, 60 volumes, plus one index volume; dual language, Latin–English; Cambridge: Cambridge University Press, 2006 [1962–76]).

6 Saint Anselm of Canterbury (1033–1109), Italian philosopher and theologian, Archbishop of Canterbury from 1093 until his death, the founder to many of scholasticism.

such as the authoritarianism of the church, or the relationship between church and state, especially where the church was accommodating to the state.

What is Anselm about? What drives Anselm? Well, first I think what I've just said is probably not appropriate, it is wrong. It is theologians in the modern era that are driven, to a degree; Anselm is not like that. But anyway, what is it that holds Anselm's – yes, holds is probably a better word to use – What is it that holds Anselm's work together? Simple: it is faith – *fides quaerens intellectum*, 'faith seeking understanding'. You see, in Anselm you have a clear presentation of the medieval two-source theory of knowledge: Revelation and reason are held in balance. This system goes back as we saw to Boethius. These are, in effect, sources of theological knowledge.

i. The Oneness of Truth

So there is one source of truth, there is oneness to truth. But then there is the two-source theory. Well, you see, there tended to be a distinction between truths that can be discovered by reason alone – that there is one God, that he exists – and those that can be known only through Revelation. By Revelation you get the Trinity and the Incarnation. A very neat dichotomy, and it is deeply in our consciousness. It is so easy to assume that if you are going to talk about God you have to get a sort of philosophical proof of *His* existence before you can go on. This is a deeply entrenched position in theological thinking today, though as you can guess, it comes from philosophy.

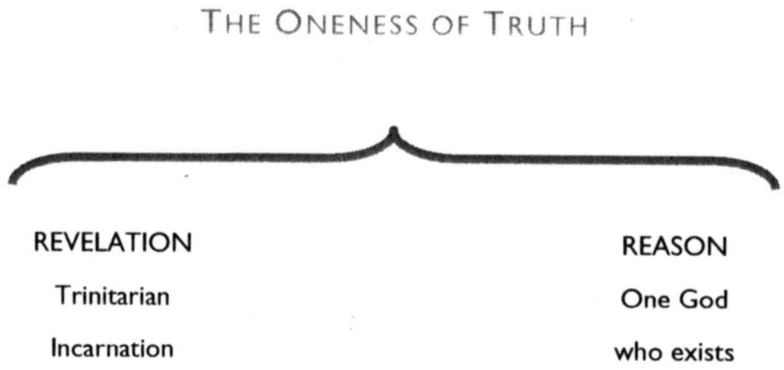

Figure 25

Yes, a very neat dichotomy, this two-source theory. In the Middle Ages this was embraced by the view of the oneness of truth: God is one, truth is one, therefore you can naturally expect reason and Revelation to produce the same result, or at least not to be incompatible. Reason is therefore seen as a semi-independent or semi-autonomous source of knowledge. This scheme broke up in the Enlightenment: reason became a fully independent source of knowledge, absolutely independent from any concept of Revelation. Reason was seen as adequate by itself – this is of course representative of the radical, early Enlightenment. Locke, as we saw last week, regarded Revelation as inferior: reason was considered superior. This led in the more anti-religious writers to the teaching that reason was supreme; the only important sources were reason and science. Revelation and faith were at best opinion, if not completely irrelevant (figure 25). Anselm is a pre-Thomist medieval: that is important to remember. He is a medieval theologian, a highly philosophical theologian who yet pre-dates Aquinas; it is Anselm who brought this Revelation–reason parallelism into such focus.

ii. Anselm's Understanding of 'Proof' in Theology

It is important to understand that it is a mistake to regard Anselm's famous demonstration of the existence of God as an ontological argument. Although philosophers, in particular those working in the philosophy of religion, will argue that the ontological argument starts with Anselm, is reaffirmed by Descartes, apparently destroyed by Kant, but revived by Hegel, and so on, it is important to remember that Barth asserts that this is not a right way to describe Anselm's argument on the existence of God. He argues it is not an ontological argument in the way that we understand the concept of proof in the modern era. The modern method of proving the existence of God is to start from nothing and arrive at what can be conceived of as evidence. The belief here is that to start from nothing is a position that reflects that of the majority. Anselm calls his argument a 'proof' – but it is not a proof in the modern sense where an argument moves people from unbelief to belief. What Anselm does is to generate *intelligere*, or understanding. This is crucial – Anselm's argument helps us to understand what we mean by God. The aim of theology for Anselm is, simply, understanding. The first title of Anselm's book on this was *fides quaerens intellectum*: 'faith seeking understanding'. So for Anselm theology is primarily faith seeking understanding. Understanding is the main thing for Anselm, it is what drives him, though as I said, we can't say that someone like Anselm is driven in the same way that modern philosophers are driven by an 'agenda' – yes, that's a word, a concept, I don't like, labelling everything with the word 'agenda'.

You see, in seeking understanding you are defending the faith against unbelief, Barth does not deny that; but understanding is the main thing for Anselm. As understanding is achieved, it issues in joy. The dominating factor in Anselm's mind is that even the Church Fathers wrote in order to give the faithful joy in believing – joy! Yes, that's the point of theology: joy. Not rationalistic explanations but by showing the *ratio* of their faith. The reason is that the understanding seeks and finds, possesses in itself, not only *utilitas*, usefulness, but also beauty. Anselm is trying to understand the proof in such a way that it results in joy – rejoicing. Anselm wants proof and joy because he wants understanding, and he wants understanding because he believes. For Anselm, to believe doesn't simply mean a striving of the will towards God, in other words an effort to believe in God, in other words not trying through effort to believe in God but a striving of the will *into* God, and so, *participation*, and yes, *joyful participation*.

For Anselm, theology is about participating in God's life. Not simply some abstract understanding. For Anselm faith means knowledge, the creed is rational in the highest sense possible. This raises the question, 'What is the status of this understanding?' Well, for a start there is an absence of crisis in Anselm's theology. Anselm, you see, is a serene theologian, he knows that you can trust the church, you can trust the past and you can trust the tradition.

iii. What is Reason in Theology?

ANSELM OF CANTERBURY ON REASON

LOWER LEVEL **Subjective Reason**	MIDDLE LEVEL **The Ratio**	HIGHEST LEVEL **The Ratio Veritatis**
The lowest form of reason here is the primary capacity for dealing with experience, formulating conceptions and judgements.	*The Ratio: that which can be known belonging to the object of faith itself*	*The rationality of the truth itself – meaning God. God is eternal rationality, reason, almost, in itself.*
That is the use of ideas and judgements – the human capacity to think, and to make general judgements: for example, this chair is green. We can use our experience and generalize from it.	So, objective reason, the object of faith. For Anselm this is the creed. The creed has an objective rationality because it is given. It is an objective recount of the words and acts/actions of God.	This is the highest reason, and there is naturally a movement down. This is also seen in the Greek λόγος – the rational order underpinning the universe.
To Anselm this is the subjective power to think	*For Anselm this is objective reason*	*For Anselm this is reason, of God*

Figure 26

Therefore, we may ask, 'What is reason in Anselm's theology?' Here it is important to see what he means by reason – again the word is *ratio.* (rational, rationalization). The word has three senses in a strict hierarchy; this is a system Barth, for instance, used and derived from Anselm which classified *ratio* across three levels, ascending (figure 26). This is not only Anselmian but is characteristic of the medieval mind. There is a definite hierarchy. This is not to undervalue the lowest level – the subjective level of reason allows us to navigate and cope with the physical world. But the level of reason which allows us to comprehend the creed is on a higher level and is ultimately from God. Therefore, the correctness of human reason does not lie in us. We can operate on the level of making subjective day-to-day judgements, but beyond this if we submit ourselves to the inherent rationality in a particular given, for example, the creed, then this is a level of reason beyond ourselves. We can say that the rationality of water is H_2O. Our *ratio* is true if indeed water consists of two parts hydrogen to one part oxygen.

Therefore, our scientific concepts are not true unless they reflect the world. Therefore, certainly for Anselm, our theological concepts are not true unless they reflect the true God. The creed won't be true unless it reflects the reality of God himself. The job of theologians is to seek that our subjective formulations, the things we say about God, actually reflect the way things are in eternity. And for Anselm the mid-point is, of course, the creed.

So that is Anselm, a straight hierarchy of reason. The correctness of our reason does not lie in itself: that is the problem with natural theology, that is the problem with trying to devise your own definitions of God. The problem then is to give human reason the capacity that it doesn't have.

Therefore, all our language is incapable in itself of telling the truth. Our language can't tell the truth, it is made meaningful by God. God must commandeer our language; it must be taken over by God if it is going to be true about God. This raises the question of the relationship between divine Revelation and this commandeering of our language.

iv. The Status of Anselm's Definition

If we look at Descartes' ontological argument he says that if I look into my mind I have an idea of God as a certain being with the following definition: God is a perfect being. Descartes gets his idea of God from his mind, 'inside his head' to put it crudely. Anselm does not believe that the idea of God is simply there in our minds: for Anselm, this idea of God is given by God. The idea of God is the gift of Revelation, it is not the product of philosophical speculation. Anselm writes in his autobiography about how he struggled, long and involved, and that the proof, as such, was the answer to prayer. He was tortured with the notion that he should be able to find one simple argument that demonstrated God's existence – not by a long and complicated chain of reasoning, but by itself in a short phrase. He argues and recounts that the so-called ontological argument was given as the response to prayer. It was a form of divine Revelation: that than which no greater can be conceived. It is not a concept but a name. And the reason is this: a concept is something that grasps something; this definition of God is exactly the opposite, you can't grasp it, you cannot grasp that 'than which no greater can be conceived'. What it is saying, in effect, is that God is beyond your intellectual grasp. God reveals himself to Anselm as being a certain kind of God but one that can't be submitted to human grasp; nothing greater than this can be imagined. So, our understanding is somewhere between faith and science. We can understand this as God allows us to, but we can't finally grasp it. There are limits. Our knowledge of God is real because after all he has told us what he is like but we can't finally tease out what it means. Therefore, his definition of God is a name rather than a definition. It is God's free gift.

v. Theology and Prayer

Anselm's *Proslogion* is couched as a prayer.[7] It is a long prayer; Anselm is therefore asking God that he will allow him to understand that *He* exists. Listen to this, there's time, listen, this is so different to anything that Enlightenment philosophers would do, is it not? –

> *Lord my God, you who formed and reformed me, tell my longing soul what else you are besides what it has seen, so that it may see clearly what it is longing for. It strives to see more, and it sees nothing beyond what it has seen except darkness. Or rather it does not see darkness, for there is no darkness in you; but it sees that it cannot see more because of its own darkness.*
>
> *Truly, Lord, this the inaccessible light in which you dwell*
>
> *I do not see this light since it is too much for me; and yet whatever I see I see by means of this light, just as my feeble sight sees what it sees by the light of the sun, but cannot look on the light of the sun in the sun itself.*
>
> *O supreme and inaccessible light! O whole and blessed truth*
>
> *How far are you from me who am so close to you! How distant you are from my sight while I am present to your sight!*
>
> *You are wholly present everywhere and I do not see you. In you I move and in you I have my being. You are within me and around me. I pray, O God, that I may know you and love you, so that I may rejoice in you.*
>
> *Let my mind meditate on you, let my tongue speak of you, let my heart love you, let my soul hunger for you, until I enter into the joy of the Lord, who is God, Three in One, blessed for ever.*[8]

At the end of this three–stage ontological argument we find a prayer, or the prayer continuing. The process of understanding penetrates into the subject matter and results in Anselm being convinced. For Anselm, theology creates understanding and understanding creates conviction. It is faith seeking understanding. You see, it is important to remember that Anselm worshipped before he theologized. How many theologians and philosophers do so today? Anselm's work is about the Revelation of joy. We can apply the same criticism: How many theology conferences today are joyful? Anselm's proof is joyful and it is about God's perfection. It is a definition of perfection, is it not?: 'that than which no greater can be conceived'. God is the perfect being.

7 Anselm of Canterbury, *The Proslogion*, in Brian Davies and G. R. Evans, *Anselm of Canterbury – The Major Works* (Oxford World Classics, Oxford: Oxford University Press, 1998.), pp. 82–104.

8 Anselm, *The Proslogion*, §. 1 A Rousing of the Mind to the Contemplation of God, in *Anselm of Canterbury – The Major Works*, pp. 84–7.

3. Duns Scotus and Ockham

i. Duns Scotus

Duns Scotus[9] followed on from what is considered the purity of the high medieval world epitomized in Aquinas (as I said, we'll look at Aquinas in a while). Scotus was the first major figure to object to the idea that the forms existed in the mind of God (the doctrine Philo had been teaching); this is because it makes God passive. It limits God because these things, these forms, are eternal. In addition, accepting, or thinking along these lines, means that Christianity is enthralled to a pagan philosophy. Christianity doesn't need these pagan concepts for its rationality. So, the idea begins to be accepted that Christianity does not need to rely on ancient pagan philosophies to justify its rationality. Scotus' theological centring of reality was not to make the forms the centre of reality. In doing so Philo and Augustine were excluding Christology. From a Christian world view, biblically, it is through Christ that God structures the world. Ironically, through much of the medieval period, the structure of the world is seen through Platonic forms. From the time of Scotus we find an attempt to structure the world Christologically. This is important – crucially important. Hence, Scotus makes it possible to bring creation and redemption back together. You see, if you structure your creation doctrine Platonically, or through Aristotle, and then structure your salvation doctrine Christologically, you are tending to put creation and redemption out into different worlds. Christianity has historically been weak on creationism. If you rely upon either Platonism or Aristotelianism for the rationality of creation then once Enlightenment science comes along this rational side of Christianity is dismissed, and an incomplete, flawed picture remains. In Scotus, the synthesis between the rational and the revelatory – between reason and Revelation – begins to fall apart. The question then arises, is Scotus a realist? Platonically he is. But what is certain is that he wants to give emphasis to the particular: that is clear! To him Genesis is about the richness and the variety of the world God makes.

ii. Ockham

Ockham was in many ways very different to Scotus, but was in some ways continuous. Ockham argues, focuses on, certain particular doctrines. How does this happen? Well, in a number of propositions:

First Proposition: If you say A causes B, you are not saying, logically, that A implies B, but that A is as a matter of fact followed by B.

9 John Duns Scotus (c.1266–1308), theologian, philosopher and logician, exponent of scholasticism, who wrote on theology and metaphysics, logic and epistemology, propounding what is termed the theory of the univocity of being.

First, for instance, if you say A causes B, you are not saying, logically, that A implies B, you are not necessarily implying a connectedness, but you are saying simply that A is as a matter of fact followed by B. Ockham is teaching that relations between things are empirically and not rationally discerned. This is a move from a view of causality as logical implication, which tends to be the Platonizing medieval doctrine, to the view that the links between things are contingent and not rational. Ockham is the great teacher of the contingency of things in the created order.[10] Things are what they are because they happen to be what they are. And therefore, he draws a distinction between logical implications and causality. This is one of the great opening outs in modern science because modern science happens when connections are observed.

Second Proposition: The Forms do not Exist

Second, the forms do not exist, even for God. For Ockham, the forms do not exist – even for God, everything is particular. This is a radical departure, even from the teaching of Ockham. There are no forms: everything is particular. Therefore, we have a constructivist or psychological view of the forms. The forms are convenient constructions by the mind to account for why, for example, something that is green is green. General concepts are simply our reading of how things are, rather than something written eternally into the structure of reality.

Third Proposition: The Proofs of God are Impossible

Therefore, despite all the scholasticism and learning that has gone before, the proofs of God are to be seen as impossible. To Ockham the proof of God is an impossibility. You cannot observe God; you cannot. If you can only observe irregularities you cannot argue logically upwards from them to the eternal world. Therefore, Revelation is by the authority and will of God alone; all right, Revelation is directly the result of the will of God.

The reason that Scotus' legacy is so mixed is because of this third proposition: proofs are impossible. Revelation is by the authority and will of God alone. This has two effects, positive and negative (figure 27). This leaves a permanent worry in the theological mind: there is no natural theology. If there are no rational grounds for theology then what do we appeal to? Do we appeal to authority alone? If so, what authority – the Pope or the Bible? This is often the charge laid at Barth, though he is not an Ockhamist. Tom Torrance wrote well on this, on Ockham, he commented how humanity is thrown back on revealed truth for its absolute power.[11]

So, we then appear to have no rationality at all. So everything is by the will of God rather than the love of God. Essentially we can now see how the modern age comes about.

[10] William of Ockham (c.1288–1348), scholastic metaphysician, theologian and epistemologist, is attributed with what is termed 'Ockham's razor' (a method of investigation) he is also noted for his work on nominalism.

[11] T. F. Torrance, *Scottish Theology: From John Knox to John Mcleod Campbell* (Edinburgh: T&T Clark, 1996).

Ockham: The Impossibility of the Proofs of God

POSITIVE	NEGATIVE
This doctrine follows Scotus in freeing theology from its dependence upon philosophy: theologians do not have to go cap in hand to the philosophers for reasons as to why they should theologize.	Negatively, however, this doctrine introduces a note of arbitrariness: God creates by sheer will, and not according to predetermined forms.

Figure 27

Chapter 6

A Historical Perspective 2: The Triumph of Reason?

1. Thomas Aquinas

So, Thomas Aquinas. To many it is Aquinas that begins to formulate the modern respect for reason.[1] I don't know that I go along with that all the way; but that is often what is said, that is how he is rated.

i. Scientia

Scientia is what is important to Aquinas.[2] This is just what we call science today. This is a mode of enquiry more than anything – think of what we were saying about Torrance last week. But yes, it relates to science today, but even more to *Wissenschaft* in German. In *scientia* there is a certainty about our knowledge; we are certain we know. We are driven to find out, to know. This is from Aristotle, of course, so Aquinas' work is in many ways all about a separation between reason

1 Saint Thomas Aquinas (c.1225–74), Italian priest in the Order of Preachers, scholastic philosopher and theologian often referred to as Doctor Angelicus, advocate of natural theology, and the founding father of the Thomistic school of philosophy. His great work, *The Summa Theologica*, which runs to 60 volumes in translation, and was left incomplete at the end of his life, focuses on metaphysics and theology, logic, a doctrine of the mind, epistemology and ethics, and is noted for his five proofs for the existence of God. See Thomas Aquinas, *Summa Theologiae* (the complete paperback set of 60 volumes, plus one index volume; dual language, Latin–English; Cambridge: Cambridge University Press, 2006 [1962–76]).

2 Thomas Aquinas, *Summa Theologiae*, the material dealing essentially with Revelation and reason can be found in P1. Q(1)–Q(43), but especially in the question 'The Nature and Extent of Sacred Doctrine': Q(1-)A(1). Thomas examines specifically, with regard to doctrine, in the ten articles, (1) Whether it is necessary (2) Whether it is a science (3) Whether it is one or many (4) Whether it is speculative or practical (5) How it is compared with other sciences (6) Whether it is the same as wisdom (7) Whether God is its subject matter (8) Whether it is a matter of argument (9) Whether it rightly employs metaphors and similes (10) Whether the sacred scripture of this doctrine may be expounded in different senses.

and Revelation. The faculty of reason, you see, is very important to Thomas. He is not a Platonist; Aquinas is not a Platonist in his thinking, he does not think that formal knowledge is prior to particular knowledge. There is nothing for Thomas in our mind that is not first in our senses; OK, there is nothing in the intellect that is not first in the senses. So for him knowledge is abstraction from what we are given though the senses: it is an abstractive process. So what about universals? The universals are real, quite real, we discover them, it is the Ockhamist who would say we produce them ; so Aquinas isn't a nominalist, he doesn't think that general names are simply names, merely as Ockham did.

Thomas did accept that certain truths were given. For him the scriptures were divinely inspired. The interesting thing is that Thomas doesn't talk about Revelation much. I don't think there is a whole section on Revelation – of God sharing *His* knowledge. Thomas would agree thus far about the value of *scientia*, but – and this is important – where modern thinkers rush to classify mind as matter and matter as mind in seeking to understand man's more perplexing thoughts and experiences, Thomas would doubtless point out the folly.

Chesterton is keen to point this out in his biography of Thomas. He is keen to point out the insanity of the materialist position and describes Thomas' conception of the syllogism as sure reasoning from sure premises.[3] Chesterton draws an analogy with the modern puzzlement over whether mind is matter or something else. Thomas does not say what the modern material rationalist would say – Thomas would say that mind is moving from matter to a higher realm.

You see, Thomas' concept of *Scientia* is a medieval one. Thomas' understanding is much more like Barth's when he talks about science and knowledge. You see for Barth theology is a science, as it is with Torrance. So the parallel is with Tom Torrance whose view is that theology is *Wissenschaft*, because it is in a way God sharing his own knowledge.[4] In one sense Torrance is very anti-Thomist, anti-Aristotelian, if you share that view. For Torrance, and to a degree with Barth, true theological knowledge is a science and it derives from God sharing his knowledge with us.

In other words, to understand what Aquinas is trying to do you have to broaden your conception of science. *Wissenschaft*, the German concept, covers what we would call the natural sciences as well as the humanities. Again, in the German, you mean any organized body of knowledge, not simply the natural sciences – it means something much broader, much, much broader.

ii. Epistemological Anxieties

It is important to remember that Aquinas did not get apprehensive about how we know; he's not like a lot of modern academics who get neurotic about whether we can know anything at all! He is not anxious about the question of knowing, how we

3 G. K. Chesterton, *St Thomas Aquinas* (Garden City, NY: Image Books, 1956).
4 T. F. Torrance, *Theological Science* (Oxford: Oxford University Press, 1969).

know – epistemology – you see, those anxieties come after Kant. In the modern age epistemology is fraught with anxiety – as Descartes said, 'Can I know anything?' I think, yes. That anxiety founded cosmology, to a degree, as an attempt to answer a doubt. Whereas for Aquinas it is simply common sense that we can know. In that sense Aquinas and Barth are at one for all their differences.

Q: Was Aquinas characterized by what can be called 'wonder aiming at wisdom', whereas the modern era is characterized by 'doubt searching for certainty'?

That is very interesting, if you look at Ingolf Dalferth's book, *Theology and Philosophy*,[5] he makes this same point, we tend to look back at Aquinas as natural theology plus revealed theology, but both of these are, for Aquinas, within a framework of a faith perspective. In part, Aquinas believes that faith and philosophy are one, because he believes in God and the unity of all truth. Simple really: all truth is one because all truth is God, all truth relates to the one truth that is God. Truth is one because God is one, for Aquinas; therefore, it is a fundamentally theological starting point. There is then the question of whether we think he is right to link Aristotle and scripture in the first place, whether we believe he is right in joining Aristotle to scripture; but the fundamental assumption is Christian.

iii. Fallenness

Yes, you see, there is a confidence in even unfallen reason for Aquinas, and we move now into places where Barthian supporters think a bit differently to Aquinas. But where Barth, and people like Barth, would agree with Aquinas is generally with the distinction between science and Revelation. However, Aquinas' next step is to say that certain things can be known with certainty apart from Revelation because the mind is to a degree 'unfallen'. The Thomist view is that the will is 'fallen', you can't do what is right, but the intellect to a degree is unfallen, you can know to a degree what is true.

You can say that our intellect and our will are fallen, which I think is the case. The will is fallen but so is the intellect, the mind. You see, the mind, the intellect, is just as fallen: for instance, you can produce all sorts of logical statements that are completely wrong! In certain respects there is nothing wrong with Hitler's logic, he argues as well as many other people; surely evil people can argue as well as good people, often better. I don't think there is anything magical about logic.

What I am saying is that a more radical Augustinian position (we'll leave Barth out of it for now), would say that both the mind and the will are fallen, and that there can be no knowledge apart from redemption. Aquinas says, 'No!'; he assumes no, the will is fallen but not the mind. Therefore, we can know quite a lot of truth about God apart from Jesus Christ, or apart from redemption. Logic in its own

5 Ingolf U. Dalferth, *Theology and Philosophy* (Oxford: Blackwell, 1988).

right is sufficient to give us knowledge of God, that is, I believe, what Aquinas is saying.

I think we have to say that the Fall affected the mind as well as the will. Why otherwise can people look at God's will and say 'This is not the product of God but a demon!', or 'There is no God!' They are thinking clearly – after all doesn't Barth make the point that it is by no means self-evident that this world is produced by a good rather than a bad God. That the world is produced by a good God is not at all self-evident, not at all. If you ask for the evidence whether it is a good one or a bad one people can fall on both sides: it is ambiguous, yes, ambiguous! That would be Barth's argument, that it is not self-evident that this is a good world. However, scripture – Genesis – *reveals* that it is: and God said that it was good. You can think clearly that this world is an evil place made by a demon, and you are still thinking clearly; you might be wrong but the atheist has a lot of very good arguments. It doesn't follow that the atheist is logically mistaken. Am I right? Is it that the atheist is logically mistaken or is it that he doesn't see things as they are? It is not a matter of logic – it is a matter of a fundamental personal orientation.

That is where the argument between the Thomist and the more pessimistic Calvinist like me would go. While one remains, it is not obvious that this world is made by a good God. It is not a question of time or effort, because some people do nothing else but think about it and still end up atheists. Some people want to believe, desperately – Isn't the world full of regretful agnostics? I want to push this because it is a very important matter, very important, it is about how we come to know God, which, of course, brings us back to Revelation and reason. But our mind as well as our will is in need of redemption; that is so important, so crucial to what we are doing here – Is it not? This is a very Tom Torrance point: Tom has a tendency to say to people who disagree with him, 'You don't have a redeemed mind'!

Paul talks a lot about our minds being darkened by Satan. And of course the whole argument in Romans 1 is that despite God showing himself we suppress that knowledge. And can it be said that even if our minds might be darkened that our faculty of reason has not broken down; well, it doesn't follow that it is broken down but it is very strange to say that, for example, although our minds are working all right we make atomic bombs, we herd people into gas ovens and blow people up by the million and we make thermo-nuclear bombs, and even in good societies like ours we allow people to live in desperation. You can go on and on like this if you want to use that kind of negative; I'm not sure you should, but it does seem to be more than a matter of unclear thinking. You can't separate the mind and the will, can you, in that way – Is it possible? Kant did, I think Kant did; this is where the two cultures thing really won't work, you know, the separation of the arts and the sciences.[6]

6 Colin Gunton is referring here to C. P. Snow's famous and influential lecture, originally published in an article for *The New Statesman*, 6 October 1956, then much expanded and developed for the 1959 Rede Lecture (delivered 7 May in the Senate House, University of Cambridge). The thesis of 'The Two Cultures' was that the breakdown of communication between the two cultures – the sciences and the humanities – was a major hindrance to

You see it is not obvious that the God of the first chapters of the *Summa Theologiae* is a Christian God. You see, certain doctrines like omnipotence and impassability need to be treated Christologically, otherwise you have problems; if they are not treated Christologically you tend to produce a rather tyrannical deity: How is it put? – Aristotle's sublime tyrant indifferent to suffering. You see, if you tie your God to Aristotle then it is no good saying he is Trinitarian; not with all these Aristotelian concepts.

You don't have to say that human powers have completely broken down because as Calvin says the existence of the sciences, politics and the arts shows that the Spirit is still active even in a fallen world. You have to allow for that and the question is where you put the boundary: how optimistic you are.

GOD IS NOT THE PROBLEM

GOD IS NOT THE PROBLEM – WE ARE!

If your thinking ceases to be coherent
in relation to the givenness of revelation,
if you produce a distorted god, different from Christ
then it is not God that is the problem – you are!

Figure 28

God isn't the problem – we are! If your theology is not making sense, if you end up with a distortion, a distorted god, different from Christ then it is not God that is the problem – you are! That is fundamental to any of you if you are attempting to be theologians: God is not the problem; we are. Read Genesis 3! (Figure 28)

iv. Christian Doctrine

Is Thomas trying too hard to establish Christian theology as *scientia*? Although philosophy does give you some sort of abstractive knowledge of God, real theology for Aquinas is another matter altogether – *sacra* doctrine is directly in the gift of God. And it is God, therefore, who has to reveal it. You see, there are similarities with the sort of argument Pannenberg uses. Pannenberg in many respects is trying to do the same as the 'Medievals', to establish the character of theology as in some sense encompassing science. Of course, you could say that Pannenberg's whole idea is an elaboration of a teleological idea. There are clearly parallels between

solving the world's problems. Snow was a trained scientist and a novelist. See C. P. Snow, *The Two Cultures* (Cambridge: Cambridge University Press, 2005 [1960]); see also C. P. Snow, *The Two Cultures: A Second Look, an Expanded Version of 'The Two Cultures and the Scientific Revolution'* (London: Cambridge University Press, 1963) (Editor).

Pannenberg's attempt to show that theology is the queen of the sciences and the medieval project, so to say.

Thomas is, I believe, arguing that faith does not take over from reason; it takes over to a degree from our sensory perception. I don't think – and this is like the absence of a neurosis about epistemological questions – and I don't see Thomas seeing the need to justify Christian doctrine: all he is doing is teaching and communicating it. He is passing on doctrine and affirming man's ability to know. It is also the case, I believe, that every medieval believed in a creedal totality that had to be passed on – this was simply a given.

v. Foundationalist?

Is Aquinas a foundationalist? I think it is right to say that he is not a foundationalist in the modern sense; but he is a foundationalist in so far as he appears to hang something on Aristotelian reason. That is to say, a capacity or ability to reason, a concept of reason that all people can accept, whether or not they are Christian: that is a sort of foundationalism.

Q: Is this to do with the existence of God?

This is nothing to do with it. The foundationalist problem is simply the doctrine that in some sense or other your intellectual enterprise, theology or whatever you are doing, requires a foundation in some sense prior to it, outside it.

Foundationalism in the post-Cartesian sense is much more radical; after Descartes – and certainly after Kant – foundationalism is much more deep-seated and far-reaching in the sense that it is a purely secular foundation that they are looking for, that is demanded. Aquinas' foundation – if he has one – isn't a purely secular one: it is a religious vision (which of course is why modern philosophers don't like Aquinas, though I suppose that is a bit of a generalization, but there is truth in it. Certainly I believe that is partly why the modern mind doesn't like Aquinas, and certainly not Thomist thinking!). But nonetheless Aquinas' work is dependent upon sources that are prior to Revelation, even if parallel with it. The final question seems to be about whether Aquinas is right to assume that man can know anything about his condition outside the knowledge given in doctrine and scripture, and again – I keep stressing this – it is because of our fallenness. That is the question, you see: 'How much of ourselves and the world can we know apart from Christ?' But we have to be wary of a modern existentialist reading of Thomas. If you read his development it is simply about the world, not about human beings.

2. Reformation and Enlightenment

i. Introduction

In some ways, the Reformation lets the 'cat' out of the bag; or should we say certain 'cats'. You see, what really shapes our culture from this time on is rationalism; though much of this comes after the Reformation.

ii. Luther and Calvin

You see, there are important differences on Revelation and reason even between the two greats, the two Reformation greats: Luther was essentially taught by the Ockhamists; Calvin was essentially taught by the Scotists. In general, the Reformation shifts the understanding of and the relationship between Revelation and reason into a more Biblical direction. In Calvin you have the ability again to engage with scripture. Scripture is relied upon, as a living entity in the way the Medievalists did not engage with it. Certainly I think it's fair to say they did not engage with it as a living entity. Luther is often quoted as objecting to reason – for rejecting reason – especially Aristotle. Luther regarded reason as a whore essentially because it had replaced the Bible and Revelation.[7] Luther is very much against Aristotle and in particular Aquinas's use of Aristotelian reason – it is the beginning of the rot setting into the church for him.

The battle cry of the Reformation was *sola scriptura*; this was, I suppose, not a statement of the only source, or a third source added to the two-source theory of Revelation and reason: thinking in the form of reason was not excluded, neither was the Revelation of the church in the form of tradition, the church's tradition, if that is Revelation. There are those who would dispute any form of ongoing Revelation after the completion of the Bible, but, you see, I think the cry of *sola scriptura* must be seen as of the final authority for the church. Is that right? – Is that how scripture was seen, particularly by Calvin? Is that how it was used by the Reformers? They don't exclude reason do they, but scripture becomes the test, the measure.

For both Luther and Calvin scripture is to be considered Revelation, certainly against the church's manipulation of tradition. So, we have scripture alone as the

[7] 'But since the devil's bride, Reason, that pretty whore, comes in and thinks she's wise, and what she says, what she thinks, is from the Holy Spirit, who can help us, then? Not judges, not doctors, no king or emperor, because reason is the Devil's greatest whore' (Vernunft ist die höchste Hur, die der Teufel hat) from, 'Martin Luther's Last Sermon in Wittenberg Second Sunday in Epiphany, 17 January 1546', Martin Luther, *Dr Martin Luther, Werke: Kritische Gesamtsusgabe* (Band 51; Weimar: Herman Boehlaus Nachfolger, 1914), p. 126.

foundation on which the church is to argue and believe. So where does that leave what we can call unbiblical traditions in the church. Calvin especially should be seen as one with roots sunk deep into the traditions of the church, as Torrance has pointed out in his book on the hermeneutics of Calvin.[8]

You see, this is tied up with membership of the church, being part of the church – you don't stand outside the church thinking in your reasonable powers, using reason to justify yourself. The church for Luther and Calvin is built on the tradition of Revelation, but the Revelation of scripture must be seen, must be used to measure and justify, to a degree.

iii. The Age of Reason and the Enlightenment

In the modern period the crisis for modern theology is because of the Enlightenment. In the mainstream Enlightenment we find two phases. The earlier phase, often called the 'Age of Reason', illustrates a great optimism about reason. The second phase, I suppose the true 'Age of Enlightenment', is dominated by Kant.

The first phase: this sees Descartes and his successors strongly confident that they can rebuild theological foundations on the wreck of failed Christianity. Many of the early Enlightenment figures were religious thinkers. What they thought was that reason had the capacity to decide most of the things we need to know about God. This culminates in deism, rational theism – the rational end to this.[9]

Locke is, you see, this proto-modern foundationalist: he has a tendency to say that if you defend religion you have to defend it on grounds other than the religious. As we have seen, with Locke you have this development that you have to defend the faith on extrinsic grounds: unless you can justify your belief rationally by appealing to things outside the faith, then it is not rational. Is faith also reduced here to a weaker, second–rate form of knowledge?

By contrast with the Age of Reason faith and reason were equally valid to Aquinas. In the Enlightenment faith begins to be pushed into the realm of mere opinion, whereas only that which is rationally justified is worthy of real belief. That is the tendency in Locke. The tendency after this is to say that faith is irrational: only reason is rational, but this was not what Locke concluded. Locke is something of an early liberal, a broad–church Anglican trying to pull off a compromise with the spirit of his age.

8 T. F. Torrance, *The Hermeneutics of John Calvin* (Edinburgh: Scottish Academic Press, 1988).

9 A seventeenth- and eighteenth-century religious philosophy, deism was popular among intellectuals and cultivated literati in Western Europe and the United States and propounded a God that is separate, independent from the world, that does not interfere at all with the natural order. There is no belief in miracles, all beliefs must be grounded in human reason and through examination of the natural world, there is no space or role for Christ in deism, nor for a personal God of love and compassion

3. René Descartes

So we have this early phase in which there is a strong belief in reason's capacity to reason about religious matters, to reason things out: Descartes to Locke. Now it is Descartes more and more that philosophers are realizing is at the heart of the triumph of reason, the victory of rationality, in some ways accidentally, inadvertently.

i. A Theistic Defence?

Descartes' doctrine of God is about what kind of God we are talking about, and how we know that God. This is central to Revelation. Was Descartes an out-and-out rationalist? In his attempt to re-forge philosophy Descartes had to doubt everything: in doubting all he knew there was something concrete that was doing the doubting, also that he was aware that there was something more perfect than himself. That perfect entity was God. This in effect completely repeats the scholastic argument that he was claiming not to be dependent upon; this is very important here.[10]

What you've got here is a kind of transmuted version, of the Aquinas argument which is applied to the world, a sort of ideal cosmological argument. Aquinas asks 'What causes motion?' The answer is 'God'. Descartes asks 'What is the cause of my particular ideas?' And the answer is 'God'. He also has a kind of ontological argument; however, Kant later was to argue by drawing on Descartes that all of the proofs depend upon the ontological argument in the sense that they all involve the intuition of a perfect being. What is happening is a transposing, a transposition of the Aquinas argument to Descartes, and later to Kant, that is a transposing into a different key. This is in many ways typical of modernity, to transpose what in antiquity was philosophy of the world – I've alluded before to

[10] René Descartes (1596–1650), French mathematician and philosopher, scientist and writer who is often regarded as the father of modern philosophy and mathematics. Most subsequent philosophy in the Western tradition is as a result of or a reaction to his work including Cartesianism, Rationalism, Foundationalism. Key works include: René Descartes, *Méditations métaphysiques* (ed. André Robinet; Paris: J. Vrin, 1976); also, René Descartes, *Les Principes de la Philosophie* (ed. Claude Picot; Rouen: Chez Jean-Baptiste Besongne, 1698. For an up-to-date edition see René Descartes, *Oeuvre Scientifique. Premiere et Deuxième Parties*: Tome V, *Les Principes de la Philosophie* (Clermont-Ferrand: Paleo, 1999). English editions: *A Discourse on the Method of Correctly Conducting one's Reason and Seeking Truth in the Sciences* (trans. and ed. Ian Maclean; Oxford: Oxford University Press, 2006); *Philosophical Essays and Correspondence* (trans. Roger Ariew; Indianapolis: Hackett, 2000); *Meditations, Objections, and Replies* (trans. and ed. Roger Ariew; Donald A Cress; Indianapolis, IN: Hackett, 2006); *The Method, Meditations and Philosophy of Descartes* (trans. John Veitch; Whitefish, MT: Kessinger, 2004); and *Descartes: Selected Writings from 'Discourse on Method', 'Meditations on the First Philosophy' and 'The Principles of Philosophy'* (trans. John Veitch; London: Collector's Library, 2004).

the change from the *systema mundi*, the system of the world, to the idea of system as essentially an intellectual construct which is what you've got here – Descartes has transposed out of the concrete, the material world, into the realm of the mind.[11]

This is a characteristically modern form of dualism. For platonic dualism there is not a mechanism in it, but there is in the modern dualism originating, it is fair to argue, in Descartes. If you distinguish so strongly between mind and matter then you do end up with a strong, even rigid, dualism. This leads to the modern tendency to make physics the archetypal science with all else dependent upon it. This leads to a philosophy of mechanism, or Newtonianism as an ideology explaining the whole of reality: everything is reducible to physics. The equivalent today is in reducing everything to genetics: causes are reduced to logical implications.

Q: Are Descartes' meditations on philosophy theodicy or atheism?

The Barthian response would be to ask whether the two options you give are at all different – Are they the same? That is actually a serious point: Are questions of theodicy – expecting God to prove he is good, to justify his actions, to explain evil and suffering in the world –a form of atheism? This raises serious questions about how we use our powers of reason does it not?

ii. Fallo ergo sum *and* cogito ergo sum

Q: Is there a similarity, a comparison between Augustine' *fallo ergo sum* and Descartes' *cogito ergo sum*? Descartes seems to follow Augustine in many respects does he not? Also does he get the idea of the memory as a storehouse from Augustine?[12]

Yes, it is more than that because he actually uses the form 'If I am deceived I exist', because the whole structure of his philosophy depends on his capacity to be deceived – even that comes from Augustine. [13]

11 The philosophical phrase, *systema mundi*, essentially 'world system' is derived from both Platonic Greek and Latin: σύστημα, τό, συστῆναι; a whole compound of parts, a system, with *mundi*, the world. Instead of seeing the world as an ordered system (Greek: κόσμος) with an intrinsic, intelligible order, the world now becomes, following Descartes, a construct of the human mind, the order of which is an imposition of rational structures on a material world, that is, for Descartes, mainly characterized by its extension in space (Latin: *res extensa*). This further entrenches the Cartesian dualism of the mind being independent of the body. The *systema mundi* is also a *systema humanae vitae*, a system of life, or human life, which runs contrary to the extreme mechanistic concept of the world. My thanks are to Christoph Schwöbel for this clarification (Editor).

12 *Fallo ergo sum*, which can be translated variously as 'I make mistakes, therefore I am' and 'what can be done wrong, exists'; *Cogito ergo sum*, 'I think therefore I am' – Descartes' famous maxim.

13 'I am not at all afraid of the arguments of the Academicians, who say, "What if you are deceived?" For if I am deceived, I am. For he who is not, cannot be deceived; and if I am deceived, by this same token I am. And since I am if I am deceived, how am I deceived in believing that I am?' Augustine, *City of God* (trans. Henry Bettenson;, Harmondsworth:

You see it is important to remember that Descartes' philosophy only makes sense in the religious context, so to speak. He admitted that there were questions that lay outside the scope of rational explanation, reasoned explanation. This has led many to conclude that his epistemology is only intelligible within a theological structure. This rationality that allows him to affirm beyond doubt, his doubts, is seen as divine. Descartes asserts that the existence of the mind and of God are the most certain things we know. This is a classic Platonic move – because Plato moved from the uncertainty of any knowledge to certainty, but again it is important to remember Plato's argument about the unreliability of sense perception. This is what I was saying about Descartes simply transposing what has been said already into a different key: he wants to start again but he is replicating over and over – which is I think a lesson. If you think you're beginning again the chances are you are not. This whole idea of the quest for originality is odd because it stops people being aware of the limits of originality: as Karl Barth used to say of Mozart, what is most original about Mozart is that he doesn't try to be original and therefore he is.[14] If you are really going to be different you need a strong grip on tradition.

iii. The Primacy of Reason

A problem with Cartesian thought is that it must exert the primacy of the human, the thinking human, to defeat scepticism; which leaves little possibility for Revelation: reason will *reveal* to us very little that is beyond ourselves.

Q: Does Descartes consider the question of the relationship of Revelation to reason?

The important question with and for Descartes is about the Incarnation: Does Descartes leave open the possibility for incarnational Revelation? He does in the *Meditations* have an understanding of continuous creation, with a conservation of the creation, he wants to say that God upholds the world from moment to moment; this is an assertion, it is not an argument though. He is buying into a tradition, you see. If you are defending Christian theism then you would have to say that it wasn't just creation in the past, there is an upholding of creation in the present. So there might be a way in there for a more incarnational form of Revelation, but he does not have the arguments for it. This is problematic, because in a mechanistic world, once the world is a mechanism, it is very difficult for God to do anything with it.

Q: Is this a Deistic conception? – God separated from the world looking on but not interfering. If so, how does he reconcile this with the perfection of this good God?

Penguin Books, 1972), pt II, bk XI, ch. 26, pp. 459–60. Op. cit. n.5, ch. 2, p. 42, for full details and quotations.

14 Karl Barth, *Wolfgang Amadeus Mozart 1756/1956* (Zürich: TVZ, 1956). English trans. *Wolfgang Amadeus Mozart* (trans. Clarence K. Pott, foreword, John Updike; Eugene, OR: Wipf & Stock, 1986).

Descartes needs clear arguments but he doesn't have them. He is trading on scholastic assumptions like the hierarchy of perfections and causal conceptions without arguing for them.

Q, [interrupting]: but if you are an evil person your idea of God or god would be an evil one would it not, something more evil than you?

No, he's not saying our ideas are a projection. He's not saying that our ideas about God, this concept he has of a perfect God that God has put in our minds as a proof of God, is a projection; he is saying it is innate. These ideas are innate.

Again, another type of Platonism that Descartes believes firmly is that in view of the fact that he discovers these things by entering the chamber of his mind – to quote Anselm – he discovers these things, they must be there ready, so God must have inserted them into his mind, when he was born or when he was conceived.[15] So Descartes is an 'innatist', and one of the things that Locke will use to get his idea off the ground is to attack the doctrine of innate ideas.

So, for Descartes, because this conception is innate, you could not have an idea of an evil God. This is Descartes' ontological argument: if you think clearly and distinctly about the idea of God that is in your mind then you will know that God is the sum of all perfections. And because the idea of God is the sum of all perfections, then he must exist and he must do all the other good things.

Q: But what can we say about the idea of evil as such? Is it an innate idea?

For Descartes evil is the result of man's use of his will beyond reason. Does this mean our reason is innately deficient? Well, we can assent to a concept through our will which we may not fully understand with our reason. This leads to a problem: if our reason is deficient and we rely upon our reason for this perfect idea of a perfect God, then can the idea be flawed? This is the idea that if reason is used properly we cannot make mistakes – there is something like that in Aquinas, but not in so radical a form – then, of course, you open the door to say 'only reason'. If 'only reason' then you exclude God *actually* – causally or metaphysically – from the world: you exclude Revelation. This is also the ground for excluding God epistemologically because if the human mind when reasoning is clearly infallible then you have no need of Revelation. Revelation is neither needed nor can it actually happen: that is the logical outcome, but he doesn't draw it. This is a flaw that can happen to all good thinkers; Descartes stops short of carrying through the full logic of his ideas. This ironically, of course, implicitly points to the limits of reason: even if you believe your reason to be infallible, you must still, in humility, recognize that there may be limits to your logic!

15 'Come now, little man! flee for a while from your tasks, hide yourself for a little space from the turmoil of your thoughts. Come, cast aside your burdensome cares, and put away your laborious pursuits. For a little while give your time to God, and rest in Him for a little. Enter the inner chamber of your mind, shut out all things save God and whatever may aid you in seeking God; and having barred the door of your chamber, seek Him. Speak now, O my heart, O my whole heart, speak now and say to your God: My face hath sought Thee: Thy face, O Lord, will I seek.' Anselm of Canterbury, *The Proslogion*, in Brian Davies and G. R. Evans, *Anselm of Canterbury – The Major Works* (Oxford World Classics, Oxford: Oxford University Press, 1998), p. 84.

You see, Descartes really does believe everything he says – he is saying, in effect, that everything he knows clearly and distinctly must be true. What does he mean by 'clearly and distinctly'? First of all, clearly means you can see what an idea entails. The example is the idea of God – for Descartes you only have to think hard enough about the idea of God to have a clear and accurate idea of God; distinct means 'to distinguish it from all other ideas'. So insofar as you can know clearly what an idea means and distinguish it from all other ideas, then your idea must be true.

This leads to a huge rationalistic confidence: Descartes' critics will assert that he may have believed he was defending the Catholic faith but he was in effect undermining it. You may believe you are defending the faith but the implications in the long run – or even in the short term – may be that you undermine it. Descartes was setting out to undermine scepticism and defend religious belief: But what was the long–term outcome? In the short term he does defend the faith but not in the long term.

If reason is infallible, then reason is all you need. And if reason leads you to distinguish between mind on the one hand which is completely self-contained and matter which is accidentally joined to it and is mechanistic, then in the end you will produce a world machine. Then you have the idea of the God of the gaps: God disappears because if the world is a machine and it can be explained in other terms than by God, then in the long term God is driven out of the world. But Descartes did not want to do that.

iv. Philosophers as Theologians: Reason or Revelation?

I think you need to understand these people in their context. At this time you do not really have a serious anti-religious, anti-Christian, movement. So the people who read Descartes as an early freethinker just haven't understood the context in which he thinks. I can illustrate this for you anecdotally. Descartes' work is taken to be an early example of what became known as 'philosophy of mind'; by contrast, Locke's work is taken to be an early example of British empiricism: how you know, and how you experience the world. That is how it was presented when I was taught philosophy, when I was taught as an undergraduate. It was only when I came to teach about these people as part of the history of philosophy, and when I was teaching philosophy of religion, that I realized that they were all theologians. Geoffrey Warnock wrote a book on George Berkeley, which treated Berkeley as an early example of a logical analyst – to Warnock, what Berkeley is doing is analysing the notion of the idea in your mind – but if you actually read Berkeley he is totally obsessed with proving the existence of God.[16] OK, you read Locke and Locke is

[16] G. J. Warnock, *Berkeley*, (Harmondsworth: Penguin Books, 1969). Geoffrey Warnock (1923-95), British philosopher and Vice-Chancellor of Oxford University (1981 to 1985), was married to Mary Warnock, moral philosopher and writer on education, the mind and existentialism. George Berkeley (1685–1753), Bishop of Cloyne, was an Irish philosopher

indeed an ideologist of early modern science, but he is also a religious thinker. Locke is a religious thinker whose concern is to argue for the place of religion in society after the religious wars, or in the light of the religious wars; but this is a conception of religion which is enthusiasm, a conception of religion which is defined by the characteristic of the enthusiastic. He is critical of a concept of religion based on enthusiasm: subjective judgements – enthusiasm is seen in subjective judgements where someone feels something strongly, therefore, they take it to be true.

You see, all good philosophers are concerned with human life in society, they are not just concerned with the sort of things many people think philosophers are concerned with – logical analysis, how words work, and so on; that is part of it. But the greatest philosophers have been social, political and religious philosophers. It is just inconceivable that anybody in Descartes' age would have considered religion to be not part of the overall understanding of things – part of the world view. It would have been inconceivable to exclude religion from the world view. People such as Hobbs – who is the nearest to scepticism, the closest there is to an utter sceptic (people are always arguing as to whether Hobbs is sceptical or not, that is an open question) – Hobbs would exclude the religious, but in general a philosopher knows in this era that part of his responsibility is to think man in society! – and that includes God! So, it is completely anachronistic, I think, to treat Descartes as an early version of a freethinker who tries to free people from the shackles of religion.

All sorts of people like Bayle in this period are often treated as sceptics; but – as one of the professors of French in this institution [King's College] pointed out to me, he wasn't, he was a Calvinist. And his sceptical arguments are in the interest of a doctrine of Revelation, not in the interests of free thought and the debunking of religion.[17]

who wrote on perception, epistemology and vision. His main achievement was a theory he called 'immaterialism', also known as 'subjective idealism', which was encapsulated in the dictum, *esse est percipi* ('to be is to be perceived'). Berkeley argued that we can only know sensations and ideas of objects, we cannot know abstractions. See *Three Dialogues between Hylas and Philonous* (1713) and *A Treatise Concerning the Principles of Human Knowledge* (1710). For Contemporary editions, see George Berkeley, *A Treatise Concerning the Principles of Human Knowledge*. Part I: *Wherein the Chief Causes of Error and Difficulty in the Sciences, with the Grounds of Skepticism, Atheism, and Irreligion, are Inquir'd into* (ed. Kenneth Winkler, Indianapolis, IN: Hackett, 1995); and George Berkeley, *Three Dialogues Between Hylas and Philonous* (New York, NY: Fordham University Press, 1995).

17 Pierre Bayle (1647–1706), a French philosopher, literary scholar and writer, who was a progressive Christian scholar from a Calvinist background who argued that reason could justify Christian belief: reason by itself could not be used to substantiate faith because God is innately incomprehensible to the human. Many philosophers today regard him as a sceptic because of his thoroughgoing assault on the use of reason in religious matters. His arguments that the coherency of faith could not be substantiated through reason alone influenced major Enlightenment thinkers that came after him but not in the way he expected or would have approved of; these arguments are still influential. Bayle was also important in his work as a forerunner of the *Encyclopédistes* – an influential and significant eighteenth-century French

v. Is Descartes a Catholic Thinker?

You see, you must place these people in their context — and the real need now is to liberate ourselves from this kind of Enlightenment ideology that treats everybody in terms of how advanced they are in freeing the human race from the shackles of religious thought. This is very important: Descartes has to be seen as a Catholic philosopher, who maybe undermines Catholic belief, perhaps inadvertently, but he is a Catholic philosopher in the same way that Locke has to be seen as a broad-church Anglican.

Q: But does Descartes talk much about Revelation itself?

The nearest he gets to Revelation is a sort of substitute for revelation in the form of scepticism. He does talk about the idea that perhaps it is a malign demon that is deluding him, but he uses this to assert that he knows through reason that he exists.[18] Suppose there are malign demons, he writes, who are conning me into believing that two-plus-two equals four when really they equal five – What is left? That is the point: it is a question of hypothetical utter scepticism. But, for Descartes, even this malign demon cannot prevent or deny the statement that I exist. This is Augustine again: even if I am deceived, I must exist in order to be deceived.[19] That is his bedrock. People are always talking in the history of theology about the modern turn inwards and this is it: uncertainty leads to rationality – the bedrock of his mind, for Descartes.

Q: Is this a form of Revelation?

It's a substitute; it's not really Revelation. But for Descartes it is, because God has revealed himself to Descartes in the idea of God that God has put into Descartes' own mind. It's a sort of Revelation, especially for the lofty-minded in the Enlightenment.

It is important to place Descartes as a Catholic thinker; he's a Roman Catholic, he's operating in the Catholic tradition. What did Aquinas hold? – the great Catholic thinker! That there are two sources for our knowledge of God: reason and Revelation. You see? – on the one hand we can know certain things by reason; on the other hand, for other things, we need Revelation. Well, Descartes as

literary and philosophical association whose members worked on the *Encyclopédie* (the *Encyclopédistes* were considered to be related to a broader intellectual grouping known as the *philosophes*, whose aim was to promote the advancement of scientific investigation and secularism through the supposed elevation of Enlightenment reason.

18 This is the third method of doubt used by Descartes in the First Meditation, where he realizes God would not deceive him. See René Descartes, *Meditations Metaphysiques* (ed. Andre Robinet; Paris: J. Vrin, 1976); also, René Descartes, *Meditations, Objections, and Replies* (trans. and ed. Roger Ariew; Donald A. Cress; Indianapolis, IN: Hackett, 2006) (Editor).

19 'I am not at all afraid of the arguments of the Academicians, who say, "What if you are deceived?" For if I am deceived, I am. For he who is not, cannot be deceived; and if I am deceived, by this same token I am. And since I am if I am deceived, how am I deceived in believing that I am?' Augustine, *City of God* (trans. Henry Bettenson; Harmondsworth: Penguin Books, 1972), pt II, bk XI, ch. 26, pp. 459–60. Op. cit. n.5, ch. 2, p. 42, for full details and quotations.

a believer is quite content to do the philosophical side: he's a philosopher. He is defending the faith but only on the philosophical side. So, we can say that he is dealing with Aquinas's left hand, leaving the right hand to the church.

Now, the way that Buckley argues is this: today, and since Descartes, developing progressively, what you are getting today is a radicalization of what was the case developing through the Age of Reason and the Enlightenment, and that is this: that you defend your belief in God in a non-Christological, non-pneumatological way.[20] In other words, you defend your belief in the Christian God in a non-Trinitarian way. So, and this is similar to what Tertullian said (Buckley quotes him if I remember correctly), these people are attempting to defend Christianity by what we can call Greek methods.[21] Jesus and the Spirit don't come into it. This is what is now so often happening and has happened, and it is essentially what Descartes is doing: he is using Greek methods – pagan philosophy; Jesus and the Spirit don't come into it. This can be seen as happening right from the Middle Ages on. What happened? – Christian apologists let the atheists in. If you are defending the Christian faith in a non-Christian way then that is what you are doing – Is that not so?

This is the key problem. But Buckley is not blaming Descartes for it; Buckley is asserting that it is in the medieval theologians who are to blame. It is Aquinas in many ways that sets the scene for the triumph of reason. Is it? Is he right? If he is right, then why? The reason is that they attempted to answer all the main questions before they got to Christology. Buckley does charge Aquinas with this.

So, Descartes as a Catholic philosopher is not interested in the right hand, so to speak, the Revelation side, he is only interested in the left hand. So he defends more and more without appeal what is at the heart of Christianity: that is the oddness of all of this. That is why it is so important for us to see what is going on here. Throughout this period you get an increasing emphasis on scepticism at the expense of Jesus and the Spirit.

Q: So is this why religion becomes theism and then deism?

Yes, of course, that is another way of putting it. That's right; eventually this leads to deism. Deism is theism without a doctrine of providence, without the church – it is the God who is simply known by reason, and is simply known as the machine maker. All the things that make Christianity interesting – Jesus, redemption, the church, the sacraments – these become irrelevant. The only thing that is left is that this 'god' creates the world from the beginning, lets it run and then gives out rewards and punishments at the end. In the middle, the world just runs itself. You see? And who runs in to fill the empty space?

Q: Can we then say that Descartes isn't a Catholic theologian? If he is not talking about Jesus, he isn't talking about the Spirit and the church, then whatever he is, he isn't a Catholic thinker?

20 Michael J. Buckley SJ (Canisius Professor of Theology, Boston College, Newton, MA). See Michael J. Buckley, *The Origins of Modern Atheism* (New Haven, CT: Yale University Press, 1987).

21 See Tertullian, *De carne Christi liber. Tertullian's Treatise on the Incarnation* The Text edited with an Introduction, Translation and Commentary (ed. Ernest Evans; London: SPCK, 1956).

Well, he belongs in the Catholic tradition of natural theology; but he is radicalizing it. As a Catholic theologian he is a loyal Catholic; he is a Catholic theologian in that he uses a lot of traditional Catholic weapons – particularly his argument about causality. But, he is not Catholic if by Catholic you mean someone who wants to set forth the whole creedal statement of the faith. What I mean by Catholic is that perhaps he is historically Catholic; and that he is Catholic in the sense that he is radicalizing certain things. That is Buckley's argument. Buckley writes – as a Jesuit (Buckley is a Jesuit) – that in radicalizing certain things that are already in the tradition, Descartes ultimately takes philosophy out of the faith.

But, he is not a Catholic theologian in the sense perhaps that John Paul II would expect or regard a Catholic philosopher to be: Is that right?

Q: Does Descartes ever address the question of purpose? Why did God bother? Why is there a creation? Does he ever address these questions?

Well, the goodness of creation is presupposed in some of his arguments; it is there in the innate idea of goodness for Descartes. Right? If you were Manichean, you would have to argue for the innate goodness and innate badness in God; so Descartes is trading, I believe, on metaphysical positivism. He is actually assuming that God is good, that God means goodness. He's not to my knowledge interested in why God created. His main argument in the *Discourses* and in the *Meditations* is to show the necessity of the existence of the mind and of God, and he does this because of the ascendancy of scepticism. You see it is interesting that at this stage teleology begins to be excluded, after all, a machine does not necessarily need to have a purpose – it just runs. A machine maker makes machines but there is not much teleology other than that. The world as a machine does not need to go anywhere, it just ticks.

William Temple, the Anglican Archbishop, described the day when Descartes meditated at his kitchen stove/oven as the worst, the most disastrous, day in the history of Europe, because it rationalizes all and turns inward away from the world and from God: ultimately it produces this great narrowness.

4. The Nineteenth Century

The second phase of the Enlightenment is essentially in the nineteenth century and is dominated by Immanuel Kant. Kant is the dominant figure in the modern period, especially in modern theology and in particular in modern Liberal Protestantism. Barth devotes a chapter to Kant in his critique of nineteenth-century Liberal Protestantism. This brings out Kant's theology, further, how Kant's Protestant background keeps appearing. Barth comments that Kant is the 'Enlightenment with a well-protected rear'. To Barth, Kant has cut away the naivety of the Enlightenment. What is cut away is the Enlightenment's confidence to know – particularly to know theologically.

Kant is therefore, in one way, cutting reason down to size. He appears to some commentators as a deeply religious man who was aware there was another world, but he was confident that we could know nothing about it – he was deeply agnostic. You see, Kant liberally quotes scripture in his writings but there are two words which he never quotes, and they are 'Jesus' and 'Christ' – that is classic deism. Kant never moved more than a couple of miles from where he was born, yet he changed the world. He was prepared to accept religion, but not any particular religion and not the particular Christian religion. Religion, to Kant, is acceptable, within the limits of the power of his thought, which means that he allows any religion that is licensed by moral reason, but no more. Religion becomes allowable at best as a back–up for ethics. Hence the human mind legislates; not the Torah. So theology becomes subordinate to moralism.

In the nineteenth century there were a number of options for people: one is to be a Kantian, though this is not really an option; Schleiermacher tried to broaden the Kantian categories from reason and ethics to experience. Schleiermacher tries to say that Kant divides the human being into reason and ethics, but it is our religiousness that enables us to bring them together. There is a lot going on here; we will talk about it in more depth.

Then there was Hegel. Hegel was seen as the third possibility. Hegel tried to find an entirely new definition for reason. Hegel is considered by some commentators as utterly rational and utterly 'Christian' at the same time. Hegel is a very interesting character. He philosophized the whole of reality – he did this through a sort of Trinitarian dialectic. He took the structure of his philosophy from the Trinity, but he totally philosophized it. Kierkegaard thought he totally reversed it!

By the time of Kant's death the general atmosphere was that you could not be a cultured person and be a religious believer. Reason and the primacy of the human intellect seemed to have broken Christianity. It is not without significance that Schleiermacher's *On Religion's Speeches to its Cultural Despisers* was published in 1799.[22] In the nineteenth century you have major theological minds trying to respond to this state of affairs: Schleiermacher and Hegel, Coleridge and Kierkegaard. After 1800 attempts to make rational sense of Christianity are dominated by Kant. Kant has said that you can't know God – and he gives reasons. Barth comments that there can be no theology after Kant without some awareness of the method of reason that you use. Kant makes us become conscious in theology of what we are doing, the methods we employ.

The movement called systematic theology arises out of this Kantian challenge: after Kant there can be no theology without method. Since Kant truth has become more subjective: since Kant there can be no knowledge that has not been framed by categories – categories that are not out there but in our minds. So our minds rule; therefore, when we use concepts like causality or substance they are objectively real but they are only shaped by the mind.

The only knowledge there can be is, as with physics, knowledge formed by the pre given concepts with which we are born. So it becomes subjective – the mind

22 Friedrich Schleiermacher, *Über die Religion: Reden an die Gebildeten unter ihren Verächtern* (1799). English trans. *On Religion: Speeches to its Cultured Despisers* (trans. Richard Crouter; Cambridge: Cambridge University Press, 1996).

forms its own capacity to know. Yet somehow, Kant knows that all minds have to think like this. Hence to be a knower, you have to think Newtonian!

However, this is knowledge of how things are; morally there is a difference. With morals we are talking about how things should be. For Kant the word is invent – for Kant we both make up and discover our morals. So in a sense the human mind becomes a divine mind. As I have mentioned before, an interesting book on this is Edward Craig's *The Mind of God and the Works of Man.*[23] This is a charting of this movement from the view that the human mind is the image of God to the modern pragmatism that human action is the action of God. Here we have a movement towards the self-deification of the human.

Barth's answer to Kant's assertion that you can't know God is that you can and we do! If God does reveal himself, then you can know God.

23 Edward Craig, *The Mind of God and the Works of Man* (Oxford: Oxford University Press, 1987).

Part Three : Aspects of Karl Barth on Faith and Reason

Chapter 7

Barth: Theological Self-Consciousness after Kant

1. Introduction

We need to look in more depth at Kant,[1] Schleiermacher and particularly Hegel. We've mentioned them in the context of the development of Revelation and reason, reason and Revelation, but – and this is important – whatever you do as a theologian after Kant is done in the man's shadow. Theology after Kant is always self-conscious. The issue regarding Revelation came up in the post-Kantian world, and it has not gone away – yet! This is particularly true of theology in the academy, in the university, that is a perennial argument.

2. Immanuel Kant: Reason without Revelation

i. Barth on Kant

Barth comments on this, theology's self-consciousness, in his chapter on Immanuel Kant: Barth devotes a chapter to Kant in his critique of nineteenth-century Liberal Protestantism.[2] Barth makes it clear that after Kant no theologian can operate

1 Immanuel Kant (1724–1804), considered the most important philosopher of the Enlightenment and crucial to the basis of modern Europe, his work centres on epistemology, metaphysics and ethics. He is primarily noted for Transcendental Idealism, the principle of the Categorical Imperative and *synthetic a priori*, among other ideas.

2 Karl Barth, *Die protestantische Theologie im 19. Jahrhundert* (Zürich: Theologischer Verlag Zürich, 1947). English trans. *Protestant Theology in the Nineteenth Century* (trans. Brian Cozens and John Bowden, intro. Colin E. Gunton; London: SCM Press, 2001 [1959]). See ch. 7 'Kant', pp. 252–98.

In these seminars, particularly Part Three on Barth, Colin Gunton uses the word 'liberal/liberalism' in the context of nineteenth-century German Liberal Protestantism. Therefore, a distinction needs to be drawn between this Liberal neo-Protestantism (the word will be capitalized when referring to the theological movement – also, Barth often referred to it as *neo-*Protestantism) and what is often euphemistically called a liberal perspective in Christian theology without a clear account of the method of reason. You see, Barth is often thought of as an irrationalist, but on the contrary, what Barth is trying to do is to develop a distinctive concept of theological rationality. Barth comments in *Dogmatics in Outline*, that where the creed is uttered, knowledge is meant to be given.[3] Christianity to Barth is not anti-rational or supra-rational (here he was taking a side swipe at Schleiermacher) but rational in the fullest sense of the word. The question has to be raised 'Is Barth attempting to create a distinct concept of theological rationality?'

You see, I've said it before, and I'll need to keep saying it, Immanuel Kant is the dominant figure in the modern period, especially in modern theology and in particular in modern Liberal Protestantism. I suppose, to Barth, Kant has cut away the naivety of the Enlightenment. What is cut away is the Enlightenment's confidence to know – particularly to know theologically.

Kant is therefore, in one way, cutting reason down to size. Kant appears to some commentators as a deeply religious man who was aware there was another world, but he was confident that we could know nothing about it – he was deeply agnostic. Yes, he was deeply agnostic and religious, like so many atheists in the academy today!

ii. Religion within the Bounds of Reason Alone

Religion, to Kant, is acceptable, within the limits of reason alone; the limits and boundaries defined by reason, by the human capacity to think, though reason is more than that, more than just thinking.[4] You see, reason alone and nothing else: which means that he allows any religion that is licensed by moral reason, but no more. Religion becomes allowable at best as a back–up for ethics. Hence the human mind legislates not the Torah; morality is not given, you see, not given as in the Torah, morality is defined by the human mind. So theology becomes subordinate to moralism. But as I've said elsewhere, this is the morality of a white Liberal Protestant man, a cultural bourgeois eighteenth-century man (remember he died in 1804, so although he is at the heart of the Enlightenment in the late eighteenth century, his influence and impact on nineteenth-century theology and philosophy is profound).

(such a perspective will be set with a lower case 'l'). Therefore, the use of the term 'liberal' is derived from Barth's use of the term, rooted in Liberal neo-Protestantism, a theological movement of the nineteenth and early twentieth centuries against which he was, to a degree, reacting.

3 Karl Barth, *Dogmatik im Grundriß* (München: Christian Kaiser Verlag, 1947). English trans. *Dogmatics in Outline – Lectures on the Creed* (trans. G. T. Thomson; London: SCM Press, 1949).

4 Immanuel Kant, *Religion innerhalb der Grenzen der bloßen Vernunft* (1793). English trans. *Religion within the Boundaries of Mere Reason and Other Writings* (trans. and eds. Allen Wood and George Di Giovanni; introduction by Robert Merrihew Adams; Cambridge: Cambridge University Press, 1998).

iii. The Critiques of Reason and Judgement

Kant's work can best be perceived in his three volumes, his three critiques: *The Critique of Pure Reason*, *The Critique of Practical Reason* and *The Critique of Judgement.* The first, *The Critique of Pure Reason*, contains Kant's attack on the ability to know, especially theologically.[5] This is an attack on metaphysical optimism. His predecessors believed you could work out a world view through reason — they were confident in the powers of reason to plumb the depths of reality. The metaphysicians constructed systems of metaphysics by reason alone; classically, they are Spinoza, Descartes, Leibniz. But as Kant pointed out, the battles of the metaphysicians are endless and empty, as they can never come to any agreement. Having read Hume, Kant came to the conclusion that there can't be metaphysics.[6] So, there cannot be a rational metaphysics. Pure reason can only be used in a very

5 Immanuel Kant, *Kritik der reinen Vernunft* (1781; 2nd edn, 1787). The most commonly used and respected English translation is of the second edition by Norman Kemp Smith (1872–1958): Immanuel Kant, *Immanuel Kant's Critique of Pure Reason* (trans. Norman Kemp Smith; New York: Macmillan, 1905). For a contemporary edition, see Immanuel Kant, *Critique of Pure Reason* (intro. Howard Caygill; trans. Norman Kemp Smith; Basingstoke: Palgrave Macmillan, 2007). Kant's, *The Critique of Pure Reason,* is regarded as probably the most widely read and the most influential and important book in the history of Western philosophy.

6 A summary of Kant's beliefs may be relevant here for some readers. For Kant, because of the limitations of reason, we can't know for certain if there is an afterlife and a 'god', or the 'God'; this philosophical agnosticism excludes the certainty of theism and atheism. Morality was acceptable and important for Kant because of social order and cohesion. Kant realized that all the efforts of reason, of what he considered to be pure philosophy, are aimed and directed towards three problems: 'god', 'soul' and 'freedom'. These three questions lead to another – 'What ought we to do?' Beyond this there is for Kant the idea or ideal of pure reason, which he argues goes beyond possible experience if it believes, or more pertinently concludes, speculates, that there is a being who is more real than anything conceivable. Such a 'god', if personified, is seen by reason to be the subject of all predicates, and possibly to be the sum total of all reality. For Kant this 'supreme being', or 'god', can be considered to be the 'ideal of pure reason' as he would put it, because 'it' exists as the highest, most absolute, of all objects, the original cause and sustenance/sustainer: this is, in other words, a 'god of reason'. When talking of ontological proof, particularly of this 'god', Kant attributes perfection: if he didn't exist, he would be less than perfect. Furthermore, this depersonalized abstract 'god of reason' could be seen as the cosmological 'prime mover' and therefore, was proof of the existence of 'god'. For Kant, speculatively, there can be three proofs of the existence of his 'god': ontological proof of 'god's' existence; cosmological (prime mover) proof of 'god's' existence and physico-theological (watchmaker) proof of 'god's' existence. Kant's 'ontological proof' was of the most real 'being' and claimed absolute necessity; the 'cosmological proof' concludes that such a 'being' has the most reality. There is then the, as it is often termed, 'physico-theological' proof of God's existence: the watchmaker. This is based on *a posteriori* experience, after the reality of nature, the world, not on *a priori* concepts. It observes the world and concludes that there is intention, order and wisdom: an intelligent power. This is one cause, one prime mover; powerful and wise, and self-sufficient. None of this postulates absolute certainty. None of this considers the self-revelation of God as triune: the idea or the Kantian doctrine of such a 'god' becoming incarnate, allowing *Himself* to be subjected to humanity's hatred on the Cross is unthinkable, it is un-reasonable, it is Christologically barren (Editor).

restricted way to understand the world of the senses as it is presented to the senses and filtered through the structures of the mind.

In the second critique, *The Critique of Practical Reason*, Kant argued that while pure or theoretical reason could do nothing except those things that he allowed it to do, practical reason can do a great deal because it can legislate.[7] Primarily it must legislate for the good. As ethical beings we are entirely free to impose and discover, and at the same time discover and impose the universal maxims on which conduct is to be based.

At the end of his ethical writings, Kant comes to this apparently contradictory belief that viewed from the outside a human being is an entirely mechanistic being, viewed as a piece of matter in motion. The human being is a determined piece of matter (and in principle this makes him a scientist); however, internally we are free to legislate according to what we ought to do. There is an apparent dualism in this position. So this is an appeal to a highly rationalistic understanding of morality that appears to be contradicted by external knowledge.

The third critique, *The Critique of Judgement*, was an attempt to bring the conclusions of the first two critiques together.[8] However, I believe – along with many others – it failed, because on Kant's presupposition you can't. Post-Kantian morality has wrestled with this problem ever since. Gordon Michaelson has done a very good study of this called *Fallen Freedom* – it ends up with a vague postmodernist hopefulness, as I would call it.[9] *The Critique of Judgement* is essentially about aesthetics. He has dealt with truth (*The Critique of Pure Reason*), then goodness (*The Critique of Practical Reason*, or *Critique of Morals*) and now beauty (*Critique of Judgement*). Kant would have liked to move to some kind of solution to the relationship between the true and the good, between pure reason and practical reason, but he didn't: Schleiermacher did it for him. Yes, I think it's fair to say Schleiermacher did it for him.

iv. The Power of Reason and Philosophical Ethics

Barth was very self-conscious of his place in the theological tradition. He clearly saw himself as trying to do something different from his predecessors, though he is

7 Immanuel Kant, *Kritik der praktischen Vernunft* (1788). See first English translation, *Kant's Critique of Practical Reason* (trans. Thomas Kingsmill Abbot; London: Longman's, Green, 1898). For a contemporary edition, see Immanuel Kant, *Kant: Critique of Practical Reason* (Cambridge Texts in the History of Philosophy; eds Mary J. Gregor, Karl Ameriks and Desmond M. Clarke, intro. Andrews Reath; Cambridge: Cambridge University Press; new edn, 1997).

8 Immanuel Kant, *Kritik der Urteilskraft* (1790); the most commonly used and respected English translation is James Creed Meredith, *Kant's Critique of Aesthetic Judgement* (trans. and intro.; Oxford, Oxford University Press, 1911). For a contemporary edition, see, *Kant's Critique of Judgement* (trans. Ruth F. Chadwick and Clive Cazeaux; London: Routledge, 1992).

9 Gordon E. Michalson, *Fallen Freedom: Kant on Radical Evil and Moral Regeneration* (Cambridge: Cambridge University Press, 1990).

not as different as he thought, or is claimed to be. He saw, yes, Kant as the climax of the Enlightenment critique of Christianity and the relegation of religion. He saw that the early Enlightenment thinkers were great optimists, they did firmly believe that between the two poles of science and reason the world could be made immeasurably better, or so they believed, and further that all problems would eventually be solved. Kant was a strong rationalist, but he also had a good dose of Lutheran and Pauline scepticism and a secularized view of sin. He was sceptical about this, but he was highly rationalist. In *Religion within the Limits of Reason Alone* he argued that we can accept only those things from Jesus which we know independently to be true by philosophical argument: this is the whole tone of Kant's approach to anything religious, and it fits in with what we have said earlier about foundationalism.[10] To Kant there were two ways to know the world: physics and ethics. Physics was based on the method of Newtonian mechanistic science; the other was an innate morality. Newtonian science was mechanistic and left no room for God, or at least excluded Revelation. Kant believed profoundly in the innate power in all individuals to know what was right, a deep ethical core of philosophical ethics, the power to decide and know what was right: moral or practical reason. This is at the heart of *The Critique of Practical Reason,* is it not?

You see, religion outside such rational philosophical ethics was considered dark and superstitious. This is a very narrow and prejudiced position. Kant in a famous saying asserts that you should have the confidence to use your own intelligence: don't listen to priests, don't listen to the church, use your own intelligence and decide for yourself. The story of Kant processing at the beginning of each university year – I often recount this story because it says so much – Kant would process with the rest of the university staff but he would turn to one side when the procession entered the cathedral, he would go off to do his philosophy by himself. So, he was the model of a good enlightened citizen and was to have nothing to do with the institution – the church – nothing to do with historic religion. Kant quoted liberally from scripture but never quoted the words 'Jesus' or 'Christ', and avoided John 1.14, simply because, I think it is fair to say, he could not cope with the idea of God becoming Incarnate. This simply did not fit into his system, his idea of a god whom he could envisage with his power of reason, such a 'god' would not become 'incarnate', one of us, it was inconceivable.

v. What is Theologically Possible?

Barth identified that, after Kant, theology and philosophy could never be the same. Any theologian had to come to terms with Kant, either to follow in his tracks, or branch out in some way from what he established. Barth laid out three options/responses to Kant in or for the scholars that followed him; after Kant the

[10] Immanuel Kant, *Religion within the Boundaries of Mere Reason and Other Writings* (trans. and eds. Allen Wood and George Di Giovanni; intro. Robert Merrihew Adams; Cambridge: Cambridge Unoversity Press, 1998).

restriction upon what was possible, theologically, was perceived by Barth in three ways:

a fundamentally Kantian framework: Ritschlian
extending the Kantian framework: Schleiermachian
an alternative Kantian framework: Hegelian

Barth assesses all post-Kantian theology under one of these three categories. This is because of the assertion by Kant that you can't know God. The power and influence of this assertion was such that all nineteenth-century theology ended up being formulated either in response, or in the wake of it.

3. A Fundamentally Kantian Framework: Ritschlian

The Kantian category encompassed theologians who attempted to operate in what we can call a broadly Kantian framework, this involved many theologians. Albrecht Ritschl is a case in point.[11] The fundamental structure of his theology is Kantian; Ritschl's theology has a strong dualism and a strong agnosticism about the knowledge of the 'word'.

i. Moralistic Bourgeois Culture

Ritschl is fundamentally a Kantian: he sees Christology arising from a value judgement as to Jesus' value to people as God. This is operating within a Kantian framework – attempting to salvage from ethics a fundamentally Kantian view of the Christian tradition. Ritschl saw Christology as the key. He selected the historical Jesus in place of the Christ of dogma; this reduced Jesus to a good moral teacher. Ritschl distinguished between nature and spirit. Ritschlianism broke down towards the end of the century. Ritschlianism was derived from a pure Kantian position, itself based on Newtonian physics, which said that the universe was a closed

11 Albrecht Ritschl (1822–89), German theologian, born in Berlin, he studied at Bonn, Halle, Heidelberg and Tübingen. Ritschl was professor of theology at Bonn and Göttingen, his work showing the influence of Kant and Schleiermacher. See, for instance, Albrecht Ritschl, *Rechtfertigung und Versöhnung*, published in English as *The Christian Doctrine of Justification and Reconciliation* (trans. J. Sutherland Black; Edinburgh, 1872). Contemporary edition: Albrecht Ritschl, *The Christian Doctrine of Justification and Reconciliation* (Kila, MT: Kessinger, 2006). See also the recently published edition of Ritschl's lectures on ethics: Albrecht Ritschl, *Vorlesung Theologische Ethik* (Rolf Schäfer; Berlin: De Gruyter, 2007). For a general study of Ritschl, see David L Mueller, *An Introduction to the Theology of Albrecht Ritschl* (Philadelphia, PA: Westminster Press, 1969); also Gerald W. McCollah, *Christ's Person and Life-Work in the Theology of Albrecht Ritschl: with Special Attention to Munus Triplex* (Lanham, MD: University Press of America, 1990); and Clive Marsh, *Albrecht Ritschl and the Problem of the Historical Jesus* (Lewiston, NY: Edwin Mellen Press, 1992).

mechanism, independent, self-sufficient, self-sustaining; but separate from this is spirit, the realm of moral freedom.

Ritschl was a Christian theologian and in order to remain a Christian he wanted to make a link between the two worlds. The key to this was Jesus. Ritschl wanted to make a link between the two worlds through Jesus – but not through Jesus of Nazareth. In many ways, Ritschl steered a path between Jesus of Nazareth and Christ by selecting, by concentrating on, Jesus as an ethical teacher. Basically Ritschl's view is that the ethical life and the teaching of Jesus, in particular his teaching of the Kingdom of God, were the key to his significance. Because of this, because of Jesus', so to speak, 'status' as a teacher – there are other things as well, of course, but this is the heart of it. This gave the reason why we might value him as God. Ritschl does not teach that Jesus is God become man, as the tradition teaches, but he sees reasons why you can value this human being as God, *as if* he were God. Ritschl does not say that Jesus is God; his followers say, I make a judgement, because of which I judge him to be of the value of God. So Ritschl's theory of the value judgement here is important, because the value judgement enables you to go a little beyond the merely historical Jesus; you see, Jesus for Ritschl wasn't just an ordinary man, he wasn't just an ordinary person who taught, a good man and all that, he was actually somebody who taught in such a way and lived in such a way that he is 'as God' to us. As such, Ritschl continued to be a theologian, and continued to be an influential theologian right into the twentieth century.

So this position allows Ritschl to go beyond the position of Jesus as just another ordinary man, but essentially packages Jesus as acceptable for a nineteenth-century Liberal Protestant mentality: Jesus was remodelled to fit in with bourgeois culture. This becomes a moralistic view of Christianity. Ritschl – and for that matter Kant also – saw the Kingdom of God as crucial to this understanding of Jesus. For Ritschl, the Kingdom of God means the Kingdom brought about through forgiveness and ethical vocation. But this was a vocation within society, so that it ended up as a bourgeois position. In England there was a similar mindset in Victorian middle-class Christianity where the Christian vocation is to be a good upright citizen. Barth would not say that this was wrong, but would object to such a sociological interpretation, which limited Christianity to the role of a form of glue holding society together, welding the social order.

ii. The Breakdown of Ritschlianism

Ritschlianism broke down towards the end of the nineteenth century. Ritschl's own son-in-law, Johannes Weiss, was instrumental in this. He wrote a key work on the Kingdom of God, *Die Predigt Jesu vom Reiche Gottes*.[12] In this he argued that the

[12] Johannes Weiss, *Die Predigt Jesu vom Reiche Gottes* (Göttingen: Vandenhoeck & Ruprecht, 1900). English trans. *Jesus' Proclamation of the Kingdom of God* (trans., ed. and intro. Richard Hyde Hiers and David Larrimore Holland; London: SCM Press, 1971).

Kingdom of God does not mean a moral kingdom, it does not mean a bourgeois ethic, it means an other–worldly, eschatological, reality breaking into our world. You see, the other–worldliness of the biblical conception of 'the Kingdom' is what was stressed. Jesus was not so much a moral teacher as an eschatological prophet. This is not a man, Jesus, in the sense of a good upright moral citizen, but a man that actually threw a bomb at the social order. That is how they began to see Jesus. And, of course, there is Schweitzer – whose famous book on the historical Jesus took this even further and showed that all of these attempts to find Jesus as a historical figure, to define Jesus as a purely historical figure. were just reflections of the nineteenth century. Schweitzer is important, very important.[13] The Catholic George Tyrrell[14] said about Ritschl's Jesus and the others, such as Harnack and so on, something like, 'the Jesus of Liberal Protestantism is but the face of Liberal Protestant man reflected in a deep well'.[15]

Ritschlianism broke down because his biblical criticism was seen as inadequate and his concept of the Kingdom of God was seen as fatally flawed. The final nail in the coffin, so to speak, came with the First World War. Here, the stability, pride and security of Liberal Protestant German religion, society and culture broke down: the Great War represented the breakdown of all of these old certainties about the bourgeois social order in Germany, and for that matter the Victorian middle–class ethic in Britain. The progressive optimism of the nineteenth century fell apart during the Great War – millions were slaughtered on both sides over very small reasons.

4. Extending the Kantian Framework: Schleiermachian

Schleiermacher is a great theologian in the way that he sees that there has to be a way forward from Kant. He takes up a suggestion laid by Kant himself, or Kant's third project, *The Critique of Judgement*. Schleiermacher's theology is predicated on the fact that the human being is more than a combination of physics and ethics. We are not, on the one hand as Kant said, scientists and then, in a completely different respect, moralists. To use the modern metaphor, Kant is schizophrenic: to Kant there are the two kinds of mind, the scientific mind and the ethical mind and they can't be combined. Schleiermacher's genius is to say that of course they can. There

13 Albert Schweitzer, *Von Reimarus zu Wrede: eine Geschichte der Leben-Jesu-Forschung* (Tübingen: Mohr P. Siebeck, 1906). English trans. *The Quest of the Historical Jesus: A Critical Study of its Progress from Reimarus to Wrede* (London: A. & C. Black, 1911).

14 Father George Tyrrell SJ (1861–1909), a priest and Modernist Catholic scholar who attempted to interpret Catholic teaching in the context of modern knowledge and was thus embroiled in the Modernist controversy within the Roman Catholic Church towards the end of the nineteenth century. See George Tyrrell SJ, *External Religion: its Use and Abuse* (St Louis, MO: Sands, 1899).

15 '*The Christ that Harnack sees, looking back through nineteen centuries of Catholic darkness, is only the reflection of a Liberal Protestant face, seen at the bottom of a deep well*' (George Tyrrell SJ, *Christianity at the Cross-Roads* (London: Longmans Green, 1909), p. 49; see also, generally, pp. 46f).

is a higher function than either science or ethics and that is religion, a religious function.[16]

i. Schleiermacher's Response to Kant

A SCHLEIERMACHIAN HIERARCHY
OF THEOLOGICAL STATEMENT

↓

Description of religious experience:
the highest form of theological statement.

↓

Description of God as mediated by that experience:
the intermediate form of theological knowledge.

↓

Description of the world as filtered through
our experiential knowledge of God:
the lowest form of theological knowledge.

Figure 29

Barth's point is that Schleiermacher wants to extend Kant to a higher viewpoint in which both the Newtonian world of determined nature and the ethical world of decision and moral reason, can be extended into something higher. So to Schleiermacher it is the religious side of the human being that brings together the otherwise sundered faculties of the human soul. This is his act of genius, that in religion we bring together what might be called the utter dependence on nature for what we are, but also our transcendence of nature as ethical beings. This implies that, for Schleiermacher, theology is a function of experience. This is the important thing to see: we can only say anything about God and the world through the filter of our experience of God and the world. Schleiermacher defines this religious sense as an absolute dependence upon God as the one who is the object of our dependence. For Schleiermacher, theology is the articulation of experience: we are not talking about God, but God filtered through experience. There is a sort of hierarchy of theological statement (figure 29). Theology is the articulation of religious experience for Schleiermacher. If you define human response to God in terms of religiosity then you are bound to have a hierarchy of religiosities. Schleiermacher sees a description of religious experience as the highest form of

[16] Schleiermacher's *magnus opus* of systematic theology is Friedrich Schleiermacher, *Der christliche Glaube* (1820–21; 2nd edn, 1830–31). English trans. Friedrich Schleiermacher, *The Christian Faith* (trans. H. R. MacKintosh, ed. J. S. Stewart; Edinburgh: T.&T. Clark, 1999).

theological statement; a description of God as mediated by that experience is seen as an intermediate form of theological knowledge. Finally, the lowest form of theological knowledge would be a description of the world as filtered through our experiential knowledge of God. Schleiermacher, in a sense, became the founder of comparative religions from a Christian perspective because he was trying to show how Christianity related to other religions. Theology is the description of states of religion – according to Schleiermacher. However, this produces a highly rationalistic understanding of philosophy.

He is one of the great modern systematizers in that he believes that he must organize religious experience in as tight a philosophical manner as possible; or more pertinently, the different states of religious experience. Schleiermacher produced a very tight system.

ii. A Religion of Feeling?

Schleiermacher believes that theology is the rational articulation of the essentially supra-rational. Religious experience is a feeling. That's certainly a fair description of what Schleiermacher is about. The early Schleiermacher was essentially a pantheist. In his early material he would write about the white heat of the soul surrendering itself to the universe. He is a romantic – romantics feel their way to the world. A particular religious experience is tested by judging the degree to which an experience is of absolute dependence. The later Schleiermacher becomes much more Christocentric and less pantheistic. Therefore, our experience is still one of dependence but it is mediated through Christ. However, for Schleiermacher the basic relation is felt rather than thought; and moreover it is at the expense of thought. Supra-rationalism, that is what this is, is above reason – it is supra-rational – but it is theology's job to rationalize it, to describe it in as tight a way as possible. Barth in *Dogmatics in Outline* criticizes this by asserting that it is not supra-rational, it is rational in the first sense because the creed is rational: it is learned.[17] Schleiermacher struggles with the inherent pantheism in his theology; he has to develop criteria, which are quite Kantian, this led Barth to accuse him of still being Kantian in his ethics. Schleiermacher therefore dismisses all religions that are not monotheistic – if they are not monotheistic then they do not exhibit absolute dependence.

Schleiermacher comments that our everyday experience is a combination of feelings of absolute dependence and also of freedom. We are dependent upon others for our feeding and upbringing, et cetera, but we are also free to make of experience and reality what we can. But go deeper than this combination and you will find a drive towards absolute dependence. In some ways this is an experiential version of Aquinas' five ways. Aquinas is arguing that if you analyse any bit of reality you will see that it points up to God. If you analyse it in terms of causality

17 Karl Barth, *Dogmatik im Grundriß* (München: Christian Kaiser Verlag, 1947). English trans. *Dogmatics in Outline – Lectures on the Creed* (trans. G. T. Thomson; London: SCM Press, 1949).

then whichever of the Aristotelian five courses you follow you will find a monotheistic God.

Schleiermacher is saying, similarly, that if you analyse any experience in depth you will see that it points not necessarily upwards but inwards. He is talking about an inward-centred theology and you find a sense of absolute dependence which shapes our being. Religions express this more or less successfully.

iii. A Feuerbachian Critique

To Schleiermacher religion is essentially about anthropology writ large. Now, there is a danger there as you may know; because of this Barth considers Feuerbach to be the natural outcome of Schleiermacher. Anthropologically it can be argued that if religion is experiential then it is only of our experience. You see, Barth saw that Feuerbach was right: this 'god' – note a lower case 'g' again, though Feuerbach would not like me saying that I suppose – is the realized wish of the heart, our heart's desire raised to certainty and fulfilment, such as theology is, Feuerbach says, really only anthropology. Further, to Barth, Schleiermacher in answering Kant asserts that there are two paths, one is experiential the other is historical. It is important to remember that Schleiermacher was the first to write a life of Jesus.

As you can see, there is a big problem theologically here: theology is basing itself not on Revelation but on experience – and human history to a degree. Feuerbach gets rid of experience: Barth commented that in running away from Feuerbach these theologians run into the arms of Strauss. Because Strauss does for biblical history what Feuerbach did for religious experience. Feuerbach and Strauss represent for Barth the two logical outcomes of Schleiermacher: atheism in various ways. For Barth, Schleiermacher is the great opponent. Much of what Barth writes is to repudiate Schleiermacher.[18]

5. An Alternative Kantian Framework: Hegelian

Hegel can be illustrated by the famous story that he is reputed to have uttered about Schleiermacher, that, if religion is a state of absolute dependence then my dog is the most religious thing I know.[19] Behind this jibe is a very serious point: Hegel is accusing Schleiermacher of an intellectual copout. Hegel considers that Schleiermacher is evading the question of truth. Schleiermacher is talking about experience rather than truth – though it is fair to say that he believes experience is a

[18] See Friedrich Schleiermacher, *Über die Religion: Reden an die Gebildeten unter ihren Verächtern* (1799). English trans. *On Religion: Speeches to its Cultured Despisers* (trans. Richard Crouter; Cambridge: Cambridge University Press, 1996).

[19] '[if the] if a sense of absolute dependency were indeed the font of religion, then the dog would be the most religious of creatures': Georg Wihelm Friedrich Hegel, *Early Theological Writings* (trans. T. M. Knox; Chicago, IL: University of Chicago Press, 1948), pp. 20–21.

way to truth. Hegel believes that this is an evasion of the question. For Hegel the question is always 'Is this rational, is this true?' Barth likes Hegel in so far as truth is the great end of philosophy and theology.

i. Salvation by Reason?

Hegel was not an orthodox Christian; Kierkegaard regarded him as an utter Gnostic because for him salvation is by reason. Barth, however, likes Hegel. The great Kierkegaard quote is that Christianity teaches that only Jesus is divine – this is what makes Christianity Christian! By comparison, Hegel teaches that every human mind is implicitly divine; this turns Christianity into paganism. Paganism is the teaching that everybody is God; Christianity teaches that only one human is God: Jesus Christ.

Barth admires Hegel on a number of counts: dedication to the concept of truth – something has to be true for you to believe it. In this sense Barth regards Hegel as a true son and disciple of the Tübingen seminary. Hegel is therefore a typical product of the nineteenth century – he began as a theologian and ended as a philosopher. However, he can be regarded as a Christian philosopher in some respects because it can be asserted that his philosophy was Trinitarian: this was not an orthodox Trinitarianism, but it was Trinitarian.

ii. Truth as Movement

Hegel's view is of truth as movement, or event, truth happening: Hegel believed that truth takes shape in history and that truth becomes itself through the movement of a divine spirit throughout time, through history. However, Hegel is criticized for making the mistake that his philosophy was the ultimate divine spirit. Robert Jenson comments that Hegel had only one clear fault, he confused himself with the last judge, but this is quite a fault. Hegel really believed that truth happened in history, and in his own philosophy, but this is not the point: to Barth truth is a happening; truth is God happening in Jesus Christ. This is why he likes Hegel, this idea that our truth can only be a response to divine truth taking place in our time and space. Therefore, Hegel extends the notion of truth, Kant's notion of truth.

There are a number of problems, essentially because Hegel believed that our mind was equivalent to the divine mind so that the way we think is ultimately the way God thinks. This is essentially a Greek idea: Hegel's view is therefore a historicized and Christianized view of the way the Greeks thought. It is Christianized because it is put in a Trinitarian form. Hegel commented that

Christianity is the absolute religion because it is the revealed religion.[20] It is the revealed religion because in Jesus Christ is taught the truth of God's humanity; except this is not restricted to Jesus, and in that way it becomes real for everybody. Hegel, for Barth, had two great points, one on the plus side, and the other on the minus side (figure 30).

BARTH'S CRITIQUE OF HEGEL

POSITIVE	NEGATIVE
Hegel believed in truth because he believed in God	The living God of Hegel is ultimately the living man

Figure 30

In many ways Hegel is the deepest of all of the philosophers and certainly the deepest of all of the Christian philosophers. However, at the same time there is much to the accusation against Hegel by Kierkegaard that he turned the faith into a philosophy. What Hegel does is acknowledge that if you are going to devise a new form of philosophy or theology after Kant then you have to devise a new form of rationality. This is also what Barth wants to do. And that is so true of Barth: it is impossible to engage with Barth without exploring the nature of theology.

6. Hegelian Dialectics and Eschatological Pantheism?

We can certainly look at Hegel in more depth, particularly because of Barth's ambivalent response to the man. Barth's ambivalence was well-stated in his chapter on Hegel. Barth knew the difficulties with the man, and how these problems were not isolated.[21]

20 See Georg Wilhelm Friedrich Hegel, *Phänomenologie des Geistes* (1807). English trans. G. W. F. Hegel, *Phenomenology of Spirit* (trans. A. V. Miller, foreword J. N. Findlay; Oxford: Clarendon Press, 1977), VII. Religion in General, §. C. Revealed Religion, pp. 750–85.

21 'Theology was just as incapable of accepting Hegel's philosophy as was modern cultural awareness. Of course it cannot be said that it rejected him at that time because it knew better and because it clearly recognized the things which were unacceptable to it in his teaching. It would only have been able to do that if it had previously allowed itself to be taught by him much more thoroughly. Ultimately theology rejected him merely for the same reasons which also made him unacceptable to modern cultural awareness. Who knows whether it was not in fact the genuinely theological element in Hegel which made it shrink back? When we come to consider Schleiermacher we shall have to ask very seriously whether his secret is a different one from that of Hegel, only that with Hegel it might be a secret which was to a great extent more respectable and at all events more instructive than that of Schleiermacher. Theology had, and still has, no occasion to throw stones at Hegel, as if it had not trodden the same path as he, only not in so firm or so logical a manner as he did.' See Karl Barth, *Die protestantische Theologie im 19. Jahrhundert*, ch. 10 'Hegel', p. 407.

i. The Drive for Unity

Primarily, I suppose, Hegel was concerned with unity, with reconciling paradoxes and polarities in life and thought. In this respect this is a Romantic reaction to rationalism in the sense that the Enlightenment era was an era of analysis and the breaking up of things. Hegel was a Romantic in the sense that he saw in the Middle Ages a sort of ideal unity, a medieval unity. In the Middle Ages social unity cohered because everybody fitted into the Christian world scheme. The point about unity is very important. Hegel is a modern in that he realizes that you can't go back to medieval unity. Some of the more nostalgic medievals did in terms of the Oxford Movement. Hegel is looking for a modern unity which yet at the same time has the same kind of theological and social coherence that the medieval synthesis had.

Like Schleiermacher, he was in many ways a romantic: a romantic seeking a unity that transcended the Enlightenment. But – and this is important – this had to be based in the rational. Hegel's dialectics were essentially new, and were in many ways eschatological: thesis must give rise to its antithesis, contradictions are necessary. This dialectical movement is sublated by a higher synthesis of reason.[22] OK? Any intellectual movement tends to generate its opposite – this is, so to speak, Socrates' method of finding out truth by 'yes' and 'no'. This is the measure of what Hegel is doing. Hegel is a rationalist: this is classic rationalism.

Where is Christianity in this? Well, Christianity to Hegel is the culmination of the historical and spiritual process. It is, to quote Hegel, Revelation that comes from outside, but the truth must become internal, it must become rational. There is an important universality in this.

Q: Is this Platonic?

Well, yes and no – there's a nice bit of Hegelian dialectic I suppose! You see, the Platonic objection to the truthfulness of the particular is that sense has no part in truth because sense goes with the particular. And for the Platonist only that which is universal and general can be a candidate for truth. But Hegel is saying that representative forms, which partake of this sensual nature of material particularity can yet be a form of universality. And, of course, this is the theory of art, a particular painting can in some ways represent the universal, or a universal claim or truth. So representations include both sensuous particularity and universality.

The point about Christianity is that it's no good the Enlightenment saying you can't get truth from particulars, which is what the Enlightenment tended to say. That you can only get truth as general philosophical truth – this is the point of Lessing's famous saying about the 'ugly broad ditch' between the contingent truth of history and the universal truth of reason.[23] Hegel is saying that there is an

22 See Georg Wilhelm Friedrich Hegel, *Phänomenologie des Geistes* (1807). English trans. G. W. F. Hegel, *Phenomenology of Spirit* (trans. A. V. Miller, foreword J. N. Findlay; Oxford: Clarendon Press, 1977).

23 Gotthold Ephraim Lessing (1729–81), German writer, philosopher, publicist and art critic, representative of the German Enlightenment and spokesperson of the bourgeoisie. His phrase 'ugly broad ditch' applied to the New Testament era: we could not trust the contingency of

intermediate, in some sense, an intermediate something that participates both in the particular and in the universal: Christianity does this, Christianity is that something.

ii. Pantheism or Panentheism: Does God Need the World?

Where does this lead? Barth could see the problems in Hegel, yet he could also see the man's genius. To Hegel religion's ultimate end must be philosophy; philosophy is itself an act of divine worship. You know the famous saying of Descartes, 'I think, therefore I am',[24] well for Hegel the equivalent is 'I think, therefore I am religious'. Hegel is essentially a thinker; to be a thinker is in some sense or other to be religious. In a way it is a deep rationalism: for Hegel, being religious means realizing God somewhere or other in one's processes of thought. This does not mean having a relationship: ultimately for Hegel the process of thought is the process of becoming divine. There is a mystic element in this – being caught up in God.

Pantheism rears its ugly head with Hegel, as it did with the early Schleiermacher: you see, Hegel is tying God to the world. He is saying that without the world, God is not God. Therefore, the inevitability of God's Revelation is to tie God to the world, this is his system (figure 31).

PANTHEISM OR PANENTHEISM:
DOES GOD NEED THE WORLD?

For Hegel, without the world,
God is not God

Hegel inevitably ties God to the world through revelation
Is this Eschatological Pantheism, or Panentheism?

Figure 31

You could therefore say that this is an eschatological pantheism. In the end God is all; in the meantime there is otherness. When God is fully realized then God will be, in a radical sense, all in all: movement then, movement for Hegel is a movement towards that realization.

history because there was this ugly broad ditch between then and now so we could not accept the New Testament accounts as fact or truth, further, this ditch lay between the contingent truth of history and the universal truth of reason. Lessing was convinced that rationalism was the universal mode of understanding that humanity had for understanding the world. Lessing concluded that the Bible was not a source of truth, let alone the truth of God, also that the church's account of Jesus was flawed with the 'scandal of particularity': only the universal was true, the universal available to all humanity through reason not the contingency of history.

24 René Descartes (1596–1650), *Cogito ergo sum.*

The word *Aufhebung* can mean both to abolish and to lift to a higher degree. Hegel is playing on this ambiguity, just as when Barth speaks of other religions. For Barth, Christianity is the *Aufhebung* of other religions; this is translated as, 'Christianity is the abolition of religion' so they say Barth is against religion. But *Aufhebung* also means the elevation of religion to become true religion.[25] Hegel uses this word and plays on its ambiguity.

Hegel is all the time using words which could be ambiguous, but I think he meant them to be taken in two ways. Therefore, you have to say that he is, and is not, a pantheist. In one respect to Hegel everything is God, because he spiritualizes everything; but in another respect there is a distinction between God and those who think God.

Q: In Hegel's theology, does God need the world?

For Hegel there is the question, Does God need the world? – that is probably right, whether you can use words like *need* in Hegel's case I don't know, well, you see, you have to get out of your mind the idea of a God out there who then creates a world. For Hegel God is then both the determinate and the end of all processes; therefore, we have to understand Hegel's God in terms of immanence of some kind or other. But this does not lead to a personal God except in so far as he is personal through the processes of thinking. So all the time he is pushing towards a pantheism, but it isn't a straight pantheism; however, it is important to remember that pantheism is a problematic concept in that it means something different to everyone. Pantheism means something different to each and every one. But then you have to raise questions about the Christological soundness of Hegel's work. For Hegel, is Jesus unique or universal?

iii. Truth: Universal or Particular

Q: What do you mean by 'Christianizing' – and is Hegel 'Christianizing'?

You see, it comes down to the nature of truth. For general truth to be realized it had to be first particularized. You can't be a Platonist and simply intuit the general truths, the universal truths – you can't just philosophize them, they have to be realized through the particular, and that is where it is Christianizing, that's where Hegel Christianizes. You could describe Hegel's philosophy as a kind of historicized neo-Platonism. Whereas for Plotinus the word emanates from God timelessly, for Hegel the world emanates from God through time, well in a way from God in terms of time dialectically, but at the same time he wants to be particular and therefore, Christianize it as well. This might be the same thing as Christianizing it; I suppose he is trying to historicize Greek philosophy as well: therefore, it is a Christianizing.

Kierkegaard is critical of Hegel for divinizing the whole human race. Kierkegaard asked the question of where Jesus fits in with Hegel's scheme; Kierkegaard has this lovely saying that in Christianity only one human being is God

25 *Aufhebung, die*: abolition; repeal; rescindment; revocation; cancellation; lifting; closure.

and that is the crucified Christ. Hegel turns this into the doctrine that all human beings are divine in some way or another, and that simply is a reversion to paganism.

So either you reject Hegel or you don't. So the point is you either reject Hegel – and many theologians and philosophers have – or you don't: for Kierkegaard there is an absolute choice between the fact that the foundation is the crucified Christ, the foundation of our faith, or the foundation is the human. The view then is that Hegel, in the end, uses the crucified Christ simply as an example of something of the divinity that all human beings are called to share. You could say that Hegel's whole programme was an appeal to modern human beings to realize their divinity.

So Jesus is not the God-man but the one who realizes the consciousness that we are all god-men. To put it another way, it is the complete Gnosticizing of Christianity. The Gnostics believed that it was the inner spiritual core that was the real within you, the inner spiritual core through which you realized your divinity. You see, Hegel is dematerializing the material and that includes the historical Jesus of Nazareth who is a symbol, a representation in historical fact of a deeper truth that has to be realized beyond this historical fact, which then transcends it. So it is almost as though Jesus is a stage on the way to human consciousness realizing its universal divinity. However, Hegel is never as crude as that.

What happens is that the left-Hegelians, like Feuerbach, look at Feuerbach's programme. You now worship God, for Feuerbach, as a symbol of the human race, and so you worship humanity. And you may say that this is taking Hegel's rationalist side to its logical conclusion. On the one hand you get these people, the left-Hegelians, who say that to be human is to be divine, on the other the right-Hegelians try to push the concrete humanity of Jesus, stressing the other side of Hegel, which was the necessity of Jesus and therefore, they try to go back to a more concrete historicity.[26]

iv. The Relationship of Reason and Revelation in Hegel

So, what can we conclude about the complex relationship of reason and Revelation in Hegel? Hegel's mistake was to think that he was the *eschaton.* Suppose you make Jesus the *eschaton* instead, you still have the whole Hegelian idea of movement and all that – history moving towards a climax.. So Hegel's mistake was that he thought that it had arrived with him. It isn't, it hasn't, it is anticipated in Jesus; it will arrive at the end. This brings us back to Pannenberg's game, which is to open out history

[26] Feuerbach's famous criticism that God is the realized wish of the heart, the wish exalted to the certainty of its fulfilment, furthermore the secret, so to speak, of theology is that it is nothing more than anthropology. See Ludwig Feuerbach, *Das Wesen des Christentums* (1841) (ed. W. Schuffenhauer, Gesammelte Werke, vol. 5; Berlin: Akademie Verlag, 1973), pp. 121 and 207. English trans. *The Essence of Christianity* (trans. George Eliot, 1853). For a contemporary edition, see *The Essence of Christianity* (Amherst, NY: Prometheus Books, 1989).

in a way that it wasn't opened out for Hegel – Hegel had closed it! So Hegel has shaped this.

Q: Are Process theologians Hegelian?

Process theologian? – well, I suppose they are kind of non-dialectical Hegelians; process theology is just a kind of soggy Hegelianism because they don't believe that there is any negation at all, just a process of accumulating, but to process theologians this is the same concept where history is a bearer of God. They are much more cosmic than Hegel; Hegel was really an Idealist. They are, however, somewhere in this, this Hegelian approach.

Barth thinks that Hegel was the most self-confident theologian ever, and, as Barth says, this is because of Hegel's confidence in God. Then he goes on to say that ultimately Hegel's living God is the living man. In the end 'you' thinking are God, you become God through thinking – not your Father in heaven (figure 32).

HEGEL'S DIVINE ANTHROPOLOGY

Thought equals God

In the end the 'you' thinking is God,
not your Father in heaven

Figure 32

Q: Is there any understanding in Hegel that he is a sinner? Is there any concept of sin?

Well, he does and he doesn't. He is a Greek, and for him the problem of reconciliation is, proper reconciliation, is much more to do with reconciling the infinite and the finite rather than God and the sinner. Another interesting thing about Hegel is pointed out in a book by Findlay, he says that in the past most theologians have borrowed their philosophical dress from philosophy, like Aristotle, this is the history of theology – theology has drawn on philosophy for its structure and its concepts. This Hegelianism is the opposite here, it is a philosopher drawing on Christianity. What is his central concept? In some ways the Trinity; this is the odd thing, here is a philosopher using these concepts.[27]

v. Hegel: Christianizing or Gnosticizing?

So the big question is 'Is this a Christianizing of philosophy or a Gnosticizing of philosophy?' And, in the end, I think that this is the latter: there is definitely a Gnosticizing tendency in Hegel's work. Whether this is, whether it involves

27 See J. N. Findlay, *Hegel: A Re-examination* (Muirhead Library of Philosophy; London: Routledge, 2002 [1958]).

Pantheism or Panentheism I'm not sure, but it is, I believe, more to do with the Gnostics than with orthodox Christianity.

Hegel does not really take seriously the radical nature of evil or the transcendence of God seriously, or that religions may be different from the way Hegel represents them. Hegel's system is, in the end, inadequate: this is I believe a fair criticism. It can be argued that Hegel saw the human epistemological process dialectically – that we learn along the lines of thesis, antithesis, synthesis. If this is so we cannot simply dismiss him entirely.

The other way we can go, the other interesting way, is with Barth and this of course is that Barth says that Hegel is a very good anti-Kantian: he is a very good anti-Kantian ally. What Kant did was to lay down in advance the conditions for knowledge. Kant's epistemological programme is to say 'Before you know, you must conform to this prior epistemology that arises out of the critiques.' What Hegel is saying is that 'You only know by getting on with it.' So in that sense he is epistemologically useful. But what Hegel is saying is that you should read the history of culture and of religion but think through it. So actually, it is an attempt to be empirical.

Hegel had to say about Kant's position that to decide what knowledge is beforehand is to miss the crucial point, because it is anti-foundationalist also. Kant's attempt, to Hegel, to decide in advance what knowledge is or is not, to decide prior, is like someone who wanted to learn to swim before going into the water. Hegel is saying just get into the water and *know*. So the epistemology is out of the immersion in it – in theory. But in practice it is very Barthian; that is why Barth's chapter on Hegel is so revealing in many ways.[28] It is surprising how much Barth's dogmatics falls into three – it is as much Trinitarian as dialectical, but then the question arises 'Is Hegel's dialectic Trinitarian?' Because Platonic dialectic is double, it is an eternal dialectic of 'yes' and 'no'. Hegel's crucial concept is spirit. It is spirit that reconciles the 'yes' and 'no' at a higher level. Now it may not be the Christian spirit.

But you can say that Hegel's theology is an attempt to do a theology of the third person of the Trinity. God is *Geist*, spirit, and the spirit is eschatological, and all that. The spirit is the eschatological God straining, you see, to enable us to realize final truth.

Q: Is Barth rejecting him creedally?

Well, scripture is important – you see, Barth's criteria would be biblical rather than creedal. It is not the creeds but the Jesus Christ of scripture he witnesses to. Hegel's final synthesis is that the Christ of scripture has to be sublated to a higher knowledge, which is a universal Christology – everybody in a sense is Christ, not just Jesus of Nazareth. Barth would say that this is just a misreading of scripture. He would say that there is nothing beyond Jesus Christ.

[28] Karl Barth, *Die protestantische Theologie im 19. Jahrhundert*. See ch. 10 'Hegel', pp. 370–407.

Chapter 8

Barth: Revelation and Reason 1 – A Theology of Demolition?

1. Introduction

Karl Barth emerges from the nineteenth century taught by one of the century's more conservative theologians: his own father, who remained something of an evangelical amidst a welter of liberalism. Barth was influenced by the liberals of his day: Adolf von Harnack and Wilhelm Herrmann.[1] By his twenties, Barth is already

[1] Johann Wilhelm Herrmann (1846–1922) was professor of systematic theology at Marburg from 1879; Adolf von Harnack (1851–1930), theologian and church historian, who taught at Marburg and Berlin, worked essentially on the influence of Greek philosophy on early church writing. Both Herrmann and Harnack were Barth's teachers at the University of Marburg – their work was often referred to as Marburg neo-Kantianism and they epitomized Liberal neo-Protestantism for Barth. This is what Barth works against, having been an avid advocate in his student days and in his first ministry in Geneva. As such Liberal Protestantism claimed freedom not only from traditional dogmas and creeds but also in the analysis of and value accorded to scripture; such theology was to a large degree formulated in the light of advances in the natural sciences and philosophy. It is vital to remember that whenever Barth wrote or spoke of liberalism in his early work it was in the context of nineteenth-century Liberal neo-Protestantism. Karl Barth had left full-time theological education in 1909 a believer in his theological heritage rooted as it was in nineteenth-century German Liberal neo-Protestantism, derived in part from the theologian Friedrich Schleiermacher and the philosopher Georg Hegel. This was mediated to Barth by his teacher Wilhelm Herrmann. Marburg was the end of Barth's theological studies (somewhere that Barth had wanted to go, much against his father's wishes) where he absorbed the liberalism of Wilhelm Herrmann. Herrmann was a follower of Kant in philosophical terms and a follower of Ritschl in theological terms. He insisted that what should be observed and taught about Jesus of Nazareth were those facts that would act upon humanity – for example, the man's moral teaching but not the story of the Virginal Conception or the Resurrection. Furthermore, Herrmann proposed that there might have been other aspects of the man 'Jesus of Nazareth' that were considered relevant and of value by the apostles but these ideas/conclusions were not of importance to late nineteenth- and early twentieth-century humanity. Essentially, he held to a Ritschlian Christology but went further – he excluded both the mysticism of personal religious experience and the metaphysical speculation that underpinned any intellectual reasoning about ultimate reality. Any value to the historical Jesus was therefore in the man's moral teaching for

beginning to see the inadequacies of the Schleiermachian tradition – he can see that it is Schleiermacher who has influenced and ruled the tradition of nineteenth-century Liberal Protestant theological thought in Germany more than the Hegelian inheritance. The fact that Barth is Swiss is one of the reasons that he can distance himself from the German tradition. Barth realized that there is a fundamental contradiction in Schleiermacher:

2. The First Phase: Destructive

The first phase of Barth's theological career is destructive – there is so much from the nineteenth century that has to be undone. Barth sees Schleiermacher as the great influence on nineteenth-century German Protestant theology. This works through to Barth in his education – at the hands of his teacher Wilhelm Herrmann. Barth had been studying from 1904 to 1909 at the universities of Berne, Berlin, Tübingen and Marburg. He began his career as an assistant minister: in Geneva and then pastor for ten years at Safenwil in the Aargau.

i. Herrmannian Immediacy

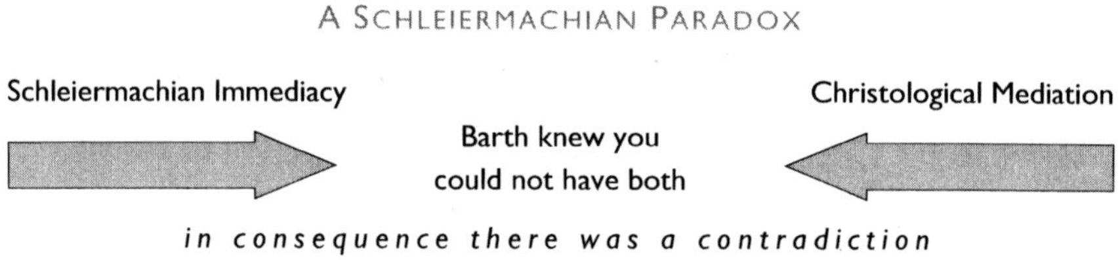

Figure 33

The first main objection to Schleiermacher and the nineteenth-century tradition was intellectual, although it becomes moral: in Herrmann's work on the communion of the Christian with Christ, there are inconsistencies. Herrmann was in the Schleiermacher tradition. Immediacy is at the heart of Schleiermacher's idea of religious experience – in religious experience you have an immediate felt link

humanity. Harnack insisted on absolute freedom in the study of church history and the New Testament – anything and everything could be questioned and refuted. His interest was in the so-called Christian religious life, he avoided anything resembling systematic theology. Harnack focused on the elements of Greek philosophy in the patristic fathers, refuting much of their doctrine. See Wilhelm Herrmann, *Der Verkehr des Christen mit Gott,* 1886; English trans. *The Communion of the Christian with God* (Philadelphia: Fortress Press, 1971); and Adolf von Harnack, *Das Wesen des Christentums* (Tübingen: Mohr Siebeck, 2005 [1900]). See also Simon Fisher, *Revelatory Positivism? Barth's Earliest Theology and the Marburg School* (Oxford: Oxford University Press, 1988); and Bernard Reardon (ed.), *Liberal Protestantism* (London: A. & C. Black, 1968) (Editor).

with the divine. Hans Frei called this relationalism in that you have a direct link with God through your feelings.[2] Herrmann attempted to combine Christology with this Schleiermachian concept of the immediacy of religious experience. It is not possible to have a notion of immediacy if you have Christology. The moment you bring Christ into the frame then you have to accept that Christ is the mediator – a direct link to God, a felt link, is not possible if Christ is mediating (figure 33). Once you get Christology then any notion of immediacy is called into question. Christ is the mediator of our knowledge of God; if you go to God through Christ, it is difficult to say that you go to God immediately. Barth came to think that these two were in the end incompatible: you can't have Schleiermachian immediacy and Herrmannian Christology.

Barth began to come to this conclusion in the 1910s, before the war. Bruce McCormack comments that Barth was in many ways prepared for the war by his own intellectual development. McCormack shows how Barth starts to write a Schleiermachian systematics early on but that he realizes that it won't hold together. This is Barth's genius – he produces an intellectual critique of it. It is the war that causes his final breach with the liberal tradition. What the war and his pastoral experience from 1911 on showed him, caused him to break with the liberal tradition.

ii. Safenwil: the Political Barth

While at Safenwil he had to face a number of things:

industrial conflict
the war
the Russian revolution

It is important to remember that politics forms the context of all of Barth's writings. Timothy Gorringe has published a work attempting to align the conclusions of Barth with the contemporary political events.[3] The political context does shape Barth: the earlier Barth, the First World War and his Romans commentary; then Hitler and the Second World War and his Dogmatics. There is clearly a political context.

Barth had been educated by the liberals to believe that the essence of Christianity was in religion, the essence was to be religious. However, he came to the view that religion does not cut any ice in an industrial dispute, or in a war where Christian nations were butchering each other. In particular, he thought that

2 Herrmann, *The Communion of the Christian with God* (1971). See also, Hans Wilhelm Frei, *The Doctrine of Revelation in the Thought of Karl Barth, 1902–1922: the Nature of Barth's Break with Liberalism* (New Haven, CT: Yale University Press, 1956); also, Hans Wilhelm Frei, George Hunsinger and William C. Placher, *Types of Christian Theology* (New Haven, CT: Yale University Press, 1994).
3 Timothy Gorringe, *Karl Barth: Against Hegemony* (Oxford: Oxford University Press, 1999).

the Schleiermacher tradition had sold out to culture. It had simply been the cement of nineteenth-century bourgeois culture and had nothing to say to it when that culture collapsed.

There are all sorts of influences behind Barth, but of particular importance were the Blumhardts. The elder was a revivalist, eschatological preacher, who was believed to produce miracles, yet this was an era when it was believed that miracles and healings could not take place. His son became an apocalyptic preacher, and was also the first preacher to become a social democrat MP.[4]

Basically religion did not have much to say where Barth had strikers and employers in the same congregation. In addition, the Russian revolution was fermenting and he had witnessed his own teachers supporting the war, much to his dismay. Barth later commented on the black day in 1914 when 93 German intellectuals, among whom were his own teachers, signed an open letter in support of the Kaiser's war policy. Barth further commented that this showed to him that he could neither follow their dogmatics nor their ethics, or their understanding of history or their biblical interpretation.[5]

The nineteenth century had had a particular view of dogmatics, the Bible and history and, of course, ethics. This had been very particular and very worked out, but it all fell apart as a result of what happened when Barth was a young minister. All of this had been disproved by what happened in the 1910s with the war, with industrial disputes and with the Russian revolution.

[4] Johann Christoph Blumhardt (1805–80) was the nephew of Christoph Gottlieb Blumhardt (1779–1838), founder of the Protestant Basel Mission. He was born at Stuttgart and studied at Tübingen, taught in Basel, but became pastor at Möttlingen in Württemberg. From 1852 till his death in 1880 he worked at Bad Boll near Göppingen, which through his involvement became a centre for missionary work. Johann Christoph died complaining that he had not witnessed the second coming. Although his work and ministry has been likened with Swabian Pietism, it is the eschatological dimension that marks his ministry as radical. Johann Christoph found himself witnessing to miracles and the supernatural during his ministry at Möttlingen in Württemberg. Johann Christoph's evangelistic work was often accompanied by physical cures. In one instance he prayed over a woman in his congregation who showed all the signs of demonic possession and she was healed. The inhuman scream that was heard to accompany the expulsion of the demon led to the coining of the slogan/motto he was to adopt, *Jesu ist Sieger* ('Jesus is Victor'). This, of course, did not fit in with nineteenth-century scientific scepticism. See Eduard Thurneysen, *Christoph Blumhardt* (München: Christian Kaiser Verlag, 1926).

Christoph Friedrich Blumhardt (1842–1919) took over the work of his father as the Director of Bad Boll after his death. He was also a fervent evangelical minister as well as a commensurate theologian. Concern for the conditions of the working classes led him to be elected as MP for the Social Democrat Party of the Württemberg Diet.

[5] See an address delivered at the meeting of the Goethegesellschaft in Hanover, 8 January 1957: Karl Barth, 'Evangelische Theologie im 19 Jahrhundert', in Karl Barth, *Evangelische Theologie im 19. Jahrhundert* (Zollikon-Zurich: Evangelischer Verlag, 1956), p. 14.

3. Barth: *Der Römerbrief*

So, where was Revelation and reason in all of this? Much of Barth's time was spent writing two huge commentaries on Romans: the first published in 1919, the second edition of this was in 1922. Now what is important is that where the apostle Paul uses the word 'law' in his Epistle to the Romans, Barth uses the word 'religion'. That is very important. In other words, God is not to be found in religion. What Barth does in *The Commentary on Romans* is to play concepts like grace and Gospel against religion: all these great Pauline terms are contrasted with religion. This is a very great, a very dynamic and a very eschatological book.[6]

BARTH'S DYNAMIC AND TRANSCENDENT ESCHATOLOGY

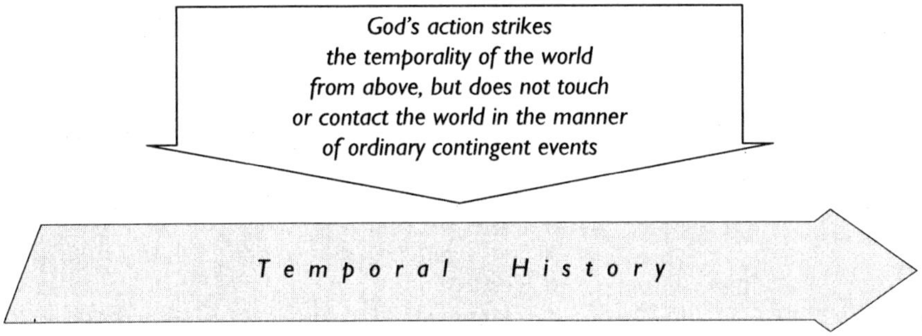

Figure 34

The other interesting thing about the nineteenth century is that eschatology had been written out of the lexicon, with the exception of characters such as the Blumhardts. The late German sceptics such as Johannes Weiss and Albert Schweitzer, whom we mentioned last week, were among those who rediscovered biblical eschatology. Eschatology now took its place as the depth of Christianity. In other words they rediscovered that Jesus wasn't a moral teacher but an eschatological prophet who went to his death mistaken; he was misunderstood (figure 34). What we have in Barth's *Commentary on Romans* is a very dynamic and transcendent God breaking into the world in a most unexpected way: this is a sort of eschatology. This is an astonishing book, which received the name 'dialectical' by its critics. It is true to say that there are a lot of dialectical expressions in it. If God is the transcendent other who breaks into the world, the absolute transcendent other, then where God breaks into the world you can only express

6 Karl Barth, *Der Römerbrief* (Erste Fassung; Zürich: Theologischer Verlag Zürich, 1985 [1919]). Karl Barth, *Der Römerbrief* (Zweite Fassung; Zürich: Theologischer Verlag Zürich, 1999 [1922]); English trans. Karl Barth, *The Epistle to the Romans* (trans. Edwyn Hoskyns; Oxford: Oxford University Press, 1933).

this in a 'yes' or a 'no'. God is there but completely unrecognizable; just as you would expect. In the same way you would only recognize a crater after a bomb has dropped. What Barth is trying to do is distance God from culture. The nineteenth century had domesticated God; it was as if a 'god' patted law-abiding Germans on the head and said, 'Very well, keep going and you will bring in the kingdom.'

So, how did the theological establishment react? This is the God of a dynamic, eschatological negative eternity: note these images of breaking into the world like lightning, or a bomb. The Catholic theologian Karl Adam described this book as a bombshell thrown into the playground of the theologians.[7] They were playing games, and then war broke out, and Barth tossed this bomb into their complacency. That is the theme that he wants to get over – to break the complacency. The view is therefore, in a sense, of an unknown God. Barth therefore poses the question 'How can you possibly know a God that hits the world at a timeless point?' God is, therefore, the unknown and the known – he is known as the unknowable.[8] Barth therefore plays with paradox. God is therefore utterly distinct.[9] This is what is revealed. This has produced a quote/phrase from him that has gone down in the annuls of twentieth-century theology as the touchstone of his theology, a quote from Kierkegaard, that there is an infinite and qualitative difference between time and eternity. [10] Barth is stressing the difference between God and all that is earthly.

To Barth, the 'Kingdom' was what contradicted all of our feeble efforts. This is a very negative eschatology. Barth is asserting that there is nothing in common between the world and God. It is as if God is the 'no' in our 'yes', and the 'yes' in our 'no'. This is pure Barth, you see, pure Barth: to every human 'advance' he calls 'halt', and to every human 'halt' he calls 'advance'. If you think you have got God tied down, as he thought the nineteenth century tried to do – did! – then you haven't got God at all. This is the negative message of that book. And this is at the heart of the difference between Revelation and reason: this goes to the heart of the problem – reason, reasonableness, is not the same as the self-revelation of the one

7 'Barth's *Römerbrief* hit immediately in its first appearance – August 1919 – like a bomb on the playground of the theologians, comparably in its effects with the encyclical on antimodernisation of Pope Pius X'. Karl Adam, 'Die Theologie der Krisis', *Hochland* XXIII (1926), pp. 271–86 (trans. Editor).

8 Barth, *Der Römerbrief* (Erste Fassung; on Romans 3.1-20), p. 77.

9 Barth, *Der Römerbrief* (Erste Fassung; on Romans 1.1-1), p. 28.

10 Søren Kierkegaard, *Einübung in Christentum* (Erste Fassung; Halle: Fricke, 1878), the first German edition Barth was working from: Christ as 'the paradox' (pp. 20, 25 and 57); the problem of 'contemporaneity' with Christ (pp. 56–60); the 'infinite qualitative distinction' (p. 124); the incarnation as the divine 'incognito' (p. 112); and the impossibility of 'direct communication' (pp. 121–28). For example, in terms of the phrase, infinite qualitative difference/distinction, the first English translation, Søren Kierkegaard, *Training in Christianity* (trans. Walter Lowrie; London: Oxford University Press, 1941), offers the following: 'endless yawning difference' (p. 67); 'qualitative infinite emphasis' (p. 72); 'it is the false invention of human sympathy which forgets the infinite difference between God and man' (p. 139); 'As God-man he is qualitatively different from every other man' (p. 142); 'infinite yawning difference which he posits between God and the emperor' (p. 169); 'infinite distinction' (p. 172).

true God. In many ways this is very existential because you can only accept this apparent contradiction by an existential leap, an existential leap of faith.

It is important to remember that Barth's Commentary on Romans occurs in a context of other works sceptical of the collapse of European culture and society: Cubism and Expressionism in the field of the visual arts, or the music of Bartók and Stravinsky. However, it is important to remember that theologically the commentary is an anti-theology. Barth described the commentary later on as being written in a context where the ship of theology was drifting onto the rocks, someone had to come along and grab the tiller and turn the ship around.[11]

Commentators would assert that in many ways it is not theology. Barth's *Commentary on Romans* is not theology, and it did not make Barth a theologian because you cannot really accept a situation where it is possible to make theology just by making a noise, by being a noisy prophet, and by being destructive.

Unfortunately, many educated British and American theologians only knew Barth through this commentary in the early to middle years of the twentieth century, as this was the only work of his in translation for some time. Many British theologians couldn't come to terms with Barth and regarded him as a noisy irrational radical. You see, the commentary is essentially saying that the way of Schleiermacher and Hegel is dead: by comparison Barth insists that where the creed is uttered there is knowledge.

In the context of Jewish–Christian relations Barth has an understanding of Paul and Palestinian Judaism, especially the relationship between Paul and the Rabbis in a way that other Western scholars fail to perceive. Many theologians and bible scholars assert that Barth's *Commentary on Romans* shows a profound understanding of the mind of Paul; some Jewish scholars, for example David Novak, can perceive a typical piece of Rabbinic exegesis in Barth's work.[12]

11 'Were we right or wrong? We were certainly right! Why? Let one read the doctrine of Tröltsch and Stephan! Let one read also the dogmatics of Lüdemann, in its way so solid, or even that of Seeburg! If all that wasn't a blind alley! Beyond doubt what was then in order was not some kind of further shifting around within the complex of inherited questions, as this was finally attempted by Wobbermin, Schaeder and Otto, but rather a *radikale Wendung*. The ship was threatening to run aground; the moment was at hand to turn the rudder an angle of exactly 180°. And in view of what is to be said later, let it immediately be stated: that which is gone does not return. Therefore there never could be a question of denying or reversing that change. It was however later on and it is today a question of "*Retraktation*"' (from Karl Barth, 'Die Menschlichkeit Gottes', in Karl Barth, *Die Menschlichkeit Gottes* (Zollikon-Zurich: Evangelischer Verlag, 1956), pp. 6–7; English trans. Karl Barth, 'The Humanity of God', in Karl Barth, *The Humanity of God* (trans. John Newton Thomas; Louisville, KY: Westminster John Knox Press, 1960), pp. 41–2).

12 David Novak, Jewish scholar, philosopher, lawyer, ethicist and rabbi, has written on Jewish–Christian relations and has worked on Jewish social ethics derived from natural law and Halakha. See David Novak, *Law and Theology in Judaism* (2 volumes; New York: Ktav, 1974); also, David Novak, *Jewish–Christian Dialogue. a Jewish Justification* (Oxford: Oxford University Press, 1989).

4. Barth and Schleiermacher

Barth's *Commentary on Romans* with its existential concept of Revelation is the beginning of an answer by him to Kant and Schleiermacher. Schleiermacher was, as we have seen, one answer to Kant. Make no mistake, Barth held Schleiermacher in high esteem – that is important to remember. He appreciated Schleiermacher's theology, but he believed the man's theology was fatally flawed. The problem is they differed on Revelation. They held opposite views you see on Revelation. In his *Commentary on Romans*, Revelation is existential and we respond to the event of this Revelation through faith. This is very existential because you can only accept this apparent contradiction by, as I said, an existential leap of faith.

i. Revelation as Relational Dependence

Schleiermacher is about absolute dependence on God. You see, by comparison, for Schleiermacher, absolute dependence means being in relation with God. Schleiermacher does attempt to systematize this by talking of different levels of religious feeling and dependence: from an animal state to this religious feeling of utter dependence – from partial feeling and partial dependence you get absolute dependence. We've looked at this before, this criticism of Schleiermacher and how Schleiermacher's theology of religion leads to a Feuerbachian dismissal, but this is so important, it will lead us to understand what drives Barth. You see, if this is so, then whatever we say about God are really only statements about our feelings: Is this Revelation? – this question is I believe at the heart of Barth's development and his conclusions, particularly in the *Church Dogmatics* (figure 35).

What Kant and Schleiermacher, and Aquinas, all share is an essentially negative starting point regarding predication: you predicate of God by abstraction, rather than directly. To Barth, both Liberal Protestantism and Roman Catholicism derive the structure of Revelation from natural theology, that is, a generalized experience of the world.

ii. Revelation as Experiential Non-Dogmatic

Schleiermacher wants to avoid any idea that Revelation is in the form of a supernatural communication to the mind. Again, like Hegel, this is essentially pantheistic. And if this is so then Revelation is no more than anthropology – as Feuerbach said. Any understanding we have of Jesus then becomes experiential not dogmatic. This is putting the whole thing into an experiential rather than a dogmatic mould. Dogma is replaced by a distillation of experience which is centred in Jesus. Jesus is no more than the impulse, which transmits this sense of feeling to us, this sense of God.

A SCHLEIERMACHIAN-FEUERBACHIAN CRITIQUE

If our feelings are the basis-ground of our understanding of God then whatever we say about God, or this 'god', are really only statements about our feelings.

This is a subjective ground for a doctrine of God.

Is this Revelation?

Does this give us the truth about God?

Figure 35

BARTH – RATIONALITY

For Barth

the Gospel is not *Irrational*

It is not *Supra-Rational*

It is not *Anti-Rational*

It is *Rational* in the Deepest Sense.

Therefore where the Creed is Uttered–
there is meant to be Knowledge.

Figure 36

They are very different, Barth and Schleiermacher. But Schleiermacher – like Barth – is trying to answer Kant, when Kant had effectively turned people into minds. By concentrating so relentlessly on the intellectual, he divided human beings along schizophrenic lines: philosophers on the one hand and moralizers on the other, and try as you may, you can't bring them together. Schleiermacher is a sign that you can't solve problems intellectually (figure 36, previous page).

iii. Revelation as Feeling

This is the whole Romantic objection to the Enlightenment, the Enlightenment movement. The Enlightenment's reliance upon analysis simply broke human beings up into fragments. The whole Romantic Movement brings together by feeling, brings the human back together: you don't think the unity of things, you feel it. The greatness of Hegel, compared to Schleiermacher, is that he thought you could think it as well – you don't cop out of reason, you find a better form of reason. So what role is there for pneumatology in Schleiermacher's scheme? Is there any pneumatology left for Schleiermacher other than the cultural *Zeitgeist*? The answer lies in how you distinguish feeling from the work of the Spirit, that's the answer. Then theology is a rational exposition of a supra-rational experience; that is almost a direct quote from Schleiermacher. Well, you see, to Barth, Christianity isn't irrational, it isn't supra-rational, it isn't anti-rational: it is rational in the deepest sense. Hence he goes on, where the creed is uttered, there is meant to be knowledge. To Schleiermacher the experience of God is supra-rational, it is above reason.

5. Existentialism: Bultmann and Heidegger

Barth's *Commentary on Romans* is – and this is widely acknowledged – heavily existential. Now, this is a new thing in some ways. You can't say Harnack and Herrmann are existential, not really – Liberal Protestantism is happily engrossed in culture, being cultivated in many ways! You see, Barth had 'let the cat out of the bag' in some ways. You have this group of young theologians or Bible scholars that gather around him – dialectical theologians is what they are called, by their detractors, which included Barth's teachers. The group included Bultmann, who takes this existential approach much further, and in ways Barth begins to disapprove of.

i. A Personal Existential Revelation?

So, what is the impact of existentialist philosophy on Rudolf Bultmann's concept of Revelation? Bultmann wrote on Revelation in the New Testament, that to know about Revelation means to know ourselves. And what do we know? – that we are dependent upon Revelation. And to know about Revelation means to know about our own authenticity, but there are limitations.[13]

You see, for Barth this is focusing too much on the human individual, and this is pure twentieth-century existentialist philosophy, you see, natural theology, philosophy, creeping in again. This is a very characteristically existentialist kind of thesis, obviously, in some way or other, the meaning of Revelation is bound up with one's subjective appropriation of it. Obviously, there are different ways of this being so.

Barth would say that Revelation is more than self-knowledge. Revelation is more than self-discovery, self-awareness: Well, is it? Bultmann's work is comparable in some ways with his one time colleague Martin Heidegger; you can find Heidegger's philosophy of being in Bultmann's theology.[14]

Bultmann says we are dependent on Revelation; this is not Revelation that is communication of knowledge by the Word. Authenticity is what Heidegger speaks of; he also talks about the polarities of existence. For both of them this is death: death is what we must confront and embrace; they then talk about existential fulfilment.

ii. Bultmann and the Cross

This allows Bultmann to talk about the Cross – Heidegger doesn't, of course. Christ embraced death, you see, decisively, that's the word, 'decisively', so the existentialists would say. I'm not sure if that is true when you read about Jesus in the Garden of Gethsemane, though. Such Revelation gives us authenticity. Is Bultmann correct?

It is interesting that we have a similar problem to what is going on in Hegel, in the sense that the same questions are being raised, or has Bultmann just given them a Christian tinge because of this existentialist vocabulary? Or, is he actually reshaping the concepts Christianly?

13 Colin Gunton is paraphrasing from Rudolf Bultmann, 'The Concept of Revelation in the New Testament', in *Existence and Faith: Shorter Writings of Rudolf Bultmann* (San Francisco, CA: Collins, 1987 [1960]), p. 67.

14 Martin Heidegger (1889–1976). German philosopher who became a supporter and member of the Nazi Party, his work focused on phenomenology, hermeneutics and existentialism. His main work is *Sein und Zeit* (*On Being and Time*) first published in 1927, in which he investigates ontology by asking about the being for whom being is a question, he names this being *dasein* focusing on mortality and temporality anxiety and historicity. See Martin Heidegger, *On Being and Time* (Chicago, IL: University of Chicago Press, 2002 [1927]).

That is always the question with him. But you can see what is happening. He is taking Heidegger's concepts and linking Heidegger's concern with death with Jesus' crucifixion. But you need a much more Christological point. It is the same sort of thing with Hegel; Christianity is mixed up with a philosophical system which is obviously Christian in its subject: a parallel anyway. Heidegger is often referred to as Bultmann's shadow.

Heidegger was a dropout from a Catholic seminary, so you would expect some Catholic input, this is not purely philosophical. For Heidegger, it was Paul's anthropology that provided him with the key to understanding life, life in its here-and-now experience. Heidegger does acknowledge some of this input; he comments that Paul led him to his use of *dasein.*[15]

Likewise there is Paul's eschatology, a Pauline eschatology, what Heidegger calls 'enacting one's life in uncertainty before the unseen God'. This is a strange concept of eschatology, more Platonic. This takes us back to the beginning of the whole of the Bultmann–Barth controversy. It is often said that Barth's *Commentary on Romans* is essentially Platonic eschatology, in the sense that it is the timeless breaking into time and not the future anticipating the present. You see, the primary meaning of Revelation for Bultmann is that God does something.

iii. Demythologizing Revelation?

Revelation for Bultmann means God does something, OK. We by comparison are sinful. This is all rather strange considering Bultmann's demythologizing of scripture. If you demythologize scripture then Revelation does only pertain to the self, to authenticity and self-understanding, which means, I think, that in Bultmann's case, Heidegger has the final word. For twentieth-century existentialists whether Christian-like Bultmann or the atheistic variety, there is always the question relating to Revelation and that is – How can man be ruled by a 'god', by cosmic forces, and yet have the ability to make choices? You see, existentialism is about making decisions, making choices. For Bultmann the tension is too great, something has to give. For him it is providence, the cosmic forces: demythologizing allows for decision, for choice. So out go the miracles in the New Testament, along with the supernatural beings – angels and demons.

So there are two points here: the form of the New Testament is not the same as its content. There is, for Bultmann, a mythical form with a non-mythical content. He is also saying that this is also a matter of apologetics, of modernizing in the sense that not only is the form different from the content, the form is also

[15] *Dasein*: 'to be there'; (*hier sein*), 'be here'; (*übrig sein*) 'to be left', to only exist. *Dasein* is also used for 'to occur' or, 'a moment has arrived'; the use is situational, though often theologians and philosophers use it to do with existence – 'to exist', 'to live' (*existieren, leben*), 'to be left'; 'to be still alive'. For Heidegger, *Dasein* (*da*, there or here; *Sein*, being: *Dasein*, existence) is 'the being for whom being is a question', 'a being who is not man but who is nothing other than man': see *On Being and Time*, §62.

made out of understanding. Therefore, for two reasons mythologizing has to be done: first, the content demands it; the second thing is that the ancient is to be seen as incredible to the modern mind. So one is the demand of the Gospel, the other is the demand of the world. If the form is inherently mythological then what is it about?

Bultmann relies on a modern scientific world view to justify this. Hence we have his famous comment about how it is not possible to use electric light and the wireless and to avail ourselves of modern medical and surgical discoveries and at the same time believe in the New Testament world of demons and spirits.[16] I think that this is one of the most stupid things ever said by a brilliant theologian. What he means is not the modern world view but the Newtonian world view, which even as he was writing was being revealed as not the whole of the world. It is just a stupid thing to say, it is manifestly false. Except it reflects the way an educated elite, or a half-educated elite, thinks. You see I do think the answer to the problem with Christianity in the modern world – if there is a problem – is theology of this kind. Your ultra–educated physicist will use the word 'God' but not in the way you or I would. But many cosmological physicists will use God language in some way or other.

I think the criticism is right that he gets a lot of this from Strauss,[17] this patronizing attitude to the ancient mind – patronizing to both the Hebrew and Greek ancient mind. His demythologizing does weld him to a Straussian dualism, a dualism between the ancient mythological mind and the modern mind, the conceptual philosopher, but what he is trying to say is that Heidegger gives you the concepts or at least what might be called the existential concepts, even though the cosmological has to be abandoned.

iv. Krisis

As with all philosophies existentialism is essentially a human thought system, that's the problem, well, it certainly is for Barth and certainly is for me. Bultmann's scheme of things places far too much emphasis on choice, on human decision. So, you see, the content becomes irrelevant. If you are so concerned to isolate the fact that it is faith and unfounded faith then it does tend to banish the decision.

If the myths are not an act of God why should the faith be an act of God, why not just have the Heideggerian approach? So, after Bultmann his pupils go just

16 Bultmann, 'The Concept of Revelation in the New Testament', p. 69.

17 David Friedrich Strauss (1808–74), German theologian who shocked European intellectuals and the church with his *Leben Jesu* (*The Life of Jesus*, 1835) whose divine nature he completely denied; later he published a follow-up volume, *Das Leben Jesu für das deutsche Volk* (*The Life of Jesus for the German People*, 1864), written in a similar vein, to extend his thesis. He revolutionized the study of the New Testament, an early Christianity and pioneered the investigations into the so-called 'historical of Jesus'. See David Friedrich Strauss, *The Life of Jesus Critically Examined* (Continuum Classic Texts; London: Continuum, 2006).

like Hegel to the left, to atheism, or like Ernst Käsemann,[18] on the right, to a much more conservative approach. Käsemann took the history much more seriously, he wanted much more to see continuities between Jesus and the faith of the early church. On the other hand there are those who developed an atheistic Christology from Bultmann!

The point is for Bultmann that the tradition had gone dead, it was not seen to cut ice. This is Tillich's experience also, they were both in the First World War – somewhere or other the tradition had gone dead. If you look at the three big names of the twentieth century, Barth, Tillich and Bultmann – or, at least, those I would see as the three big names of the twentieth century – they all try to say why the tradition had gone dead. This is a problem for each generation; you must not absolutize the ancient view or the modern world view. No matter how important we think our view is it will disappear. I suspect the future generations, if there are any, will wonder why – Why were we so hung up on science all the time? Science is as culturally conditioned as any enterprise. Bultmann was not right in absolutizing his own era.

[18] Ernst Käsemann (1906–98), Lutheran theologian and professor of New Testament Studies at the universities of Mainz, Göttingen and finally Tübingen, completed his doctoral studies under Rudolf Bultmann from the University of Marburg in 1931. See Ernst Käsemann, *An die Römer* (Tübingen: Mohr, 1973); Ernst Käsemann, *Exegetische Versuche und Besinnungen* (Göttingen: Vandenhoeck und Ruprecht, 1964); Ernst Käsemann, *Paulinische Perspektiven* (Tübingen: Mohr, 1969); and Ernst Käsemann, *Das Neue Testament als Kanon* (Göttingen: Vandenhoeck und Ruprecht, 1970).

Chapter 9

Barth: Revelation and Reason 2 – A Theology of Construction?

1. Introduction

So, the early phase in Barth's theological career was to break down what the nineteenth century had created – to separate what the nineteenth century had put together. From this point on Barth is seeking what is to be the right method for Christian theology. He is critically aware that after Kant theology cannot be other than self-conscious about how it does theology, but importantly, how it relates Revelation and reason.

2. The Second Phase: Constructive

Because of his notoriety, caused by his commentary on Romans, Barth was offered a chair at a German university: Göttingen. Barth then held professorships successively at Münster, where he was appointed professor of systematic theology, then at the University of Bonn and finally at Basel back in Switzerland.[1]

i. Content Led

On the strength of the first edition of this *Commentary on Romans*, Barth was appointed on 22 October 1921 as Honorary Professor of Reformed Theology at the University of Göttingen. Göttingen was difficult, teaching theology was difficult for him at first because, you see, you can't simply throw prophecy at them all the time – brilliant though it was – not if you are actually going to teach dogmatics! So, he had to dig deep, he had to read theology – all these old

1 Professorships held successively at: University of Göttingen (1921–5), University of Münster (1925–30), University of Bonn (1930–35) and University of Basel (1935–62).

Reformed theologians who had been forgotten by the liberals. He had much to catch up on. Barth became strong on the Reformers. Anything prior to the modern era tended to be dismissed by the liberal tendency. Barth read deeply on the Reformers and the dogmatics of the Protestants between the Reformation and the nineteenth century – the so-called, Protestant scholasticism or orthodoxy.

What Barth produces in the 1920s are a series of papers trying to pick his way to a theological method. There have been a number of interpretations of what this was. Until recent times, the most popular or fashionable interpretation was that in the 1920s you get a development, which came to a completion in Barth's book on Anselm in 1931.[2] This view has recently been attacked by Bruce McCormack.[3] He argues that Barth's position was complete much earlier. During the 1920s Barth is influenced by the content of the Gospel. To McCormack, if Barth thinks the theology is not adequate to the Gospel then he changes the theology. Therefore, all of Barth's changes are content-led. You see, I think that is very important. Barth is content-led. This is certainly true of the mature Barth. If there is one rational principle, so to speak, underlying the whole of Barth's later work it is that form must be shaped by content. That is why he does not like natural theology, because natural theology predisposes theology to have a content that isn't of the Gospel (figure 37).

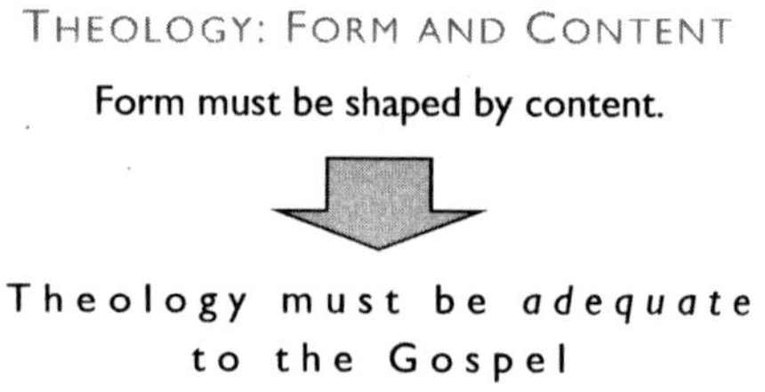

Figure 37

So what you see in the 1920s is a quite complex development where Barth wrestles with a number of problems. He wrote some Christian dogmatics, which he rejected because he thought they were still too reliant upon existentialism.[4] In the 1920s Barth is moving all the time towards a position where he can construct a theology, which is not dependent upon a philosophy of any sort. This is because in the nineteenth century he observes a situation where theology became something more akin to philosophy. To avoid the problems of the state theology had arrived at by

2 Karl Barth, *Fides quaerens intellectum – Anselms Beweis der Existenz Gottes im Zusammenhang seines theologischen Programms* (München, Christian: Kaiser Verlag, 1931). English trans. Karl Barth, *Anselm: Fides Quaerens Intellectum* (London: SCM Press, 1960).

3 Bruce McCormack, *Karl Barth's Critically Realistic Dialectical Theology: Its Genesis and Development 1909–1936* (Oxford: Oxford University Press, Clarendon Paperbacks, 1995).

4 Karl Barth, *Die Christliche Dogmatik im Entwurf – Erste Band Die Lehre vom Worte Gottes, Prolegomena zur christlichen Dogmatik 1927* (Gesamtausgabe 14; Zürich: Theologischer Verlag Zürich, 1982).

the end of the nineteenth century then philosophy, or reliance upon a philosophy, must be avoided.

ii. 'Schicksal und Idee'

A number of Barth's papers written during this period engage with the question of philosophy: if you don't want your theology to be dependent upon a philosophy then this raises the question – What is your relation with philosophy? The most interesting paper in this series is 'Schicksal und Idee' ('Fate and Idea') – a series of three lectures delivered at the Hochschulinstitut in Dortmund between February and March 1929.[5] Fate and idea represent the two poles between which all philosophies move, and in relation to which all theology must move. Fate in this sense may mean fate, objectivism or realism. So, objectivism on the one hand, you see; on the other hand, you have idealism. Objectivism or realism means the priority of the object over and against the subject. So we have a distinction between being dominated either by objectivism (*Schicksal* – fate) or subjectivism (*Idee* – idea) (figure 38).

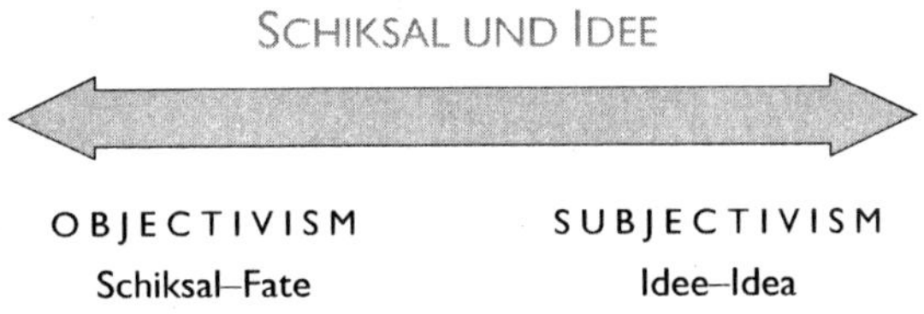

Figure 38

If you are dominated by fate you are simply swallowed up by some objective world and you lose your subjectivity, on the other hand you could swallow up the object in your subjectivity, and this is the big danger that he sees in the nineteenth century. Idealism was the nineteenth century. But nonetheless there is something in them both. Only theology, he believes, can adequately handle them both, because only theology has an object that is personal – only theology has God, so to speak, a God that becomes personally present in Revelation, and only theology can handle the subjective side in proper relation to this.

The relationship between theology and philosophy is an important one. Barth will assert that theology and philosophy operate on the same ground, and the sort of questions that philosophy raises in this whole area of realism and idealism are also questions that theology deals with:

> **In what sense is the object of our thinking real?**
> **In what sense do our minds really come to terms with this?**

[5] Karl Barth, 'Fate and Idea in Theology', pp. 25-62.

Theology is equally concerned with the truth of the object and also the subject's proper apprehension of it.

iii. Theology and Philosophy

In many ways Barth sees theology and philosophy contending for the same space. This he believes gives it an advantage over natural theology. Natural theology tries to work within a framework of reason, upon which it then pastes theology. True theology, to Barth, will stand by its own subject matter (Revelation) and in the light of this it is able to engage in a proper dialogue with philosophy (reason): theology must attend to its subject matter from Revelation; philosophy from reason.

Therefore, it is by virtue of their different bases that the two disciplines take their distinct character. Ironically he gets this from Kant: what Kant said sceptically we can take seriously – philosophy is a discipline that depends upon reason; theology is a discipline that depends upon Revelation (figure 39). The emphasis on the ideal means that theology needs the concepts of the philosopher: theology is always dependent upon philosophy for its concepts. Theology gets its language from the philosophers. However, what is important is what it makes of these concepts. There is a well-known Barth saying that they may be commandeered by Revelation. We use the language of the world but we must relate them to the object of Revelation.[6]

Theology is not a free-flowing discipline like philosophy; it is dependent upon submission and obedience to its object – to Revelation. Barth realized this; he realized that it was important to understand theology's relationship with and dependence upon Revelation and how things could not be as clear, free-flowing and neatly tied-up as with philosophy.

3. Barth on Anselm

At around the same time that Bultmann is pursuing his demythologizing agenda, and drawing heavily on Heidegger's existential philosophy Barth is drawing back from his colleagues in the so-called group of dialectical theologians: he is going back to older theologians, he is more interested in pre-Thomistic theology. This is where he discovers Anselm. We've discussed Anselm in the context of the development of theology's use of Revelation and reason, how theologians relate Revelation and reason in the history of theology. However, we now need to consider what Barth took from Anselm. What did Barth get in reading Anselm? It is in dialogue with Anselm that Barth develops his theological method. This

[6] See Karl Barth, *The Church Dogmatics* (eds. G. W. Bromiley and T. F. Torrance; Edinburgh: T&T Clark, 1957), Vol. I/1, §.4. 'The Word of God in its Threefold Form', pp. 88–124 and §5 'The Nature of the Word of God', pp. 125–86.

dialogue culminated in his book on Anselm, this can be seen from Barth's work published in 1931, *Fides Quaerens Intellectum* (*Faith Seeking Understanding*).[7]

i. The Ontological Argument

Anselm's ontological argument is given much treatment by Barth. For that matter, Anselm's ontological argument is given much treatment by many theologians and philosophers in the modern period. Charles Hartshorne is a case in point.[8]

Barth wants to argue that Anselm gives him a concept of theological method, which takes him right back beyond the Thomist and Enlightenment traditions of reason and Revelation. The Thomist tradition gives reason an equal status with Revelation, whereas the Enlightenment places reason as more important than Revelation.

What Anselm does is to give faith and/or Revelation priority over reason. For example, the so-called ontological argument by Anselm is prefaced by a prayer; indeed the whole of Anselm's attempts to prove God's existence is prefaced by a prayer. It is not only prefaced by a prayer but Anselm asks that God will grant to him understanding of what was accepted by him in faith. According to Barth, Anselm's theological programme is to begin with faith and on the basis of faith to move to theological understanding. You could say that Anselm is a Barthian before Barth, though of course there is, unlike Barth, an absence of crisis in Anselm's theology. But anyway, you see, Barth would respond to Anselm's principle, that is why we do theology. Anselm's principle is that he does not do theology primarily so that he may understand, he does theology in order that he may believe: Anselm believes in order that he may understand (figure 40, overleaf). Barth argues that it is Anselm's faith that makes him wish to understand. The basis of our rational interest is our faith. So reason is not set against faith. Reason is then seen as the fruit of faith. Christian faith encourages reason. It is no accident that the first Christian theologians happened to be Greek – as is seen in John's Gospel.

7 Karl Barth, *Fides quaerens intellectum – Anselms Beweis der Existenz Gottes im Zusammenhang seines theologischen Programms* (München, Christian: Kaiser Verlag, 1931). English trans. Karl Barth, *Anselm: Fides Quaerens Intellectum* (London: SCM Press, 1960).

8 Charles Hartshorne (1897–2000), prominent American philosopher who focused on philosophy of religion and metaphysics, is attributed with developing what has been termed the neo-classical concept of God. He developed Anselm's ontological argument to produce what is termed a modal proof of the existence of God. See Charles Hartshorne, *Anselm's Discovery* (La Salle, IL: Open Court, 1965); and Charles Hartshorne, *The Divine Relativity: A Social Conception of God*, (New Haven, CT: Yale University Press, 1983 [1948]). See also, Charles Hartshorne, *Beyond Humanism: Essays in the New Philosophy of Nature* (Chicago, IL: Willett, Clark, 1937).

A PHILOSOPHY–THEOLOGY DIALECTIC

True theology will stand by its own
subject matter (Revelation) and engage in
dialogue with philosophy (reason)

Philosophy as a Discipline depends upon Reason

Theology as a Discipline depends upon Revelation

Theology is not a free-flowing discipline like philosophy
it is dependent upon submission
and obedience to its object –

to Revelation

Figure 39

THE ANSELMIAN PRINCIPLE

I believe in order that I may understand.

I do not understand in order that I may believe,

I believe in order
that I may understand.

Figure 40

BARTH ON REASON
IN ANSELM

ratio veritatis

The reason/rationality of the truth, which means God – God is reason itself.

Rationality of the Object of Faith

For Anselm this means the creed. The creed is divine reason encapsulated in the words of the tradition. Anselm is a Medievalist – Barth often comments on the absence of crisis in Anselm's thought. Anselm as a Medievalist simply accepts individual concepts as parts of the whole.

Subjective Reason

This deals with the human capacity to make generalizations and to make judgements, to articulate truth. If we say X and Y are both blue we are exercising our basic human capacity to affirm truth. This is the lowest concept.

Figure 41

THE EPISTEMOLOGICAL PRIORITY OF GOD

For Barth, theology is an exploration

of the inner rationality of God

In so far
as God allows

Figure 42

ii. Barth on Reason in Anselm

In the late 1920s Barth, therefore, examines three concepts of reason which occur in Anselm; these are essential to Barth's later work: these three concepts are, primarily, the *ratio veritis*; second, the rationality of the object of faith and third, subjective reason (figure 41, previous page). Barth perceives in Anselm that God is reason itself: *ratio veritatis*. The creed for Anselm is then the rationality of the object of faith. The creed is divine reason encapsulated in the words of the tradition. Subjective reason is then Anselm's definition of the human capacity to make judgements, to articulate perceived truth. You see, the second level, the rationality of the creed, depends upon the first level, the rationality of truth, and our subjective reason has to depend on the rationality of the creed if it is going to be sound reason.

So there is a strict hierarchy of descent: our words must depend upon, say, the authority of scripture, which in turn must depend upon the authority of God as truth. Natural theology does not work because it operates the other way round. Natural theology wants to decide the meaning of the words first, and then apply them to God and the creed. Proper theological method depends upon the downward movement so that our words must be conformed to Revelation – that is certainly how Barth sees it.

So the key to theology is in maintaining/retaining the epistemological priority of God; our theology must conform to God rather than conforming to others (figure 42, previous page). Some readers of Barth are put off by the apparent lack of argument in this theology: this is a very assertive theology. The reason may be musical – there is an analogy with music here. Just as a composer explores themes by allowing the inner meaning to come out, the musician accepts this and just plays. Yes, I think that is right, you see, Barth is dominated by the Mozartian. One of my criticisms of the McCormack book was that there was no mention of Mozart in it, and I don't think you can understand Barth's theological method without some allusion. Barth's theology is more like theme and variations and then returning to the theme enriched. Argument is not the key: exploration is the key, exploration of the Gospel.

To a certain kind of rationalist it makes it seem that it is assertive, self-confident, even pushy, his theology is so assertive. You see, Anselm seeks the beauty of theology – so does Barth. It is an aesthetic task in the sense that Anselm wants an apprehension in his words of the overall beauty of God; the beauty of God, you see, that is so important.

Barth is setting out his own understanding of the matter: in place of Anselm's definition of God as that than which no greater can be conceived, Barth shifts the emphasis onto scripture. Barth shifts the emphasis from three-fold reason over to a biblical interpretation. Anselm's ontological argument goes as far as asserting that even if he could wish not to believe, he couldn't. Anselm writes of his thanks to God that he has given him proof of *His* existence.

4. Barth and Brunner on Natural Theology

And then, of course, around the time that Barth's book on Anselm was published, there was the big debate between Barth and Brunner – Brunner who used to be one of the group that gathered around Barth after the publication of his *Commentary on Romans*, after the impact that changed theology in Germany because the old liberal establishment just couldn't cope with what Barth had done, what he had said in that commentary. There was a falling out between Barth and Brunner – a big, public, falling out, which went to the heart of the relationship between systematic theology and philosophy, between Revelation and reason.

What was at stake was natural theology. In 1934 Brunner published a polemical tract against Barth entitled *Nature and Grace*. Barth felt it necessary to reply with a simple but forceful *No.*[9] Barth, very much as a result of his studies of Anselm, rejected all natural theology on the grounds that God reveals himself in his Word: if you can know God through his Word, then why bother with natural theology? It was, therefore, pointless to look elsewhere for Revelation. Brunner thought Barth had overstated the case. Brunner commented, listen to this –

> *It is the task of our theological generation to find a way back to a true theologia naturalis.*[10]

Barth in his reply quotes this back at Brunner and then proceeds to repudiate, point by point, blow by blow, systematically – you see, that's the sort of man we are dealing with. Within this refutation Barth defines natural theology as

> *Every positive or negative formulation of a system which claims to be theological, that is to interpret divine revelation, whose subject, however, differs fundamentally from the revelation in Jesus Christ, and whose method therefore differs equally from the exposition of Holy Scripture.*[11]

You see, Barth is not totally against natural theology but believes it undermines the actual knowledge of God mediated through Christ: as ever, he is content-driven.

9 Karl Barth, *Natural Theology – Comprising 'Nature & Grace' by Professor Dr Emil Brunner and the reply 'No!' by Dr Karl Barth* (translation by John Baillie of *Nein!* a pamphlet originally published in 1934 by Barth; and *Natur und Guade*, by Brunner likewise a pamphlet from 1934; London: The Centenary Press, 1946.

10 Karl Barth, *Natural Theology – Comprising 'Nature & Grace' by Professor Dr Emil Brunner and the reply 'No!' by Dr Karl Barth* (translation by John Baillie of *Nein!* a pamphet originally published in 1934 by Barth; and *Natur und Guade*, by Brunner likewise a pamphlet from 1934; London: The Centenary Press, 1946), p. 59

11 Karl Barth, *Natural Theology – Comprising 'Nature & Grace' by Professor Dr Emil Brunner and the reply 'No!' by Dr Karl Barth*, p. 78f.

God revealed in Christ; that's what is important for him, God revealed in Jesus Christ. Natural theology will so often work against it, against Christ.

To Barth the task of his generation was to re-learn what Revelation was, and the grace in Revelation; natural theology was mostly false. To counter Barth, Brunner offers six counter theses: first, the *imago dei*; second; general and specific Revelation; third, the question of God's gracious preservation; fourth, ordinances; fifth, contact; and sixth, that grace can perfect nature.

The *imago dei*: Barth acknowledges that the task of humanity is to be responsible but regards divine grace as part of Revelation and separate from his world. General and specific Revelation: the state of sin is 'un-natural', so humanity finds itself in an un-natural state, you see, and it takes Revelation to make us know God. The sinner is unnatural therefore the sinner can't know God, not without Revelation – that's the key for Barth, you see – not without Revelation.

Barth actually begins to see Brunner as idolatrous because the function of the revealing God in creation is not simply to lead from one religious step to another. He is saying that there is only one theology and that is a theology that is Christological and by grace. Barth questions Brunner's subdividing of grace, he questions Brunner on the existence of this other grace, he asks does this precede the grace of Christ?

Ordinances: Brunner speaks of ordinances – for example, marriage – Barth regards this as madness, he questions whether we have any standard or gauge for measuring these sociological ordinances of creation. To Barth all Revelation, all contact, is miraculous. There is no need to go through it all now, read it, read what Brunner says, read how Barth counters: this is important, you see, it gets right to the heart of what this course is about.

You see, for Barth, by grounding itself in the natural order and not in a free sovereign act of God natural theology can't demonstrate a method that is truly Trinitarian. The problem is starting with humanity and not from God: you see Barth, as ever, is content-led. Revelation must be a unity (figure 43).

Q: regarding Moltmann writing about the Cross revealing God's heart and creation, God's handiwork; Is this so?

Barth would say 'So are there two God's then – Is Revelation a unity? This is the point, 'Is revelation a unity?' If Jesus Christ is the Revelation then he is the criterion – that is the point; that is what would bother him. For Barth, you see, he does not have to deny that Christ is present in all sorts of religions, and in non-religious beliefs. You see for Barth religion is the problem not the solution. Religion is the way by which people project their own deities to escape from uncomfortable reality. That is why he does not like religion as a general category, because that is what Schleiermacher centred on – and this led to this virtual equation of Christianity and liberal culture. For Barth, religion is generally a bad thing.

If you look at the *Commentary on Romans* where Paul uses the word 'law' Barth uses 'religion'. You can see what Barth is getting at: in stating it so boldly, by saying 'law equals religion', Barth is showing the way by which we actually use the deepest side of our nature, our religious side, as an evasion of God (figure 44).The central question all the time for Barth is 'Where do you get your knowledge of God from?

BARTH, BRUNNER AND NATURAL THEOLOGY

REVELATION	NATURAL THEOLOGY
Revelation is grounded in a Free Sovereign Act of God	Grounded in the Natural Order and in thought

Figure 43

BARTH: RELIGION, LAW AND NATURAL THEOLOGY

Where Paul uses the word *'law'*,
Barth uses *'religion'*

↓

Law and philosophy go hand-in-hand
Natural theology is one form of philosophy

↓

Religion, law and natural theology are an evasion:
we project our own deities to escape
from uncomfortable reality.

↓

We use religion, law and natural theology to evade God's self-revelation in Christ

Figure 44

What worries him is that Brunner wants to build a whole structure without Jesus Christ. For Barth, philosophy is that discipline which lives by reason, theology is that discipline which lives by Revelation. Natural theology for Barth is one form of philosophy.

5. The Word of God

So, Barth learned from Anselm the primacy of faith and Revelation. Reason has its place, but belief comes first. There is a lot in Barth's writings in the early 1930s where he is wrestling with this question of natural theology, then – as we have seen – there is the argument, the very public argument in print, with Brunner. And then Barth gets thrown out of Germany by the Nazis, he is expelled from his chair at the University of Bonn because he will not subscribe to the Nazis', their National Socialist religion of blood and soil. So he returns to Switzerland – as soon as the news is out he is offered a chair at the University of Basel – and he spends the next 30 years writing his monumental *Church Dogmatics*.[12]

i. God Reveals Himself as the Lord

So, if the book on Anselm, or more pertinently Barth's study – some would say appropriation – of Anselm, if this was so important to him, something of a watershed in terms of theological method, then what did he do with this understanding?

Barth shifts this into an axiom: God reveals himself as the Lord. Scripture witnesses to thefact that God reveals himself as the Lord. This means, to Barth, that God demonstrates his inescapable reality historically in Jesus Christ.

So, this is what Barth means by Revelation. To Barth this is not propositional Revelation, this is self-revelation: God revealing himself, God unveiling himself in Jesus Christ. Therefore, all theology must consist in some way or other, in all directions, theology must be a response to this fundamental reality that God demonstrates *Himself* in history through Jesus Christ.

This is a very strongly anti-Kantian position. Kant said God can't be known from history because the material world is entirely closed off, God can't be known by the proofs of his existence nor can he be proved from Revelation. Barth says that if God does make himself known through history then he can. So, to Barth, the Christian faith is an assertion.

[12] Colin Gunton specifically recommended Karl Barth, *The Church Dogmatics* (eds. G. W. Bromiley and T. F. Torrance; Edinburgh: T&T Clark, 1936–77), Vol. I/1, §.8 'God in His Revelation', pp. 295–347; and Vol. II/1, §.26 'The Knowability of God', pp. 63–178.

ii. Actuality Implies Possibility

Theology, therefore, allows an answer to who is the God in whom we believe. The answer is a triune God: Schleiermacher put the Trinity at the end; Barth at the beginning. Barth's principle is that actuality does indeed imply possibility. You see, what can happen does happen – in the Incarnation – actuality implies possibility. Some theologians regard this as trivial. Robert Jensen criticizes this as hovering between obfuscation and triviality: but obviously what does happen can happen. According to Barth the whole of nineteenth-century theology and philosophy was a denial of this. According to nineteenth-century theologians and philosophers you had to start with human experience.

6. Christ Jesus: The Word of God Revealed

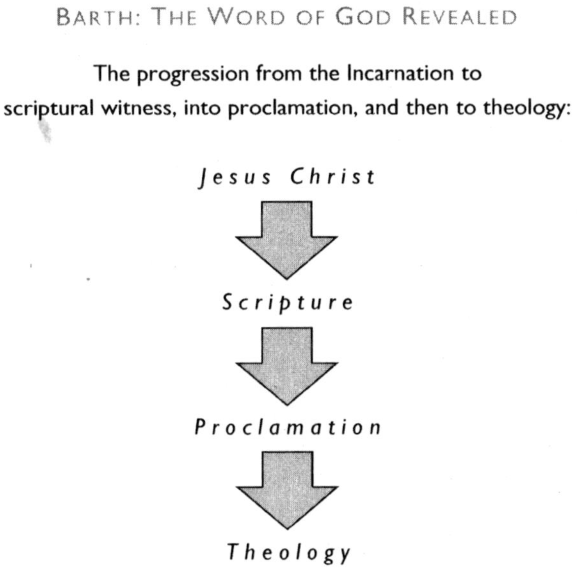

Figure 45

Barth argues that Christian theology begins in God, with God and God's Revelation. He understands scripture as witnessing to God's self-revelation. Barth states this early on in *The Church Dogmatics*, which has caused immense problems. This is the doctrine of the three forms of God, which allows theologians to hold together a liberal and evangelical position regarding scripture.

i. The Word of God Revealed

First, ***The Word of God Revealed***: the Word of God revealed is the prior reality. Jesus Christ is the Word of God, the Word of God revealed, this is that from which all else depends, all else flows.

ii. The Word of God Written

Second, ***The Word of God Written***: The word of God written is scripture; yes? This is where Barth has deeply offended certain evangelicals and fundamentalists: scripture is only the Word of God in so far as it represents Jesus Christ who is the Word of God. Scripture *becomes* the Word of God as, and in so far as, it represents the Word of God: Jesus Christ. This is a highly Christocentric interpretation of scripture. This is a very modern doctrine as it is designed to accept a historical–critical approach, which would argue that scripture is a human production. He will agree with the sceptics that scripture, the Bible, is a human book, but in so far as it mediates Jesus it is also a divine book.

iii. Human Proclamation

Third, ***Human Proclamation***: Human Proclamation, including preaching and theology, can become divine truth in so far as it remains true to the scriptural witness to the Word of God. So we have a progression (figure 45). So, the hierarchy runs from Jesus Christ the event of Revelation, through scripture, which witnesses to this act of Revelation, to proclamation then to theology. To Barth, theology is a servant of the church's proclamation of the Word of God. Theology's task is not to convince the world through apologetics. Barth is sceptical of apologetics; this is theology on the world's terms. Theology must be true to its content: the Gospel.

7. Conclusion: Barth on Revelation and Reason

What is Barth's position on Revelation and reason? How does this progression of the Word of God revealed work out in the world? Well, the crucial concept is to be found in the first volume of his *Church Dogmatics*: §4, 'The Word of God in its Threefold Form'.[13] This is a theology of the Word of God, but the question then arises – What do you mean by the Word of God? Barth presents the answer in a

[13] Karl Barth, *The Church Dogmatics* (eds. G. W. Bromiley and T. F. Torrance; Edinburgh: T&T Clark, 1936–77), Vol. I/1, §.4, 'The Word of God in its Threefold Form', pp. 88–124.

three-fold form, in three concepts: i. The Word of God Preached; ii. The Word of God Written; iii. The Word of God Revealed. These three concepts correspond to Anselm's view of the three levels of rationality – so, you see, the influence of Anselm is there.

i. Preached: Barth's Doctrine of Proclamation

The Word of God preached: this involves proclamation does it not? And, of course, such proclamation may not always be verbal. For Barth, proclamation in the church is simply and visibly there just as bread and wine are; OK, you see, a very interesting way of putting it. Though they are simply and visibly there, they are also not simply and visibly there: so, dialectic. Because they may be obvious to us, they may be obvious to believers in the church as proclamation bearers, but not everybody perceives them.

What we have here is an involvement in the realities of Revelation and faith. They are simply there, but they have to become there. Such dialectic is characteristic of Barth: they are given but they are not. This can be interpreted as meaning that they are re-given in every generation. Central to this is that there is no proclamation without, or apart from, a prior reality: proclamation is only there if there is something prior – and that is God. Proclamation is a commission given by God. Human talk about God is on the basis of God's own direction, which transcends all human causation. This implies that all talk about God is directed by God, not simply taken on by human beings but in a way that transcends our own human causation. It simply takes place and has to be acknowledged as a fact.

First of all we have God's self-revelation, God's self-objectification, so we can know and see him. This is God's judgement and it is never under our control. It is God's own speech, and it is inevitably superior to all others. If it is true proclamation it is going to be given by God. You must judge it, otherwise we are speaking our own words. We may speak human words but if they are really to become proclamation then they must be God's words. Therefore, human words become God's words in so far as God enables them to become God's words. But this is not to set aside the human part: Christ was human, became human. He was fully divine *and* fully human. Christology is essential here: Christ is true man; Christ is truly human, therefore, human words can become the words of God because of the Incarnation. Christologically Barth, therefore, sees everything on the divine and the human level: Jesus Christ is human as well as God's Word. Therefore, this is the first form of the three-fold Word of God. This is not very contentious, at least not for people in the Reformation tradition. But it is important to remember that the preacher's words or actions are not automatically God's Words. Preaching is not automatically God's Word: if it is, it is by grace.

ii. Written: Barth's Doctrine of Scripture

Here we have the beginning of Barth's doctrine of scripture. This is not an actual doctrine of scripture, but it is the beginning – it is about how scripture mediates God's Word. Proclamation depends upon scripture, but preaching or proclamation must depend upon the Word of God written. Proclamation happens in recollection of past Revelation and then expectation of coming Revelation: and this is why the canon of scripture is constituted.

The canon of scripture constitutes proclamation because it imposes itself on the church. It is here that Barth comes into relationship with modern criticism; this is also where he comes into conflict with modern biblical criticism: faith in God can so easily be replaced by faith in the historical–critical method. Barth accepts that scripture has been critically treated and will continue to be so, Barth's doctrine allows for this, as long as one is aware of one's presuppositions. He does not deny the humanity of the text. In certain respects scripture is just like any other ordinary book, but this is only the beginning – theology takes over from this starting point. In scripture God's event becomes God's Word through human words. The Bible is God's Word to the extent that he causes it to be God's Word. 'Scripture' is therefore, to Barth, a human word and can remain a human word unless God actually makes it a divine word.

This is an actualistic view; for Barth the 'Bible' is a human word that must and forever become God's Word. Scripture then becomes the Word of God today when it is read and it is said to be the Word of God, in so far as God declares it as such. Barth possibly places too much stress on how scripture becomes the Word of God today and too little stress on how it was received as the Word of God when it was originally written down, or how it was inspired to be the Word of God, by God, when it was originally written down. What Barth is trying to do is not put false values on scripture and thereby diminish God's truth.

iii. Revealed: The Event of Salvation

The Bible is not as such God's past Revelation but it bears witness to it: Jesus Christ is Revelation. Scripture is not Revelation except in so far as it points to Jesus who is Revelation – though scripture is, of course, revealing. He would not say it was not. Jesus as the Word is Revelation and scripture points to him. It is not scripture you worship, it is God. Scripture is there simply to point to Christ. So Christ is the Word of God. Scripture is, or becomes, the Word of God in so far as it points to Christ – and by that he means both the Old and the New Testaments. Scripture as witness is Barth's main concept: scripture witnesses to God's act in Christ.

On the one hand, he says, *Deus dixit* ('God spoke') on the other *Paulus dixit* ('Paul spoke'): these two become one and the same in the event of the Word of God. So the Word of God is the presence of the Word of God to the world in

Jesus. That is the Word of God revealed. The other forms of the Word of God are derivative from it. Scripture points to Jesus as the Word of God – it is this that is the Revelation. Jesus Christ as Revelation, witnessed to, attested to by scripture is the criterion for all theology.

iv. Barth Proclaims Jesus as Revelation

So that is Revelation – it is not just an event and knowledge – it is an event of salvation. So Revelation doesn't just mean information for Barth. You see, it means God happening in a saving but also informative way, a way we can understand. This happened, and this is what the Old Testament as the Word of Prophecy and the New Testament as the Word of Fulfilment both proclaim as having happened.

It has happened, conclusively totally and sufficiently. He was with us and the New Testament and the Old Testament are the Word of God, in so far as they proclaim this as having happened. And as I have said these three forms are rather like Anselm's hierarchy of reason. Reason is important but the event of Revelation comes first. Reason is important in that we realize this, we comprehend and we proclaim.

Let me just repeat that Revelation is God happening in Christ! God taking place in time! God taking place in time in the way in which I have just said: that is Revelation. Then you need to ask how you can unpack it, what it means to say that God happened in time, and so on. Barth then writes theology to explain this: all the volumes of *The Church Dogmatics*.

Appendix

Course C401 Revelation and Reason and a Session of the Research Institute for Systematic Theology, Department of Theology and Religious Studies, King's College London, from which this material was transcribed.

In this lecture and seminar programme, from which this work is transcribed, Colin Gunton gave 2-hour lectures for weeks 1–3. The academic papers given on weeks 4-11 were presented by MA students, each paper a maximum of 20 minutes duration. Although there was scope for questions Colin Gunton spent most of the remaining 40 minutes commenting on the subject of the paper and expanding on many of the related issues.

Michaelmas Term 1999

The Research Institute in Systematic Theology

Tuesday 28 September	AM: Colin Gunton, paper entitled 'I Know that my Redeemer Lives'

MA in Systematic Theology, course C401

Tuesday 28 September	PM: Colin Gunton, lecture, from 'Reason and Revelation' to 'Revelation and Reason'
Tuesday 5 October	PM: Colin Gunton, lecture, 'The Modern Problem in Historical Context'
Tuesday 12 October	PM: Colin Gunton, lecture, 'Aspects of Barth on Faith and Reason'
Tuesday 19 October	PM: Papers: a) Hans Urs von Balthasar, and b) John Locke
Tuesday 26 October	PM: Papers: a) dei verbum – Vatican II, and b) Jonathan Edwards
Tuesday 2 November	PM: Papers a) Torrance & Revelation, and b) Pannenberg & Revelation

Tuesday 9 November	No seminars
Tuesday 16 November	PM: Papers a) Barth & Brunner on Revelation, and b) The Bible & Revelation
Tuesday 23 November	PM: Papers a) Barth on Schleiermacher, and b) Foundationalism
Tuesday 30 November	PM: Papers a) Hegel, and b) Bultmann & Heidegger
Tuesday 7 December	PM: Papers a) Tradition, and b) Aquinas
Tuesday 14 December	PM: Papers a) Revelation & Relationship, and b) Lindbeck

Michaelmas Term 2000

MA in Systematic Theology, course C401

Tuesday 31 October	PM: Paper a) Karl Rahner
Tuesday 14 November	PM: Paper a) René Descartes

BIBLIOGRAPHY

I. Revelation and Reason – Related Works

This bibliography contains works cited by Colin Gunton and works listed as recommended reading for the course C401, cited either at the beginning of the course or given out at the end of each session. In addition are all the works referenced in the text even if referred to obliquely by Colin Gunton. In addition, I have also added related works where deemed relevant, particularly those published in the intervening years since Colin Gunton gave this course.

Books

A Declaration of Faith (London: The Congregational Union of England and Wales, 1967).

Abbott, Walter, *The Documents of Vatican II* (New York, NY: Guild Press, 1966).

Akeroyd, Richard H., *Reason and Revelation: from Paul to Pascal* (Macon, GA: Mercer University Press, 1991).

Anselm of Canterbury, St, *The Proslogion*, in Brian Davies and G. R. Evans, *Anselm of Canterbury – The Major Works* (Oxford World Classics, Oxford: Oxford University Press, 1998.)

Aquinas, St Thomas, *Summa Theologiae* (the complete paperback set: 60 volumes, plus one index volume; dual language, Latin–English; Cambridge: Cambridge University Press, 2006 [1962–76]).

Augustine, *City of God* (trans. Henry Bettenson; Harmondsworth: Penguin Books, 1972).

Augustine, *Confessions* (Oxford World Classics; trans. Henry Chadwick; Oxford: Oxford University Press, 1991).

Augustine, *Of True Religion* (Washington, DC: Regnery Publishing, 1991).

Baillie, John, Hugh Martin and Gustaf Aulén, *Revelation* (London: Faber and Faber, 1937).

Baillie, John, *Our knowledge of God* (New York: Scribner, 1959).

Baillie, John, *The Idea of Revelation in Recent Thought* (New York: Columbia University Press, 1956).

Balthasar, Hans Urs von, *Karl Barth, Darstellung und Deutung seiner Theologie* (Köln: Verlag Jakob Hegner, 1951). English trans. *The Theology of Karl Barth –*

Exposition and Interpretation (trans. Edward T. Oates SJ; San Francisco: Ignatius Press, Communio Books, 1991).

Balthasar, Hans Urs von, *The Glory of the Lord* (*Herrlichkeit*, trans. Andrew Louth, Francis McDonagh and Brian McNeil 1982–91; 7 vols; the first part of his 16-volume trilogy of systematics: *Herrlichkeit*, 1961–9, *Theodramatik*, 1973–83 and *Theologik*, 1985; London: Continuum, T&T Clark, 2003).

Banner, Michael C., *The Justfication of Science and the Rationality of Religious Belief* (Oxford: Clarendon Press, 1990).

Barth, Karl, *Der Römerbrief* (Erste Fassung; Zürich: Theologischer Verlag Zürich, 1985 [1919]).

Barth, Karl, *Der Römerbrief* (Zweite Fassung; Zürich: Theologischer Verlag Zürich, 1999 [1922]). English trans. *The Epistle to the Romans* (trans. Edwyn Hoskyns; Oxford: Oxford University Press, 1933).

Barth, Karl, *Die Christliche Dogmatik im Entwurf – Erste Band Die Lehre vom Worte Gottes, Prolegomena zur christlichen Dogmatik 1927* (Gesamtausgabe 14; Zürich: Theologischer Verlag Zürich, 1982).

Barth, Karl, *Die protestantische Theologie im 19. Jahrhundert* (Zürich: Theologischer Verlag Zürich, 1947). English trans. *Protestant Theology in the Nineteenth Century* (trans. Brian Cozens and John Bowden, intro. Colin E. Gunton; London: SCM Press, 2001 [1959]).

Barth, Karl, *Dogmatik im Grundriß* (München: Christian Kaiser Verlag, 1947). English trans. *Dogmatics in Outline – Lectures on the Creed* (trans. G. T. Thomson; London: SCM Press, 2001 [1949]).

Barth, Karl, *Evangelische Theologie im 19. Jahrhundert* (Zollikon–Zurich: Evangelischer Verlag AG, 1956).

Barth, Karl, *Fides quaerens intellectum – Anselms Beweis der Existenz Gottes im Zusammenhang seines theologischen Programms* (München: Christian Kaiser Verlag, 1931). English trans. *Anselm: Fides Quaerens Intellectum* (London: SCM Press, 1960).

Barth, Karl, *Natural Theology – Comprising 'Nature & Grace' by Professor Dr Emil Brunner and the reply 'No!' by Dr Karl Barth* (trans. by John Baillie of *Nein!* a pamphet originally published in 1934 by Barth; and *Natur und Guade*, by Brunner, likewise a pamphlet from 1934; London: The Centenary Press, 1946).

Barth, Karl, *Wolfgang Amadeus Mozart 1756/1956* (Zürich: TVZ, 1956). English trans. *Wolfgang Amadeus Mozart* (trans. Clarence K. Pott, foreword, John Updike; Eugene, OR: Wipf & Stock, 1986).

Berkeley, George, *Three Dialogues between Hylas and Philonous, in Opposition to Sceptics and Atheists* (1713) (London: Dent, 1910).

Bernstein, R., *Beyond Objectivism and Relativism: Science, Hermeneutics, and Praxis* (Philadelphia, PA: University of Pennsylvania Press, 1983).

Bettoni, Efrem, *Duns Scotus; The Basic Principles of his Philosophy* (trans. B. Bonansea; Westport, CT: Greenwood Press, 1978).

Blumenberg, Hans, *The Legitimacy of the Modern Age* (trans. R. M. Wallace; Cambridge, MA: MIT Press, 1983).

Boethius, *The Consolation of Philosophy* (trans. V. E. Watts; Harmondsworth: Penguin Books, Penguin Classics, 1999).

Brunner, Emil, *Revelation and Reason: The Christian Doctrine of Faith and Knowledge* (trans. Olive Wyon; Philadelphia, PA: The Westminster Press, 1946).

Brunner, Emil, *The Mediator.A Study of the Central Doctrine of the Christian Faith* (Philadelphia, PA: Westminster Press, 1947), p. 262.

Buckley, Michael J., *The Origins of Modern Atheism* (New Haven, CT: Yale University Press, 1987).

Butler, Basil Christopher, *The theology of Vatican II* (London: Darton, Longman & Todd, 1967).

Cantor, Geoffrey, *Michael Faraday: Sandemanian and Scientist. A Study of Science and Religion in the Nineteenth Century* (London: Macmillan, 1991).

Chadwick, Henry, *Boethius, The Consolations of Music, Logic, Theology, and Philosophy* (Oxford: Oxford University Press, Clarendon Press, 1981).

Chesterton, G. K., *Orthodoxy* (Peabody, MA: Hendrickson Publishers, new edn, 2006).

Chesterton, G. K., *St Thomas Aquinas* (Garden City, NY: Image Books, 1956).

Chung, Sung (ed.), *Karl Barth and Evangelical Theology: Convergences and Divergences* (Milton Keynes: Paternoster Press, 2006).

Coleridge, Samuel Taylor, *Biographia Literaria: or, Biographical Sketches of My Literary Life and Opinions* (ed. and intro. George Watson, Everyman's library 11; London: Dent, 1956).

Coleridge, Samuel Taylor, *Collected Letters of Samuel Taylor Coleridge*, Vol. II: *1801–1806* (ed. E. L. Griggs; Oxford: Clarendon Press, 1956), p. 388.

Coleridge, Samuel Taylor, *Confessions of an Inquiring Spirit* (1840) (Stanford, CA: Stanford University Press, 1957).

Coleridge, Samuel Taylor, *The Complete Works of Samuel Taylor Coleridge* (Ann Arbor, MI: Scholarly Publishing Office, University of Michigan Library, 2006).

Coleridge, Samuel Taylor, *The Table Talk of S. T. Coleridge* (intro. H. Morley; London: Routledge, 1884).

Craig, Edward, *The Mind of God and the Works of Man* (Oxford: Oxford University Press, 1987).

Currey, Cecil B. *Reason and Revelation: John Duns Scotus on Natural Theology* (Chicago: Franciscan Herald Press, 1977).

Cyprian, St, of Carthage, *On the Church* (Vol. I. *Select Letters*, Vol. II. *Select Treatises*) (trans. with intro. and commentary, Allen Brent; Popular Patristics Series, no 32 and 33; Crestwood, NY: St Vladimir's Seminary Press, 2007).

Dalferth, Ingolf U., *Theology and Philosophy* (Oxford: Blackwell, 1988).

Dawson, Robert Dale, *The Resurrection in Karl Barth* (Barth Studies Series; Aldershot: Ashgate Publishing, 2007).

DeHart, Paul J., *The Trial of the Witnesses – The Rise and Decline of Postliberal Theology* (Series: Challenges in Contemporary Theology: Oxford: Blackwell, 2006).

Descartes, René, *A Discourse on the Method of Correctly Conducting One's Reason and Seeking Truth in the Sciences* (trans. and ed. Ian Maclean; Oxford: Oxford University Press, 2006).

Descartes, René, *Descartes: Selected Writings from 'Discourse on Method', 'Meditations on the First Philosophy' and 'The Principles of Philosophy'* (trans. John Veitch; London: Collector's Library, 2004).

Descartes, René, *Les Principes de la Philosophie* (ed. Claude Picot; Rouen: Chez Jean-Baptiste Besongne, 1698.

Descartes, René, *Méditations métaphysiques* (ed. André Robinet; Paris: J. Vrin, 1976).

Descartes, René, *Méditations, Objections, and Replies* (trans. and ed. Roger Ariew; Donald A. Cress; Indianapolis, IN: Hackett, 2006).

Descartes, René, *Oeuvre Scientifique. Premiere et Deuxieme Parties*: Tome V, *Les Principes de la Philosophie* (Clermont-Ferrand: Paleo,1999).

Descartes, René, *Philosophical Essays and Correspondence* (trans. Roger Ariew; Indianapolis: Hackett, 2000).

Descartes, René, *The Method, Meditations and Philosophy of Descartes* (trans. John Veitch; Whitefish, MT: Kessinger, 2004).

Dodd, C. H., *According to the Scriptures. The Substructure of New Testament Theology* (London: Collins, 1965 [1952]).

Dodd, C. H., *The Apostolic Preaching and its Developments: Three Lectures with an Appendix on Eschatology and History* (London: Hodder and Stoughton, 1936).

Downing, Francis Gerald, *Has Christianity Revelation?* (London: SCM Press, 1964).

Einstein, Albert, *The World as I See It* (trans. Alan Harris; London: John Lane The Bodley Head, 1935).

Elert, Werner, *Der Ausgang der altkirchlichen Chrzstologie* (Berlin: Lutherisches Verlagshaus, 1957).

Fackre, Gabriel, *The Doctrine of Revelation a Narrative Interpretation* (Edinburgh: Edinburgh University Press, 1997).

Feuerbach, Ludwig, *Das Wesen des Christentums* (1841) (ed. W. Schuffenhauer, Gesammelte Werke, vol. 5; Berlin: Akademie Verlag, 1973). English trans. *The Essence of Christianity* (Amherst, NY: Prometheus Books, 1989).

Fichte, Johann Gottlieb, *Attempt at a Critique of all Revelation* (Cambridge: Cambridge University Press, 1978).

Findlay, J. N., *Hegel: A Re-examination* (Muirhead Library of Philosophy; London: Routledge, 2002 [1958]).

Fisher, Simon, *Revelatory Positivism? Barth's Earliest Theology and the Marburg School* (Oxford: Oxford University Press, 1988).

Flannery, Austin, *Documents of Vatican II* (Grand Rapids, MI: Eerdmans, 1975).

Flannery, Austin, *Vatican Council II: the Conciliar and Post Conciliar Documents* (Northport, NY: Costello, 1984).

Forsyth, P. T., *The Principle of Authority* (London: Independent Press, 1952 [1913]).

Frei, Hans Wilhelm, George Hunsinger and William C. Placher, *Theology and Narrative: Selected Essays* (Oxford: Oxford University Press, 1993).

Frei, Hans Wilhelm, George Hunsinger and William C. Placher, *Types of Christian Theology* (New Haven, CT: Yale University Press, 1994).

Frei, Hans Wilhelm, *The Doctrine of Revelation in the Thought of Karl Barth, 1902–1922: the Nature of Barth's Break with Liberalism* (New Haven, CT: Yale University Press, 1956).

Frei, Hans Wilhelm, *The Eclipse of Biblical Narrative: A Study in Eighteenth and Nineteenth Century Hermeneutics* (New Haven, CT: Yale University Press, 1974).

Frei, Hans Wilhelm, *The Identity of Jesus Christ: the Hermeneutical Bases of Dogmatic Theology* (Philadelphia, PA: Fortress Press, 1975).

Funkenstein, Amos, *Theology and the Scientific Imagination from the Middle Ages to the Seventeenth Century* (Princeton: Princeton University Press, 1986).

German, Terence J., *Hamann on Language and Religion* (Oxford: Oxford University Press, 1981).

Gilson, Etienne, *Reason and Revelation in the Middle Ages* (New York: C. Scribner's Sons, 1938).

Gorringe, Timothy, *Karl Barth: Against Hegemony* (Oxford: Oxford University Press, 1999).

Gunton, Colin E., *A Brief Theology of Revelation* (Edinburgh: T&T Clark, 1995). This work contains the series of six lectures Colin Gunton gave at Princeton Theological Seminary in 1993, the Warfield Lectures.

Harding, Anthony John, *Coleridge and the Inspired Word* (Kingston, ON: McGill-Queen's University Press, 1985).

Harnack, Adolf von, *Das Wesen des Christentums* (Tübingen: Mohr Siebeck, 2005 [1900]).

Harnack, Adolf von, *History of Dogma*, Vol. VI (trans. W. McGilchrist; London: Williams & Norgate, 1899).

Hart, Ray L., *Unfinished Man and the Imagination: Toward an Ontology and a Rhetoric of Revelation* (New York, NY: Herder and Herder, 1968).

Hart, Trevor A., *Faith Thinking: the Dynamics of Christian Theology* (Downers Grove, IL: InterVarsity Press, 1996).

Hartshorne, Charles, *Beyond Humanism: Essays in the New Philosophy of Nature* (Chicago, IL: Willett, 1937).

Hartshorne, Charles, *The Divine Relativity: A Social Conception of God* (New Haven, CT: Yale University Press, 1983 [1948]).

Harvey, Van Austin, *The Historian and the Believer; the Morality of Historical Knowledge and Christian Belief* (New York, NY: Macmillan, 1966).

Hauerwas, Stanley, *A Community of Character: Toward a Constructive Christian Social Ethic* (Notre Dame and London: University of Notre Dame Press, 1981).

Haymes, Brian, *The Concept of the Knowledge of God* (New York, NY: St Martin's Press, 1988).

Hegel, Georg Wilhelm Friedrich, *Early Theological Writings* (trans. T. M. Knox; Chicago, IL: University of Chicago Press), pp. 20–21.

Hegel, Georg Wilhelm Friedrich, *Phänomenologie des Geistes* (1807). English trans. *Phenomenology of Spirit* (trans. A. V. Miller, foreword J. N. Findlay; Oxford: Clarendon Press, 1977).

Heidegger, Martin, *On Being and Time* (Chicago, IL: University of Chicago Press, 2002 [1927].

Helm, Paul, *The Divine Revelation: The Basic Issues* (Westchester, IL: Crossway Books, 1982).

Herrmann, Wilhelm, *The Communion of the Christian with God* (Philadelphia: Fortress Press, 1971).

John Hick, *An Interpretation of Religion: Human Responses to the Transcendent* (Basingstoke: Macmillan, 1989).

Hillerdal, Gunnar, *Reason and Revelation in Richard Hooker* (Lund: CWK Gleerup, 1962).

Hodge, Charles, *Systematic Theology*, Vol. 1 (reprinted, Grand Rapids, MI: Eerdmans, 1989).

Holmes, Richard, *Coleridge: Darker Reflections* (London: HarperCollins, 1998).

Jasper, David, *Coleridge as Poet and Religious Thinker: Inspiration and Revelation* (London: Macmillan, 1985).

Jenson, Robert W., *God After God: The God of the Past and the God of the Future, Seen in the Work of Karl Barth* (Indianapolis and New York: Bobbs Merrill, 1969).

Jenson, Robert W., *Systematic Theology* (Oxford: Oxford University Press, 1997).

Jenson, Robert W., *Unbaptized God: The Basic Flaw in Ecumenical Theology* (Minneapolis, MN: Fortress Press, 1992).

Kant, Immanuel, *Critique of Pure Reason* (intro. Howard Caygill; trans. Norman Kemp Smith; Basingstoke: Palgrave Macmillan, 2007).

Kant, Immanuel, *Kant: Critique of Practical Reason* (Cambridge Texts in the History of Philosophy; eds. Mary J. Gregor, Karl Ameriks and Desmond M. Clarke, intro. Andrews Reath; Cambridge: Cambridge University Press, new edn, 1997).

Kant, Immanuel, *Kant's Critique of Judgement* (trans. Ruth F. Chadwick and Clive Cazeaux; London: Routledge, 1992).

Kant, Immanuel, *Religion within the Boundaries of Mere Reason and Other Writings* (trans. and eds. Allen Wood and George Di Giovanni; introd. by Robert Merrihew Adams; Cambridge: Cambridge University Press, 1998).

Käsemann, Ernst, *An die Römer* (Tübingen: Mohr, 1973).

Käsemann, Ernst, *Das Neue Testament als Kanon* (Göttingen: Vandenhoeck und Ruprecht, 1970).

Käsemann, Ernst, *Exegetische Versuche und Besinnungen* (Göttingen: Vandenhoeck und Ruprecht, 1964).

Käsemann, Ernst, *Paulinische Perspektiven* (Tübingen: Mohr, 1969).

Kelsey, David H., *The Uses of Scripture in Recent Theology* (Philadelphia, PA: Fortress Press, 1975).

Kerr, Fergus, *The Later Wittgenstein and Theology* (Oxford: Blackwell, 1986).

Kierkegaard, Søren, *Concluding Unscientific Postscript to Philosophical Fragments* (ed. and trans. Howard V. Hong and Edna H. Kong; Princeton, NJ: Princeton University Press, 1992).

Kierkegaard, Søren, *Philosophical Fragments: Johannes Climacus* (ed. and trans. Howard V. Hong and Edna H. Kong; Princeton, NJ: Princeton University Press, 1985).

Kierkegaard, Søren, *Purity of Heart is to Will One Thing* (New York, NY: Harper and Row, 1938).

Kierkegaard, Søren, *The Sickness Unto Death* (trans. Alistair Hannay; Harmondsworth: Penguin Books, 1989).

Kierkegaard, Søren, *Training in Christianity* (trans. Walter Lowrie; Oxford: Oxford University Press, 1941).

Lane, William L., *Hebrews 9–13 Word Biblical Commentary*, Vol. 47 (Dallas, TX: Word Books, 1991).

Lindbeck, George A., *The Nature of Doctrine: Religion and Theology in a Postliberal Age* (London: SPCK, 1984).

Locke, John, *An Essay Concerning Human Understanding* (ed. R. S. Woolhouse; Harmondsworth: Penguin Books, Penguin Classics, 1997).

Locke John, *The Reasonableness of Christianity: as Delivered in the Scriptures* (Clarendon Edition of the Works of John Locke, ed. John C. Higgins-Biddle; Oxford: Oxford University Press, Clarendon Press; 2000).

Loughlin, Gerard, *Telling God's Story: Bible, Church, and Narrative Theology* (Cambridge: Cambridge University Press, 1996).

Luther, Martin, *Dr Martin Luther, Werke: Kritische Gesamtsusgabe* (Band 51; Weimar: Herman Boehlaus Nachfolger, 1914), p. 126.

McCollah, Gerald W., *Christ's Person and Life-Work in the Theology of Albrecht Ritschl: with Special Attention to Munus Triplex* (Lanham, MD: University Press of America, 1990).

McCormack, Bruce, *Karl Barth's Critically Realistic Dialectical Theology: Its Genesis and Development 1909–1936* (Oxford: Oxford University Press, Clarendon Paperbacks, 1995).

McDonald, H. D., *Ideas of Revelation: An Historical Survey 1700–1860* (London: St. Martin's Press, 1959).

MacDonald, Neil B., *Karl Barth and the Strange New World Within the Bible: Barth, Wittgenstein and the Metadilemmas of the Enlightenment* (Milton Keynes: Paternoster Theological Monographs, Paternoster Press, 2005).

McFague, Sallie, *Metaphorical Theology: Models of God in Religious Language* (London: SCM Press, 1983).

McGrath, Alister, *The Genesis of Doctrine: a Study in the Foundations of Doctrinal Criticism* (Cambridge, MA: Blackwells, 1990).

MacIntyre, Alasdair C., *Hegel: a Collection of Critical Essays* (Garden City, NY: Anchor Books, 1972).

MacIntyre, Alasdair C., *Marxism and Christianity* (New York, NY: Schocken Books, 1968).

MacIntyre, Alasdair C., *New Essays in Philosophical Theology* (New York: Macmillan, 1964).

MacIntyre, Alasdair C., *After Virtue: A Study in Moral Theory* (London: Duckworth, 1981).

Marsh, Clive, *Albrecht Ritschl and the Problem of the Historical Jesus* (Lewiston, NY: Edwin Mellen Press, 1992).

Martin, Bernard, *The Existentialist Theology of Paul Tillich* (New York: Bookman Associates, 1963).

Maximus the Confessor, *Centuries*, 1108A–B. See, St Maximus the Confessor, *The Ascetic Life, The Four Centuries on Charity* (ed. Polycarp Sherwood; Series, Ancient Christian Writers; Mahwah, NJ: Paulist Press, 1955).

Michalson, Gordon E., Jn, *Fallen Freedom: Kant on Radical Evil and Moral Regeneration* (Cambridge: Cambridge University Press, 1990).

Moltmann, Jurgen, *Theology of Hope* (trans. J. W. Leitch: London: SCM Press, 1965).

Mueller, David L., *An Introduction to the Theology of Albrecht Ritschl* (Philadelphia, PA: Westminster Press, 1969).

Murphy, Nancey C., *Theology in the Age of Scientific Reasoning* (Ithaca, NY: Cornell University Press, 1990).

Nebelsick, Harold, *The Renaissance, the Reformahon and the Rise of Science* (Edinburgh: T&T Clark, 1992).

Aland, Barbara, Kurt Aland, Johannes Karavidopoulos (eds.), *Nestle-Aland Novum Testamentum Graece* (Stuttgart: Deutsche Bibelgesellschaft, 1995 [1979]), p. 410.

Newell, R. W., *Objectivity, Empiricism and Truth* (London: Routledge & Kegan Paul, 1986).

Newman, John Henry, *An Essay on the Development of Doctrine* (1845) (Harmondsworth: Penguin Books, 1974).

Niebuhr, H. R., *The Meaning of Revelation* (New York, NY: Macmillan, 1941).

Niebuhr, H. Richard, *Revelation and the Meaning of History. Being the Dudleian Lecture for the Academic Year 1941–1942, delivered in Andover Chapel, April 14, 1942* (Cambridge, MA: Harvard Divinity School, 1943).

Nimmo, Paul T. *Being in Action. The Theological Shape of Barth's Ethical Vision* (London: Continuum, T&T Clark, 2007).

Norris, Christopher, *Uncritical Theory: Postmodernism, Intellectuals and the Gulf War* (London: Lawrence & Wishart, 1992).

Novak, David, *Jewish–Christian Dialogue: a Jewish Justification* (Oxford: Oxford University Press, 1989).

Novak, David, *Law and Theology in Judaism* (2 vol; New York: Ktav, 1974).

O'Collins, Gerald, *Fundamental Theology* (New York, NY: Paulist Press, 1981).

O'Collins, Gerald and René Latourelle, *Problems and Perspectives of Fundamental Theology* (New York, NY: Paulist Press, 1982).

O'Dell Bullock, Karen, *Shepherd's Notes: Writings of Justin Martyr* (Nashville, TN: B&H, 1999).

Origen of Alexandria, *On First Principles: Being Koetschau's Text of the De Principiis Translated into English* (trans. G. W. Butterworth; intro. Henri De Lubac; Goucester, MA: Peter Smith new edn, 2002 [1985]).

Overbeck, Franz, *How Christian is Our Present-Day Theology?* (trans. Martin Henry; London: Continuum, T&T Clark, 2005).

Overbeck, Franz, *On the Christianity of Theology* (trans. John Elbert Wilson; San Jose, CA: Pickwick Publications, 2002).

Owen, Huw Parri, *Revelation and Existence: a Study in the Theology of Rudolf Bultmann* (Cardiff: University of Wales Press, 1957).

Pannenberg, Wolfhart (ed.), *Revelation as History* (trans. E. Quinn; London: Macmillan, 1968).

Pannenberg, Wolfhart, *Jesus – God and Man* (trans. Lewis L. Wilkins and Duane A. Priebe; Philadelphia, PA: Westminster Press, 1968).

Pannenberg, Wolfhart, *Metaphysik und Gottesgedanke* (Göttingen: Vandenhoeck & Ruprecht, 1988); English trans. *Metaphysics and the Idea of God* (trans. Philip Clayton; Grand Rapids, MI: Eerdmans, 1990).

Pannenberg, Wolfhart, *Systematic Theology* (3 vols. trans. Geoffrey W. Bromiley; London: Continuum, T&T Clark, 2004 ([1919]).

Pannenberg, Wolfhart, *Theology and the Philosophy of Science* (Philadelphia, PA: Westminster Press, 1976).

Persson, Per Erik, *Sacra Doctrina: Reason and Revelation in Aquinas* (Philadelphia, Fortress Press, 1970).

Philo of Alexandria, *The Works of Philo: Complete and Unabridged* (trans. Charles Duke Yonge; foreword, David M. Scholer; Peabody, MA: Hendrickson, 1993).

Pieper, Josef, *Scholasticism; Personalities and Problems of Medieval Philosophy* (trans. Richard and Clara Winston; London: Faber & Faber, 1960).

Plantinga, Alvin (ed.), *Faith and Philosophy* (Grand Rapids, MI: Eerdmans, 1964).

Plantinga, Alvin, *God and Other Minds* (rev. 2nd edn; Ithaca, NY: Cornell University Press, 1990 [1967]).

Plantinga, Alvin, *God, Freedom, and Evil* (Grand Rapids, MI: Eerdmans, 1974).

Plantinga, Alvin (ed.), *The Ontological Argument* (Garden City, NY: Doubleday, 1965).

Plantinga, Alvin, and Nicholas Wolterstorff (eds) *Faith and Rationality: Reason and Belief in God* (Notre Dame, IN: University of Notre Dame Press, 1983).

Polanyi, Michael, *Knowing and Being* (Chicago, IL: University of Chicago Press,1969).

Polanyi, Michael, *Personal Knowledge: Towards a Post-Critical Philosophy* (Chicago, IL: University of Chicago Press, 1958).

Polanyi, Michael, *Science, Faith, and Society* (Chicago, IL: University of Chicago Press, 1966 [1946]).

Polanyi, Michael, *The Logic of Liberty: Reflections and Rejoinders* (Chicago, IL: University of Chicago Press, 1951).

Polanyi, Michael, *The Tacit Dimension* (Gloucester, MA: Peter Smith, 1983 [1967]).

Polkinghorne, John C., *Belief in God in an Age of Science* (New Haven, CT: Yale University Press, 1998).

Polkinghorne, John C., *Faith, Science, and Understanding* (New Haven, CT: Yale University Press, 2000).

Polkinghorne, John C., *Science and the Trinity: the Christian Encounter with Reality* (New Haven, CT: Yale University Press, 2004).

Polkinghorne, John C., *The End of the World and the Ends of God: Science and Theology on Eschatology* (Harrisburg, PA: Trinity Press International, 2000).

Rae, Murray, *Kierkegaard's Vision of the Incarnation: by Faith Transformed* (Oxford: Clarendon Press, Oxford University Press, 1997).

Rahner, Karl, *Foundations of the Christian Faith* (London: Darton, Longman and Todd, 1978).

Rahner, Karl, *Grundkurs des Glaubens: Einführung in den Begriff des Christentums* (Freiburg: Herder, 1976).

Rahner, Karl, *Hearers of the Word* (trans. Joannes Baptist Metz; London: Sheed and Ward, 1969).

Rahner, Karl, *Theological Investigations*, vol. 1 (Baltimore, MD: Helicon Press, 1969).

Reardon, Bernard (ed.), *Liberal Protestantism* (London: A. & C. Black, 1968).

Rescher, Nicholas, *Cognitive Systematization. A Systems–Theoretic Approach to a Coherentist Theory of Knowledge* (Totowa, NJ: Rowman and Littlefield, 1979).

Ritschl, Albrecht, *The Christian Doctrine of Justification and Reconciliation* (Kila, MT: Kessinger, 2006).

Ritschl, Albrecht, *Vorlesung Theologische Ethik* (Rolf Schäfer; Berlin: De Gruyter, 2007).

Roberts, Alexander, James Donaldson, Philip Schaff and Henry Wace (eds), *Ante-Nicene Fathers* (10 volumes) (Peabody, MA: Hendrickson Publishers, new edn, 1994).

Rorty, Richard McKay, *Objectivity, Relativism, and Truth* (Cambridge: Cambridge University Press, 1991).

Rorty, Richard McKay, *Philosophy and the Mirror of Nature* (Princeton, NJ: Princeton University Press, 1979).

Sakenfeld, Katharine Doob, Samuel E. Balentine and Brian K. Blount (ed), *The New Interpreter's Dictionary of the Bible* (Nashville, TN: Abingdon Press, 2006).

Schleiermacher, Friedrich, *Der christliche Glaube* (1820–21; 2nd edn, 1830–31). English trans. *The Christian Faith* (trans. H. R. MacKintosh, ed. J. S. Stewart; Edinburgh: T. & T. Clark, 1999).

Schleiermacher, Friedrich, *Über die Religion: Reden an die Gebildeten unter ihren Verächtern* (1799). English trans. *On Religion: Speeches to its Cultured Despisers* (trans. Richard Crouter; Cambridge: Cambridge University Press, 1996).

Schweitzer, Albert, *Von Reimarus zu Wrede: eine Geschichte der Leben-Jesu-Forschung* (Tübingen: Mohr P. Siebeck, 1906). English trans. *The Quest of the Historical Jesus: A Critical Study of its Progress from Reimarus to Wrede* (London: A. & C. Black, 1911).

Schwöbel, Christoph, *God, Action and Revelation* (Kampen: Kok Pharos, 1992).

Sherwood, Polycarp (ed.), *St Maximus the Confessor: The Ascetic Life, The Four Centuries on Charity* (Ancient Christian Writers; Mahwah, NJ: Paulist Press, 1955).

Snow, C. P., *The Two Cultures* (Cambridge: Cambridge University Press, 2005 [1960]).

Snow, C. P., *The Two Cultures: A Second Look, an Expanded Version of 'The Two Cultures and the Scientific Revolution'* (London: Cambridge University Press, 1963).

Strauss, David Friedrich, *The Life of Jesus Critically Examined* (Continuum Classic Texts; London: Continuum, 2006).

Surin, Kenneth, *The Turnings of Darkness and Light* (Cambridge: Cambridge University Press, 1989).

Swinburne, Richard, *Revelation: From Metaphor to Analogy* (Oxford: Oxford University Press, Clarendon Press, 1992).

Taylor, Charles, *Sources of the Self: the Making of the Modern Identity* (Cambridge, MA: Harvard University Press, 1989).

Tertullian, *De carne Christi liber. Tertullian's Treatise on the Incarnation.* The Text edited with an Introduction, Translation and Commentary (ed. Ernest Evans; London: SPCK, 1956).
Thiemann, Ronald F., *Revelation and Theology: the Gospel as Narrated Promise* (Notre Dame, IN: University of Notre Dame Press, 1985).
Thiselton, Anthony C., *Interpreting God and the Post-modern Self: On Meaning, Manipulation and Promise* (Grand Rapids, MI: Eerdmans, 1995).
Thunberg, Lars, *Man and the Cosmos: The Vision of St Maximus the Confessor* (New York: St Vladimir's Seminary Press, 1985).
Thurneysen, Eduard, *Christoph Blumhardt* (München: Christian Kaiser Verlag, 1926).
Tillich, Paul, *Systematic Theology*, Vol. 1 *Reason and Revelation: Being and God* (Chicago, IL: University of Chicago Press, 1951).
Tillich, Paul, *Systematic Theology*, Vol. 2 *Existence and the Christ* Chicago, IL: University of Chicago Press, (1957).
Tillich, Paul, *Systematic Theology*, Vol. 3 *Life and the Spirit: History and the Kingdom of God* (Chicago, IL: University of Chicago Press, 1963).
Torrance, T. F., *God and Rationality* (Oxford: Oxford University Press, 1971).
Torrance, T. F., *Karl Barth: An Introduction to his Early Theology 1910–1931* (Edinburgh: T&T Clark, 1962).
Torrance, T. F., *Scottish Theology: From John Knox to John Mcleod Campbell* (Edinburgh: T&T Clark, 1996).
Torrance, T. F., *The Ground and Grammar of Theology* (Belfast: Christian Journals, 1980).
Torrance, T. F., *The Hermeneutics of John Calvin* (Edinburgh: Scottish Academic Press, 1988).
Torrance, T. F., *Theological Science* (Oxford: Oxford University Press, 1969).
Torrance, T. F., *Transformation and Convergence within the Frame of Knowledge. Explorations in the Interrelations of Scientific and Theological Enterprise* (Belfast: Christian Journals, 1984).
Tyrrell, George, SJ, *Christianity at the Cross-Roads* (London: Longmans Green, 1909).
Tyrrell, George, SJ, *External Religion: its Use and Abuse* (St Louis, MO: Sands, 1899).
Vanhoozer, Kevin J., *Is there Meaning in this Text? The Bible, the Reader and the Morality of Literary Knowledge* (Leicester: Apollos, 1998).
Vidu, Adonis, *Postliberal Theological Method: A Critical Study* (Milton Keynes: Paternoster Theological Monographs, 2005).
Ward, Keith, *Religion and Revelation* (Oxford: Oxford University Press, 1994).
Warnock, Geoffrey J., *Berkeley* (Harmondsworth: Penguin Books, 1969).
Watson, Francis, *Text, Church and World: Biblical Interpretation in Theological Perspective* (Edinburgh: T&T Clark, 1994).
Weiss, Johannes, *Die Predigt Jesu vom Reiche Gottes* (Göttingen: Vandenhoeck & Ruprecht, 1900). English trans. *Jesus' Proclamation of the Kingdom of God* (trans., ed. and intro. Richard Hyde Hiers and David Larrimore Holland; London: SCM Press, 1971).
Whitehouse, W. A., *The Authority of Grace. Essays in Response to Karl Barth* (ed. Ann Loades; Edinburgh: T&T Clark, 1981).

Williams, Stephen N., *Revelation Reconciliation: A Window on Modernity* (Cambridge: Cambridge University Press, 1995).
Wolterstorff, Nicholas, *Divine Discourse: Philosophical Reflections on the Claim that God Speaks* (Cambridge: Cambridge University Press, 1995).
Wolterstorff, Nicholas, *John Locke and the Ethics of Belief* (Cambridge: Cambridge University Press, 1996).
Wright, N. T., *Jesus and the Victory of God* (London: SPCK, 1996).
Wright, N. T., *The New Testament and the People of God* (London: SPCK, 1992).
Wright, N. T., *The Resurrection of the Son of God* (London: SPCK, 2003).

Articles and Essays

Allen, P., 'Upholding The Humanum: Science and Theology's Foundational Character', in *The Heythrop Journal* 47.3 (2006), pp. 367–86.
Armstrong, Charles I., 'The Absolute Implied: Coleridge on Wordsworth and the Bible', in *Literature and Theology* 14.4 (2000), pp. 363–72.
Barr, James. 'The Problem of Fundamentalism Today', in *Explorations in Theology 7: The Scope and Authority of the Bible* (London: SCM Press, 1980), pp. 65–90.
Barth, Karl, 'Die Menschlichkeit Gottes', in Karl Barth, *Die Menschlichkeit Gottes* (Zollikon-Zurich: Evangelischer Verlag, 1956), pp. 6–7. English trans. 'The Humanity of God', in Karl Barth, *The Humanity of God* (trans. John Newton Thomas; Louisville, KY: Westminster John Knox Press, 1960), pp. 41–2.
Barth, Karl, 'Fate and Idea in Theology' (English trans. 'Schicksal und Idee', a series of three lectures delivered at the Hochschulinstitut in Dortmund, February to March, 1929), in H. Martin Rumscheidt (ed.), *The Way of Theology in Karl Barth: Essays and Comments* (intro. Stephen W. Sykes; Allison Park, PA.: Pickwick Publications, 1986).
Bertalot, R., 'Revelation and Manifestation', in *Scottish Journal of Theology* 15 (1962).
Brazier, P. H., 'C. S. Lewis and Christological Prefigurement', in *The Heythrop Journal* 48.5 (September 2007), pp. 742–75.
Bruce L. McCormack, 'Divine Revelation and Human Imagination', in *Scottish Journal of Theology* 37 (1984).
Bultmann, Rudolf Karl, 'The Concept of Revelation in the New Testament', in *Existence and Faith: Shorter Writings of Rudolf Bultmann* (San Francisco, CA: Collins, 1987 [1960]), pp. 67–106.
Clausen, Matthias, 'Proclamation and Communication: Apologetics after Barth?', in *International Journal of Systematic Theology* 1.2 (1999), pp. 203–19.
Crowe, B. D., 'Nietzsche, The Cross, and The Nature of God', in *The Heythrop Journal* 48.2 (2007), pp. 243–59.
Davidson, J. E., 'Can God Speak a Word to Man? Barth's Critique of Schleiermacher', in Sco*ttish Journal of Theology* 37 (1984).
D'Costa, Gavin, 'The Impossibility of a Pluralist View of Religion', in *Religious Studies* 32 (1996).
Dobie, Robert J., 'Reason and Revelation in the Thought of Meister Eckhart', in *The Thomist* 67.3, (2003): pp. 409–15.

Fields, S., 'The Beauty of the Ugly: Balthasar, the Crucifixion, Analogy and God', in *International Journal of Systematic Theology* 9.2 (2007), pp. 172–83.

Frankel, Steven, 'Spinoza's Dual Teachings of Scripture: His Solution to the Quarrel between Reason and Revelation', in *Archiv für Geschichte der Philosophie* 84.3 (2002), pp. 273–96.

Fudge, E. C., 'Language, Revelation and Illumination', in *Scottish Journal of Theology* 26 (1973).

Hall, Stuart G., 'Synoptic Transfigurations: Mark 9:2-10 and Partners', *King's Theological Review* X (1978), pp. 41–4.

Janz, P. D., 'Divine Causality and the Nature of Theological Questioning', in *Modern Theology* 23.3 (2007), pp. 317–48.

Langford, T. A, 'T. F. Torrance's Theological Science: A Reaction', in *Scottish Journal of Theology* 15 (1971).

Lowe, W., 'The Intensification of Time: Michael Wyschogrod and the Task of Christian Theology', in *Modern Theology*, 22.4, pp. 693–9.

McCall, T. 'Ronald Thiemann, Thomas Torrance and Epistemological Doctrines of Revelation', in *International Journal of Systematic Theology* 6.2 (2004), pp. 148–68.

Malesic, J., 'A Secret both Sinister and Salvific: Secrecy and Normativity in Light of Kierkegaard's Fear and Trembling', in *Journal of the American Academy of Religion* 74.2 (2006), pp. 446–68.

Michalson, Gordon E., Jr, 'The Response to Lindbeck', in *Modern Theology* 4.2 (January 1988), pp. 107–20.

Molnar, P. D., 'Love of God and Love of Neighbour in the Theology of Karl Rahner and Karl Barth', in *Modern Theology* 20.4 (2004), pp. 567–99.

Mooney, T. B. and A. Imbrosciano, 'The Curious Case of Mr Locke's Miracles', in *International Journal for Philosophy of Religion* 57.3 (2005), pp, 147–68.

Moule, C., 'Revelation', in George Arthur Buttrick, *The Interpreters' Dictionary of the Bible: an Illustrated Encyclopaedia Identifying and Explaining all Proper Names and Significant Terms and Subjects in the Holy Scriptures, including the Apocrypha, with Attention to Archaeological Discoveries and Researches into the Life and Faith of Ancient Times* (New York, NY: Abingdon Press, 1962]).

Orr, Susan and Germaine Paulo Walsh, 'Jerusalem and Athens: Reason and Revelation in the Works of Leo Strauss', in *The Journal of Politics* 58.2, (1996) pp. 589–601.

Paddison, A., 'Scriptural Reading and Revelation: A Contribution to Local Hermeneutics', in *International Journal of Systematic Theology* 8.4 (2006), pp. 433–48.

Roberts, J., 'Wordsworth's Apocalypse', in *Literature and Theology* 20.4 (2006), pp. 361–78.

Robinette, B., 'A Gift to Theology? Jean-Luc Marion's "Saturated Phenomenon" in Christological Perspective', in *The Heythrop Journal* 48.1 (2007), pp. 86–108.

Rowland, C., 'Blake and the Bible: Biblical Exegesis in the Work of William Blake', in *International Journal of Systematic Theology* 7.2 (2005), pp. 142–54.

Schwöbel, Christoph, 'God: Action and Revelation "Doing Systematic Theology"', in *King's Theological Review* X (1987), pp. 51–7.

Schwöbel, Christoph, 'Particularity, Universality and the Religions: Towards a Christian Theology of Religions', in *Christian Uniqueness Reconsidered: The Myth of a Pluralistic Theology of Religions* (ed. Gavin D'Costa; New York: Orbis Books, 1990).

Spence, Alan, 'Christ's Humanity and Ours', in Christoph Schwöbel and Cohn E. Gunton (eds.), *Persons, Divine and Human: King's College Essays in Theological Anthropology* (Edinburgh: T&T Clark, 1992), pp. 74–97.

Spence, Alan, 'Inspiration and Incarnation: John Owen and the Coherence of Christology', in *King's Theological Review* XII (1989), pp. 52–5.

Szerszynski, B., 'Rethinking the Secular: Science, Technology, and Religion Today', in *Zygon* 40.4 (2005), pp. 813–22.

Torrance, T. F., 'The Deposit of Faith', in *Scottish Journal of Theology* 36.1, 1983.

Vandrunen, D., 'Iconoclasm, Incarnation and Eschatology: Toward a Catholic Understanding of the Reformed Doctrine of the "Second" Commandment', in *International Journal of Systematic Theology* 6.2 (2004), pp. 130–47.

Watson, Francis, 'Trinity and Community: A Reading of John 17', in *International Journal of Systematic Theology* 1.2 (July, 1999), pp. 168–84.

Wolterstorff, Nicholas, 'Is it Possible and Desirable for Theologians to Recover from Kant?', in *Modern Theology* 14.1 (1998), pp. 1–18.

II. Karl Barth – Church Dogmatics

Barth, Karl, *The Church Dogmatics* Vol. I/1: The Doctrine of the Word of God (Prolegomena to Church Dogmatics), Part 1 – Introduction: Doctrine of the Word of God – The Revelation of God (ed. G. W. Bromiley and T. F. Torrance; Edinburgh: T&T Clark, 1956).

Barth, Karl, *The Church Dogmatics* Vol. I/2: The Doctrine of the Word of God (Prolegomena to Church Dogmatics), Part 2 – The Revelation of God; Holy Scripture; The Proclamation of the Church (ed. G. W. Bromiley and T. F. Torrance; Edinburgh: T&T Clark, 1956).

Barth, Karl, *The Church Dogmatics* Vol. II/1: The Doctrine of God Part 1 – The Knowledge of God (ed. G. W. Bromiley and T. F. Torrance; Edinburgh: T&T Clark, 1957).

Barth, Karl, *The Church Dogmatics* Vol. II/2: The Doctrine of God, Part 2 – The Election of God; The Command of God (ed. G. W. Bromiley and T. F. Torrance; Edinburgh: T&T Clark, 1957).

Barth, Karl, *The Church Dogmatics* Vol. III/1: The Doctrine of Creation, Part 1 – The Work of Creation (ed. G. W. Bromiley and T. F. Torrance; Edinburgh: T&T Clark, 1960).

Barth, Karl, *The Church Dogmatics* Vol. III/2: The Doctrine of Creation, Part 2 – The Creature (ed. G. W. Bromiley and T. F. Torrance; Edinburgh: T&T Clark, 1960).

Barth, Karl, *The Church Dogmatics* Vol. III/3: The Doctrine of Creation, Part 3 – The Creator and His Creature (ed. G. W. Bromiley and T. F. Torrance; Edinburgh: T&T Clark, 1960).

Barth, Karl, *The Church Dogmatics* Vol. III/4: The Doctrine of Creation, Part 4 – The Command of God the Creator (ed. G. W. Bromiley and T. F. Torrance; Edinburgh: T&T Clark, 1960).

Barth, Karl, *The Church Dogmatics* Vol. IV/1: The Doctrine of Reconciliation, Part 1 – The Subject-Matter and Problems of the Doctrine of Reconciliation; Jesus Christ, the Lord as Servant (ed. G. W. Bromiley and T. F. Torrance; Edinburgh: T&T Clark, 1961).

Barth, Karl, *The Church Dogmatics* Vol. IV/2: The Doctrine of Reconciliation, Part 2 – Jesus Christ, the Servant as Lord (ed. G. W. Bromiley and T. F. Torrance; Edinburgh: T&T Clark, 1961).

Barth, Karl, *The Church Dogmatics* Vol. IV/3i: The Doctrine of Reconciliation, Part 3i – Jesus Christ, the True Witness (ed. G. W. Bromiley and T. F. Torrance; Edinburgh: T&T Clark, 1961).

Barth, Karl, *The Church Dogmatics* Vol. IV/3ii: The Doctrine of Reconciliation, Part 3ii – Jesus Christ, the True Witness (ed. G. W. Bromiley and T. F. Torrance; Edinburgh: T&T Clark, 1961.

Barth, Karl, *The Church Dogmatics* Vol. IV/4: The Christian Life (Fragments), Part 4 – The Christian Life: Baptism as the Foundation of the Christian Life (Edinburgh: T&T Clark, 1981).

III. Colin E. Gunton: A Chronological Bibliography of Works

This bibliography of Colin Gunton's works was compiled primarily using academic library databases such as ATHENS, secondarily using publishers' online catalogues; however, valuable obscure non-mainstream published work, often church-based, was gleaned from related websites.

1970s

1972

Gunton, Colin E., 'Karl Barth and the Development of Christian Doctrine', in *Scottish Journal of Theology* 25, May 1972, pp. 171–80.

Gunton, Colin E., 'Rudolf Bultmann and the Location of Language about God' (review), in *Theology* 75, October 1972, pp. 535–9.

1973

Gunton, Colin E., 'Process Theology's Concept of God: An Outline and Assessment', in *Expository Times* 84, July 1973, pp. 292–6.

1974

Gunton, Colin E., 'Karl Barth's Doctrine of Election as Part of his Doctrine of God', in *Journal of Theological Studies* 25, October 1974, pp. 381–92.

Gunton, Colin E., 'The Theologian and the Biologist', in *Theology* 77, October 1974, pp. 526–8.

Gunton, Colin E., 'Re-making of Christian Doctrine' (review), in *Theology* 77, December 1974, pp. 619–24.

1975

Gunton, Colin E., 'Knowledge of God according to Two Process Theologians: A Twentieth-century Gnosticism', in *Religious Studies* 11, March 1975, pp. 87–96.

Gunton, Colin E., 'Christian Belief Today: God, Creation and the Future', in *New Fire* III, 1975, pp. 434–41.

1976

Gunton, Colin E., 'Rejection, Influence, and Development: Charles Hartshorne in the History of Philosophy', in *Process Studies* 6, Spring 1976, pp. 33–42.

1977

Gunton, Colin E., 'The Biblical Understanding of Reconciliation: Paul and Jacob before God', in *Free Church Chronicle* XXXII, 1977, pp. 17–22.

1978

Gunton, Colin E., *Becoming and Being: The Doctrine of God in Charles Hartshorne and Karl Barth*, Oxford: Oxford University Press, 1978.

1979

Gunton, Colin E., 'The Political Christ: Some Reflections on Mr Cupitt's Thesis', in *Scottish Journal of Theology* 32.6, 1979, pp. 521–40.

1980s

1980

Gunton, Colin E., 'Transcendence, Metaphor, and the Knowability of God', in *Journal of Theological Studies* 31, October 1980, pp. 501–16.

Gunton, Colin E., 'The Truth of Christology', in T. F. Torrance (ed.), *Belief in Science and in Christian Life: The Relevance of Michael Polanyi's Thought for Christian Faith and Life* (Edinburgh: Handsel Press, 1980), pp. 91–107.

1982

Gunton, Colin E., 'Time, Eternity and the Doctrine of the Incarnation', in *Dialog* 21, Autumn 1982, pp. 263–8.

1983

Gunton, Colin E., *Yesterday & Today: A Study of Continuities in Christology* (London: Darton, Longman and Todd), 1983.

1984

Gunton, Colin E., 'Barth and God's Story' (review), in *Scottish Journal of Theology* 37, 1984, pp. 373–80.

1985

Gunton, Colin E., 'Christus Victor Revisited: A Study in Metaphor and the Transformation of Meaning', in *Journal of Theological Studies* 36, April 1985, pp. 129–45.

Gunton, Colin E., *The One, the Three, and the Many: An Inaugural Lecture in the Chair of Christian Doctrine*, 1985 (given on 14 May 1985, King's College London, pamphlet, limited publication).

Gunton, Colin E., *Enlightenment and Alienation: An Essay Towards a Trinitarian Theology* (Basingstoke: Marshall Morgan and Scott), 1985.

Gunton, Colin E., 'The Justice of God', *Free Church Chronicle* XL, 1985, pp. 13–19.

Gunton, Colin E., 'Creation and Re-Creation: An Exploration of Some Themes in Aesthetics and Theology', in *Modern Theology* 2.1, October 1985, pp. 1–19.

1986

Gunton, Colin E., 'Barth on the Eastern Intellectual Tradition: Towards a Theology After Christendom', in John Thompson (ed.), *Theology Beyond Christendom: Essays on the Centenary of the Birth of Karl Barth, May 10, 1886* (Allison Park, PA: Pickwick Press, 1986), pp. 285–301.

Gunton, Colin E., 'The Christian Doctrine of God: Opposition and Convergence', in Andrew Linzey and Peter J. Wexler (eds), *Heaven and Earth: Essex Essays in Theology and Ethics* (Worthing: Churchman Publishing, 1986), pp. 11–22.

Gunton, Colin E., 'Barth, the Trinity, and Human Freedom', in *Theology Today* 43.3, October 1986, pp. 316–30.

1987

Gunton, Colin E., 'The Playwright as Theologian: Peter Shaffer's *Amadeus*', in *King's Theological Review* 10.1, Spring 1987, pp. 1–5.

Gunton, Colin E., 'Revelation', in Alastair V. Campbell (ed.), *A Dictionary of Pastoral Care* (London: SPCK, 1987), pp. 240–41.

Gunton, Colin E., 'Christ the Sacrifice: Aspects of the Language and Imagery of the Bible', in L. D. Hurst and N. T. Wright (eds), *The Glory of Christ in the New*

Testament: Essays in Memory of George Bradford Caird (Oxford: Clarendon Press, 1987), pp. 229–38.

Gunton, Colin E., 'Reinhold Niebuhr: A Treatise of Human Nature', in *Modern Theology* 4.1, October 1987, pp. 71–81.

1988

Gunton, Colin E., 'Christianity Among the Religions in the Encyclopaedia of Religion', in *Religious Studies* 24, March 1988, pp. 11–18.

Gunton, Colin E., *The Actuality of Atonement: a Study of Metaphor, Rationality, and the Christian Tradition* (Edinburgh: T&T Clark, 1988).

Gunton, Colin E., *The Transcendent Lord: The Spirit and the Church in Calvinist and Cappadocian Fathers*, Congregational Memorial Hall Trust, 1988.

Gunton, Colin E., 'The Spirit as Lord: Christianity, Modernity and Freedom', in Andrew Walker (ed.), *Different Gospels* (London: Hodder & Stoughton for the C. S. Lewis Centre, 1988), pp. 169–82.

Gunton, Colin E., 'No Other Foundation: One Englishman's Reading of Church Dogmatics, Chapter V', in Nigel Biggar (ed.), *Reckoning with Barth: Essays in Commemoration of the Centenary of Karl Barth's Birth* (London: Mowbray, 1988), pp. 61–79.

Gunton, Colin E., 'Two Dogmas Revisited: Edward Irving's Christology', in *Scottish Journal of Theology* 41.3, 1988, pp. 359–76.

1989

Gunton, Colin E., 'A Far-off Gleam of the Gospel: Salvation in Tolkien's The Lord of the Rings', in *King's Theological Review* 12, Spring 1989, pp. 6–10.

Gunton, Colin E. and Hardy, Daniel W., *On Being the Church: Essays on the Christian Community* (Edinburgh: T&T Clark, 1989).

Gunton, Colin E., 'The Triune God and the Freedom of the Creature', in Stephen W. Sykes (ed.), *Karl Barth: Centenary Essays* (Cambridge: Cambridge University Press, 1989), pp. 46–68 (a reprint of 'Barth, the Trinity and Human Freedom', 1986).

Gunton, Colin E., 'The Church on Earth: The Roots of Community', in *On Being the Church*, 1989, pp. 48–80 (translation published in 'Kosciol na Ziemi. Korzenie wspólnoty', Studia I Documenti Ekumenicze, Warsaw, 1989, pp. 11–28).

Gunton, Colin E., 'The Church on Earth: The Roots of Community', in *On Being the Church: Essays on the Christian Community* (Edinburgh: T&T Clark, 1989).

Gunton, Colin E., 'The Sacrifice and the Sacrifices: From Metaphor to Transcendental?', in Ronald J. Feenstra and Cornelius Plantinga (eds), *Trinity, Incarnation, and Atonement: Philosophical and Theological Essays* (Notre Dame, IN: Notre Dame University Press, 1989), pp. 210–29.

Gunton, Colin E., 'When the Gates of Hell Fall Down: Towards a Modern Theology of the Justice of God', in *New Blackfriars*, 1989, pp. 488–96.

Gunton, Colin E., *Service Book* (Corp. author: United Reformed Church in the United Kingdom – Doctrine and Worship Committee) (Oxford: Oxford University Press, 1989).

1990s

1990

Gunton, Colin E., 'Augustine, the Trinity and the Theological Crisis of the West', in *Scottish Journal of Theology* 43.1, 1990, pp. 33–58.

Gunton, Colin E., 'Baptism and the Christian Community', in Christian D. Kettler and Todd H. Speidell (eds), *Incarnational Ministry: The Presence of Christ in Church, Society, and Family – Essays in Honor of Ray S. Anderson* (Colorado Springs, CO: Helmers and Howard, 1990), pp. 98–109.

Gunton, Colin E., 'Newman's Dialectic: Dogma and Reason in the 73rd Tract for the Times', in Alan G. Hill and Ian Ker (eds), *Newman After a Hundred Years* (Oxford: Oxford University Press, 1990), pp. 309–22.

Gunton, Colin E., 'The Idea of Dissent and the Character of Christianity', in *Reformed Quarterly* 1.5, 1990, pp. 2–6.

Gunton, Colin E., 'Using and being Used: Scripture and Systematic Theology', in *Theology Today* 47.3, October 1990, pp. 248–59.

1991

Gunton, Colin E., 'Immanence and Otherness: Divine Sovereignty and Human Freedom in the Theology of Robert W. Jenson', in *Dialog* 30, 1991, pp. 17–26.

Gunton, Colin E., *The Promise of Trinitarian Theology* (Edinburgh: T&T Clark, 1991).

Gunton, Colin E., 'Trinity, Ontology and Anthropology: Towards a Renewal of the Doctrine of the Imago Dei', in Colin E. Gunton and Christoph Schwöbel (eds), *Persons, Divine, and Human: King's College Essays in Theological Anthropology* (from the Research Institute in Systematic Theology, King's College London) (Edinburgh: T&T Clark, 1991).

Gunton, Colin E. and Schwöbel, Christoph (eds), *Persons, Divine, and Human: King's College Essays in Theological Anthropology* (from the Research Institute in Systematic Theology, King's College London) (Edinburgh: T&T Clark, 1991).

Gunton, Colin E., 'The Spirit in the Trinity', in Alasdair I. C. Heron, *The Forgotten Trinity* (a selection of papers presented to the BCC Study Commission on Trinitarian Doctrine Today) (Corp. author(s): British Council of Churches; Study Commission on Trinitarian Doctrine Today; Council of Churches for Britain and Ireland) (London: BCC/CCBI, 1991), pp. 123–35.

Gunton, Colin E., 'Mozart the Theologian', in *Theology* 94, September–October 1991, pp. 346–9.

Gunton, Colin E., 'Immanence and Otherness: Divine Sovereignty and Human Freedom in the Theology of Robert W. Jenson', in *Dialog* 30, Winter 1991, pp. 17–26.

1992

Gunton, Colin E., *Christ and Creation* (The Didsbury Lectures, 1990) (Carlisle: Paternoster Press, 1992).

Gunton, Colin E., 'Proteus and Procrustes: A Study of the Dialectic of Language in Disagreement with Sallie McFague', in Alvin F. Kimel Jr (ed.), *Speaking the Christian God – The Triune God and the Challenge of Feminism* (Grand Rapids, MI: Eerdmans, 1992), pp. 65–80.

Gunton, Colin E., 'Knowledge and Culture: Towards an Epistemology of the Concrete', in Hugh Montefiore (ed.), *The Gospel and Contemporary Culture* (London: Mowbray, 1992), pp. 84–102.

Gunton, Colin E., 'Universal and Particular in Atonement Theology', in *Religious Studies* 28, December 1992, pp. 453–66.

1993

Gunton, Colin E., 'Foreword', in Thomas G. Weinandy, *In the Likeness of Sinful Flesh* (London: T&T Clark), 1993.

Gunton, Colin E., *The One, the Three and the Many: God, Creation and the Culture of Modernity* (The 1992 Bampton Lectures) (Cambridge: Cambridge University Press, 1993).

Gunton, Colin E., 'All Scripture is Inspired…', in *Princeton Seminary Bulletin* 14.3, 1993, pp. 240–53.

Gunton, Colin E., 'An English Systematic Theology', in *Scottish Journal of Theology* 46.4, 1993, pp. 479–96.

1994

Gunton, Colin E., 'Marriage Address', in Susan Durber (ed.), *As Man and Woman Made: Theological Reflections on Marriage* (Corp. author: United Reformed Church) (London: United Reformed Church, 1994), pp. 148–51.

1995

Gunton, Colin E., 'Editorial Introduction', pp. 1–12 and 'God, Grace and Freedom', pp. 119–33, in Colin E. Gunton (ed.), *God and Freedom: Essays in Historical and Systematic Theology* (Edinburgh: T&T Clark, 1995).

Gunton, Colin E., 'Relation and Relativity: The Trinity and the Created World', in Christoph Schwöbel (ed.), *Trinitarian Theology Today: Essays on Divine Being and Act* (Edinburgh: T&T Clark, 1995).

Gunton, Colin E., 'The Being and Attributes of God: Eberhard Jüngel's Dispute with the Classical Philosophical Tradition', in John Webster (ed.), *The Possibilities of Theology: Studies in the Theology of Eberhard Jüngel* (Edinburgh: T&T Clark, 1995), pp. 7–22.

Gunton, Colin E., 'The Community of the Church in Communion with God', in Colin E. Gunton, P. Réamonn and Alan P. F. Sell (eds), *The Church in the Reformed Tradition: Discussion Papers Prepared by a Working Party of the European Committee* (Corp. author: United Reformed Church in the United Kingdom) (Series: European Studies from the World Alliance of Reformed Churches) (Geneva: World Council of Reformed Churches, 1995).

Gunton, Colin E., 'The Real as the Redemptive: P. T. Forsyth on Authority and Freedom', in Trevor Hart (ed.), *Justice the True and Only Mercy. Essays on the Life and Theology of P. T. Forsyth* (Edinburgh: T&T Clark, 1995), pp. 37–58.

Gunton, Colin E., P. Réamonn and Alan P. F. Sell (eds), *The Church in the Reformed Tradition: Discussion Papers Prepared by a Working Party of the European Committee* (Corp. author: United Reformed Church in the United Kingdom) (Series: European Studies from the World Alliance of Reformed Churches) (Geneva: World Council of Reformed Churches, 1995).

Gunton, Colin E., 'The Trinity', in Peter Byrne and Leslie Houlden (eds), *A Companion Encyclopaedia of Theology* (London: Routledge, 1995), pp. 937–57.

Gunton, Colin E., *A Brief Theology of Revelation: The 1993 Warfield Lectures* (Edinburgh: T&T Clark, 1995).

Gunton, Colin E., 'Universal and Particular in Atonement Theology', in Robin Gill (ed.), *Readings in Modern Theology* (London: SPCK, 1995), pp. 147–62 (a reprint from *Religious Studies* 28, 1992).

1996

Gunton, Colin E., 'Christology', in Paul A. B. Clarke and Andrew Linzey, *Dictionary of Ethics, Theology and Society* (London: Routledge, 1996), pp. 133–7.

Gunton, Colin E., 'Foreword', in Graham McFarlane (ed.), *Christ and the Spirit: The Doctrine of the Incarnation According to Edward Irving* (Carlisle: Paternoster Press, 1996).

Gunton, Colin E., 'The Indispensable God? The Sovereignty of God and the Problem of Modern Social Order', in Hilary D. Regan and Rodney B. Horsfield (eds), *Beyond Mere Health: Theology and Health Care in a Secular Society* (Melbourne: Australian Theological Forum, 1996).

Gunton, Colin E., 'Indispensability of Theological Understanding: Theology in the University', in Daniel W. Hardy, David Ford and Dennis L. Stamps (eds), *Essentials of Christian Community* (Edinburgh: T&T Clark, 1996).

Gunton, Colin E., 'Persons', in Paul A. B. Clarke and Andrew Linzey (eds), *Dictionary of Ethics, Theology and Society* (London: Routledge, 1996), pp. 638–41.

Gunton, Colin E., 'Pneumatology', in Paul A. B. Clarke and Andrew Linzey (eds), *Dictionary of Ethics, Theology and Society* (London: Routledge, 1996), pp. 644–7.

Gunton, Colin E., 'Sin, Death and the Resurrection of the Body: Towards an Eschatology of Personhood', in Hilary D. Regan and Rodney B. Horsfield (eds), *Beyond Mere Health: Theology and Health Care in a Secular Society* (Melbourne: Australian Theological Forum, 1996).

Gunton, Colin E., 'Toleration', in Paul A. B. Clarke and Andrew Linzey (eds), *Dictionary of Ethics, Theology and Society* (London: Routledge, 1996), pp. 826–9.

Gunton, Colin E., 'Trinity, Natural Theology, and a Theology of Nature', in Kevin J. Vanhoozer (eds), *The Trinity in a Pluralistic Age: Theological Essays on Culture and Religion* (from the Edinburgh Conference in Christian Dogmatics) (Grand Rapids, MI: Eerdmans, 1996).

Gunton, Colin E., *Theology through the Theologians: Selected Essays 1972–1995* (Edinburgh: T&T Clark, 1996).

Gunton, Colin E., 'Response to Hard Copy or Good News? Genetic Engineering and the Gospel, by John Henley', in Hilary D. Regan and Rodney B. Horsfield (eds), *Beyond Mere Health: Theology and Health Care in a Secular Society* (Melbourne, Australia: Australian Theological Forum, 1996), pp. 22–37.

Gunton, Colin E., 'Indispensable Opponent: The Relations of Systematic Theology and the Philosophy of Religion', in *Neue Zeitschrift für systematische Theologie und Religionsphilosophie* 38.3, 1996, pp. 298–306.

Gunton, Colin E., 'Atonement and the Project of Creation: An Interpretation of Colossians 1:15-23', in *Dialog* 35, Winter 1996, pp. 35–41.

Gunton, Colin E., 'Bruce McCormack's *Karl Barth's Critically Realistic Dialectical Theology: Its Genesis and Development 1909–1936*' (review), *Scottish Journal of Theology* 49.4, 1996, pp. 483–91.

1997

Gunton, Colin E., 'The Doctrine of Creation', in *The Cambridge Companion to Christian Doctrine* (Cambridge: Cambridge University Press, 1997), pp. 141–57.

Gunton, Colin E., 'The End of Causality? The Reformers and their Predecessors', in Colin E. Gunton (ed.), *The Doctrine of Creation: Essays in Dogmatics, History and Philosophy* (Edinburgh: T&T Clark, 1997), pp. 63–82.

Gunton, Colin E., 'The Atonement', in Edward Craig, *Encyclopaedia of Philosophy*, vol. 1 (London: Routledge, 1997), pp. 536–41.

Gunton, Colin E. (ed.), *The Doctrine of Creation: Essays in Dogmatics, History and Philosophy* (Edinburgh: T&T Clark, 1997).

Gunton, Colin E., 'Between Allegory and Myth: The Legacy of the Spiritualising of Genesis', in Colin E. Gunton (ed.), *The Doctrine of Creation: Essays in Dogmatics, History and Philosophy* (Edinburgh: T&T Clark, 1997), pp. 47–62.

Gunton, Colin E., 'Introduction', in Colin E. Gunton (ed.), *The Doctrine of Creation: Essays in Dogmatics, History and Philosophy* (Edinburgh: T&T Clark, 1997), pp. 1–15.

Gunton, Colin E., 'Historical and Systematic Theology', in *The Cambridge Companion to Christian Doctrine* (Cambridge: Cambridge University Press, 1997), pp. 3–20.

Gunton, Colin E., *The Promise of Trinitarian Theology* (2nd enlarged edn) (Edinburgh: T&T Clark, 1997).

Gunton, Colin E., *The Cambridge Companion to Christian Doctrine* (Cambridge: Cambridge University Press, 1997).

Gunton, Colin E., *Yesterday & Today: A Study of Continuities in Christology* (2 nd enlarged edn with new epilogue; London: SPCK, 1997).

Gunton, Colin E., 'The God of Jesus Christ', in *Theology Today* 54, October 1997, pp. 325–34.

1998

Gunton, Colin E., 'Dogma, the Church and the Task of Theology', in *Neue Zeitschrift für systematische Theologie und Religionsphilosophie* 40.1, 1998, pp. 66–79 (reprinted: 'Dogma, the Church and the Task of Theology', in Victor Pfitzner and Hilary Regan, *The Task of Theology Today: Doctrines and Dogmas*; Adelaide: Australian Theological Forum, 1998), pp. 1–24.

Gunton, Colin E., *The Triune Creator: A Historical and Systematic Study* (Edinburgh: Edinburgh University Press, 1998).

Gunton, Colin E., 'Martin Kähler Revisited: Variations on Hebrews 4:15', *Ex auditu* 14, 1998, pp. 21–30.

1999

Gunton, Colin E., 'A Rose by any Other Name? From Christian Doctrine to Systematic Theology', in *International Journal of Systematic Theology* 1.1, March 1999, pp. 4–23.

Gunton, Colin E., 'Editorial', in *International Journal of Systematic Theology* 1.2, July 1999, pp. 113–18.

Gunton, Colin E., 'Christ, the Wisdom of God: A Study in Divine and Human Action', in Stephen C. Barton, *Where Shall Wisdom Be Found? Wisdom in the Bible, the Church, and the Contemporary World* (Edinburgh: T&T Clark, 1999).

Gunton, Colin E., 'A Far-off Gleam of the Gospel: Salvation in Tolkien's *The Lord of the Rings*', in Joseph Pearce, *Tolkien: a Celebration: Collected Writings on a Literary Legacy* (London: Fount, 1999; reprint from *King's Theological Review*, 1989).

Gunton, Colin E., 'Dogma, the Church and the Task of Theology', in Victor Pfitzner and Hilary Regan (eds), *The Task of Theology Today: Doctrines and Dogmas* (Edinburgh: T&T Clark, 1999), pp. 1–22 [1998].

Gunton, Colin E., 'Martin Kähler Revisited: Variations on Hebrews 4:15', in *The Theological Significance of the Earthly Jesus* (Papers from the North Park Symposium on Theological Interpretation of Scripture, North Park Theological Seminary, Chicago, Illinois, 23–25 October 1998) (Allison Park, PA: Pickwick Publications, 1999).

Gunton, Colin E., 'The Cross and the City. R. W. Dale and the Doctrine of the Atonement', in Clyde Binfield (ed.), *The Cross and the City: Essays in Commemoration of Robert William Dale* (Supplement to the *Journal of the United Reformed Church History Society*, Vol. 6, Supplement to the *Congregational History Circle Magazine*, Vol. 4) (Cambridge: United Reformed Church History Society, 1999).

Gunton, Colin E., 'Incarnation and Imagery: Words, the World and the Triune God', *Philosophy of Religion 4* (Oxford: Farmington Papers; Oxford: Farmington Institute for Christian Studies, 1999).

2000s

2000

Gunton, Colin E., and Flora A. Keshgegian, 'Responses', in *Insights* 115.2 (The Faculty Journal of Austin Seminary), Spring 2000, pp. 24–32 (response to 'Are you Saved? Receiving the Full Benefits of Grace', by Cynthia L. Rigby, pp. 27–9).

Gunton, Colin E., 'Election and Ecclesiology in the Post-Constantinian Church', in *Scottish Journal of Theology* 53.2, 2000, pp. 212–27.

Gunton, Colin E., 'Three Pitfalls in Preaching Creation', in *Living Pulpit* 9.2, April–June 2000, pp. 14–15.

Gunton, Colin E., 'Authority', in Adrian Hastings, Hugh Pyper and Alistair Mason (eds), *Oxford Companion to Christian Thought* (Oxford: Oxford University Press, 2000).

Gunton, Colin E., 'Protestantism', in Adrian Hastings, Hugh Pyper and Alistair Mason (eds), *Oxford Companion to Christian Thought* (Oxford: Oxford University Press, 2000).

Gunton, Colin E., 'Salvation', in John Webster (ed.), *Cambridge Companion to Karl Barth* (Cambridge: Cambridge University Press, 2000), pp. 143–58.

Gunton, Colin E., 'The Atonement and the Triune God', in George P. Schner and J. B. Webster, *Theology after Liberalism: A Reader* (Oxford: Blackwell, 2000), pp. 113–31.

Gunton, Colin E., 'The Church as a School of Virtue? Human Formation in Trinitarian Framework, Faithfulness and Fortitude', in Stanley Hauerwas, Mark Nation and Samuel Wells (eds), *In Conversation with the Theological Ethics of Stanley Hauerwas* (Edinburgh: T&T Clark, 2000), pp. 211–31.

Gunton, Colin E. (ed.), *Trinity, Time and Church: A Response to the Theology of Robert W. Jenson*, (Grand Rapids, MI: Eerdmans, 2000), pp. 80–93.

Gunton, Colin E., 'Creation and Mediation in the Theology of Robert W. Jenson: An Encounter and a Convergence', in Colin E. Gunton (ed.), *Trinity, Time and Church: A Response to the Theology of Robert W. Jenson* (Grand Rapids, MI: Eerdmans, 2000), pp. 80–93.

Gunton, Colin E., 'Dogmatic Theses on Eschatology', in David Fergusson and Marcel Sarot (eds), *The Future as God's Gift: Explorations in Christian Eschatology* (Edinburgh: T&T Clark, 2000).

Gunton, Colin E., 'Holy Spirit', in Adrian Hastings, Hugh Pyper and Alistair Mason, *Oxford Companion to Christian Thought* (Oxford: Oxford University Press, 2000).

Gunton, Colin E., *Intellect and Action: Elucidations on Christian Theology and the Life of Faith* (Edinburgh: T&T Clark, 2000).

Gunton, Colin E., *The Christian Faith: An Introduction to Christian Doctrine* (Oxford: Blackwell, 2000).

Gunton, Colin E., *Theology through Preaching Sermons for Brentwood* (Edinburgh: T&T Clark, 2000).

2001

Gunton, Colin E., *Becoming and Being: The Doctrine of God in Charles Hartshorne and Karl Barth* (2nd edn including 'Epilogue'; London: SCM Press, 2001).

Gunton, Colin E., 'Until He Comes: Towards an Eschatology of Church Membership', in *International Journal of Systematic Theology* 3.2, July 2001, pp. 187–200.

Gunton, Colin E., 'And in One Lord Jesus Christ … Begotten Not Made', in *Pro Ecclesia* 10.3, Summer 2001, pp. 261–74.

Gunton, Colin E., *Commentary on the Lectionary* (3-volume set) (London: Continuum, 2001).

Gunton, Colin E., 'Introduction', in Karl Barth, *Protestant Theology in the Nineteenth Century* (new edn) (London: SCM Press, 2001), pp. xv–xx.

Gunton, Colin E., 'Can We Know Anything about God Anyway? Introductory Essay', in Colin E. Gunton, Stephen R. Holmes and Murray Rae (eds), *The Practice of Theology: A Reader* (London: SCM Press, 2001), pp. 219–23.

Gunton, Colin E., 'Creeds and Confessions, Introductory Essay', in Colin E. Gunton, Stephen R. Holmes and Murray Rae (eds), *The Practice of Theology: A Reader* (London: SCM Press, 2001), pp. 101–05.

Gunton, Colin E., 'Doing Theology in the University Today', in Colin E. Gunton, Stephen R. Holmes and Murray Rae (eds), *The Practice of Theology: A Reader* (London: SCM Press, 2001), pp. 441–55.

Gunton, Colin E., 'Preface', in Karl Barth, *Dogmatics in Outline* (London: SCM Press, 2001).

Gunton, Colin E., 'The Place of Reason in Theology, Introductory Essay', in Colin E. Gunton, Stephen R. Holmes and Murray Rae (eds), *The Practice of Theology: A Reader* (London: SCM Press, 2001), pp. 149–53.

Gunton, Colin E., *Commentary on the Lectionary*: Vol. 1 *The Old Testament and Acts* (London: Continuum, 2001).

Gunton, Colin E., *Nicene Christianity: The Future for a New Ecumenism* (Carlisle: Paternoster Press, 2001).

Gunton, Colin E., Stephen R. Holmes and Murray Rae (eds), *The Practice of Theology: A Reader* (London: SCM Press, 2001).

Gunton, Colin E., 'Until He Comes: Towards an Eschatology of Church Membership', in John Colwell (ed.), *Called to One Hope: Perspectives on the Life to Come* (The Drew Lectures on Immortality, delivered at Spurgeon's College) (Carlisle: Paternoster Press, 2001), pp. 252–66.

Gunton, Colin E., *Commentary on the Lectionary*: Vol. 2 *Acts and the New Testament Epistles* (London: Continuum, 2001).

Gunton, Colin E., *Commentary on the Lectionary*: Vol. 3 *The Gospels* (London: Continuum, 2001).

2002

Gunton, Colin E., 'The Spirit Moved Over the Face of the Waters: The Holy Spirit and Created Order', in *International Journal of Systematic Theology* 4.2, July 2002, pp. 190–204.

Gunton, Colin E., 'We Believe in … the Holy Spirit, who with the Father and the Son is Worshiped and Glorified', in Joseph D. Small, *Fire and Wind: The Holy Spirit in the Church Today* (Louisville, KY: Geneva Press, 2002).

Gunton, Colin E., 'Trinity and Trustworthiness', in Paul Helm and Carl R. Trueman (eds), *The Trustworthiness of God: Perspectives on the Nature of Scripture* (Grand Rapids, MI: Eerdmans, 2002).

Gunton, Colin E., 'Theology in Communion', in Darren C. Marks, *Shaping a Theological Mind: Theological Context and Methodology* (Burlington, VT: Ashgate, 2002).

Gunton, Colin E., *Act and Being: Towards a Theology of the Divine Attributes* (London: SCM Press, 2002).

2003

Gunton, Colin E., *Father, Son and Holy Spirit: Essays Toward a Fully Trinitarian Theology* (London: T&T Clark, 2003).

Gunton, Colin E., 'Introduction', in Colin E. Gunton (ed.), *The Theology of Reconciliation* (London: T&T Clark, 2003).

Gunton, Colin E., 'Towards a Theology of Reconciliation', in Colin E. Gunton (ed.), *The Theology of Reconciliation* (London: T&T Clark, 2003).

Gunton, Colin E., *The Theology of Reconciliation* (London: T&T Clark, 2003).

2004

Gunton, Colin E., 'Preaching from the Letters', in David Ford, Colin E. Gunton and Roger Van Harn (eds), *Exploring and Proclaiming the Apostles' Creed* Vol. 2 (Grand Rapids, MI: Eerdmans, 2004), pp. 621–6.

Gunton, Colin E., 'A Sermon: The Almighty God', in David Ford, Colin E. Gunton and Roger Van Harn (eds), *Exploring and Proclaiming the Apostles' Creed* Vol. 1 (Grand Rapids, MI: Eerdmans, 2004).

Gunton, Colin E., 'Sermon: 1 Corinthians 15:51-58', in David Ford, Colin E. Gunton and Roger Van Harn (eds), *Exploring and Proclaiming the Apostles' Creed* Vol. 2 (Grand Rapids, MI: Eerdmans, 2004), pp. 228–31.

Gunton, Colin E., 'The Truth … and the Spirit of Truth: The Trinitarian Shape of Christian Theology', in Michael Welker and Cynthia A. Jarvis (eds), *Loving God with our Minds: The Pastor as Theologian – Essays in Honour of Wallace M. Alston* (Grand Rapids, MI: Eerdmans, 2004).

Ford, David, Colin E. Gunton and Roger Van Harn (eds), *Exploring and Proclaiming the Apostles' Creed* (London: Continuum, 2004).

2007

Gunton, Colin E., 'Persons & Particularity', in Douglas Knight (ed), *The Theology of John Zizioulas: Personhood and the Church* (Aldershot: Ashgate, 2007).

Gunton, Colin E., 'Revelation: do Christians know something no one else knows?', in, Angus Morrison (ed.), *Tolerance and Truth: The Spirit of the Age or the Spirit of God?* (Papers from the Edinburgh Dogmatics Conference 1999; Edinburgh: Rutherford House, 2007).

Gunton, Colin E., *The Barth Lectures* (transcribed and edited by P. H. Brazier; London: Continuum, T&T Clark, 2007).

Gunton, Colin E., *Theologian as Preacher: Further Sermons from Colin Gunton* (ed. Sarah Gunton and John Colwell; intro. Stephen R. Holmes) (London: Continuum, T&T Clark, 2007).

INDEXES

Index of Names

Index of Subjects